About the Authors

Helen Garlick qualified as a solicitor and subsequently specialised in family law and became the matrimonial partner of a practice in London. As a member of the Solicitors Family Law Association, she has lectured on various topics including cohabitation, child access and matrimonial finance. She co-produced the video *For Better For Worse?* with the Institute of Family Therapy in 1986 and her first book *The Separation Survival Handbook* was published in 1989. She is an adviser to the Consumers' Association on family law matters and Vice Chair of the National Council for One Parent Families.

She is now a freelance writer and speaker and broadcasts regularly on radio and TV. She is married and lives in Chiswick.

Jane Stuart Sheppard qualified as a solicitor and specialised in property law, and, briefly, divorce law. She then set up a company providing training courses in self-expression and performance skills while becoming herself increasingly involved in individual counselling work. Having trained as an analytical psychotherapist, she now divides her time between writing and her private psychotherapy practice. She lives in North London with her husband and small daughter.

Babies! A Parent's Guide to Surviving (and Enjoying!) Baby's First Year
Christopher Green

The First Five Minutes You May Never Get a Second Chance to
Make a First Impression
Norman King

The Food Pharmacy Dramatic New Evidence that Food is Your Best
Medicine
Jean Carper

The Good Marriage A Guide to Getting Wed and Enjoying Marriage in
Modern Times
Helen Garlick and Jane Stuart Sheppard

Intangible Evidence Exploring the Paranormal World and Developing
Your Psychic Skills
Bernard Gittelson

Loveshock How to Recover From a Broken Heart and Love Again
Stephen Gullo Ph.D. and Connie Church

Necessary Losses The Loves, Illusions, Dependencies and Impossible
Expectations That All of Us Have to Give Up in Order to Grow
Judith Viorst

The Power of Your Subconscious Mind
Dr Joseph Murphy

60-Second Shiatzu How to Energise, Erase Pain and Conquer Tension
in One Minute
Eva Shaw

Talk Language How to Use Conversation for Profit and Pleasure
Allan Pease with Alan Garner

The Tao of Health, Sex and Longevity A Modern, Practical
Approach to the Ancient Way
Daniel Reid

Unlimited Power
Anthony Robbins

Who Needs God
Harold Kushner

The Working Mother's Survival Guide
Jill Black

SELF-HELP FROM SIMON & SCHUSTER

THE
GOOD
MARRIAGE

A guide to getting wed
and enjoying marriage
in modern times

HELEN GARLICK
and
JANE STUART SHEPPARD

SIMON & SCHUSTER

LONDON·SYDNEY·NEW YORK·TOKYO·SINGAPORE·TORONTO

First published in Great Britain by
Simon & Schuster Ltd in 1990

Simon & Schuster Ltd
West Garden Place
Kendal Street
London W2 2AQ

Simon & Schuster of Australia Pty Ltd
Sydney

British Library Cataloguing-in-Publication Data available
ISBN 0-671-71503-8

Typeset in Baskerville No.2 by Selectmove Ltd, London
Printed and bound in Great Britain by
Richard Clay Ltd, Bungay, Suffolk

Contents

Contents

Part IV
Towards a good marriage

To Richard and to Rick

Then the princess kissed the ugly frog who straight away
turned into a handsome prince and asked her to be his bride.
They had a wonderful wedding and there was celebration
and rejoicing throughout the Kingdom.
They lived happily ever after.

Traditional

Acknowledgements

Jointly, we would like to thank Nick Brealey, our editor, for his enthusiasm and considerable input, not least in putting forward a male viewpoint, and Nancy Duin, our copy editor, for the great care with which she sculpted and checked. Dasha Shenkman, as ever, has been a tower of strength and a source of good humour and objectivity.

We would like to extend our warmest thanks to all the couples we interviewed, who so generously gave of their time and energy, as well as our own families (not least our husbands) and numerous friends, acquaintances and strangers who contributed their own thoughts and insights. Particularly, we would like to thank Jean MacIntyre for her help and patient guidance with the Tax Appendix, Robin Skynner, the people at AGIP (especially Seema Ariel), Reverend Peter McCrory, Jeffrey Blumenfeld of the JMC and the CMAC, particularly Margaret Grimer, for their advice and contributions.

Helen would dearly love to be able to acknowledge her (wished-for but so far non-existent) secretary. Instead, she is grateful to her much abused Amstrad for never having spitefully wiped off any copy, even on Friday 13th. To her newsagent, Pete, and her cats, she is also thankful for their company during her hermit period during the preparation of this book. And last but not least, her husband and ally, Richard, who lived through the making of each chapter with great fortitude (the one on infidelity may well have been the toughest) and who was there to provide support when necessary and to crack open a bottle when the occasion arose.

Introduction

Why are we arguing so much now we've decided to get married?
Would a church service be a bad idea if I'm not a practising Christian?
Why do I feel so distant from my mother and so at odds with my father since we started planning the wedding?
How will my legal status and tax situation change once I'm married?
What are the options and implications of changing my name?
How might having a baby affect our relationship as a couple?
What if one of us is tempted to have an affair?

For both of us, for our respective partners and for most of the couples we interviewed in the course of writing this book, the decision to get married was not an automatic one. Being already in steady relationships, the alternative of just carrying on living together and even having children 'without benefit of holy wedlock' (as they used to say) seemed perfectly feasible. Why, then, marry? Might we be putting at risk more than we would gain? Or vice versa? And having made the decision to go ahead, why did we at times feel so adrift and uncertain about what we were doing? All of these questions and wonderings (and they were just the tip of the iceberg) floated round our heads and kept us awake at nights. Where could we find answers to them, or at least guides through the maze?

Not, it seemed, among the arrays of wedding books gathering dust in every bookshop. Jane's main companion through her trials and traumas was a wedding etiquette book (thoughtfully procured by her mother) featuring on the cover a bride with a bouffant hairdo and three inches of false eyelashes, escorted by a trendy groom in a kipper tie. The advice inside was similarly up-to-the-minute – useful enough as far as it went, if you need to discover the correct seating plan for the bridal table and upon whose arm the groom's widowed mother should walk out of church. There is a place for these things, but to be honest they were not really the issues that seemed to matter most as the wedding day loomed ever nearer, arrived – and then receded as marriage began for real.

At the other end of the scale, and a far cry from the obsession with bridal protocol and orange blossom idealization of the wedding day, we read gloomy predictions about the failure of relationships and marriage: the feminist tracts about marriage as an instrument of oppression, and all the self-help books about relationship breakdown, separation and divorce

with their focus on whom to blame and what to do when relationships go
messily wrong. None of these was much of a help either.

We have tried to write the book we each wanted to read and could
not find as we contemplated getting wed and then experienced our own
weddings and the early years of our marriages. This book is based on our
own experiences of the process of getting married (at the time of going
to press, Jane has been married for three years and Helen one), on our
interviews with other couples, marital counsellors and the like, and also
on our own professional work.

Together, we wanted to write a different kind of book. First, we had in
mind a very particular timespan. The subject of marriage is huge: what
we were interested in was the period around the birth of a marriage –
the period when, for better or for worse, the *modus operandi* which will
subsequently prevail in the relationship is being worked out. We did
not wish to leave you, gentle reader, newly wed at the altar. The deed
is done, the Wedding March strikes up, the photographer steps out of
the shadows to freeze you into immortality – and you face the same
scenario which ended so many fairy stories: the prince and the princess
got married and lived happily ever after. And there the book ends and
you are suddenly left on your own. But hold on a minute! What on earth
is supposed to happen next?

It seems to us that the first few years of a marital relationship – roughly
from the time that the decision to marry is made to the time when the
first child arrives – is a massively important one, and this is the period
we decided to focus on. It involves a change in basic identity and unit
status, from thinking of oneself as one, then as two and finally, perhaps,
as three. Legally you may get married in an instant; psychologically, most
people find that it all takes a bit longer.

Second, while presenting factual matters simply and separately where
appropriate, we did not wish to make artificial distinctions between legal,
practical and emotional issues. In our own experiences, life is not like this
– such issues as whether to change your name on marriage and the size of
your post-marital credit card bill have a great bearing on the state of the
heart and vice versa.

Finally, we wanted this to be a book that would involve readers – not
another dry academic tome about other people's lives. To this end, we
have included exercises, suggestions and individual accounts which we
hope may, together with the text, give you some new perspectives on your
own relationship as you continue to explore it together. The book does not
necessarily have to be read at one sitting; it may be dipped into and tasted
in smaller helpings as the desire arises.

Most of all, we wanted to create a book which can be a friend and guide
to those facing marriage and those caught up in its tumultuous first years.
We hope it may serve you well.

While criticizing the sad lack of research and study about marriage while it is still alive and kicking (rather than expiring on its death bed), we want to make a specific exception of the excellent work of the Marriage Research Centre, directed by Dr Jack Dominian, which has made enormous strides in lifting the lid off what really goes on in marriages in latter-day Britain. Penny Mansfield and Jean Collard, two sociologists working at the Marriage Research Centre, have been conducting studies on 65 married couples and a follow-up study, up to six years on, is due out in the near future. For those interested, we recommend perusal of their books – it is always fascinating to peek behind usually closed doors. Information about all the books and authors mentioned in *The Good Marriage* is contained in the 'Further reading' section on pages 253–4.

We have sometimes needed to be specific about forms of marriage ceremony and have often referred to the Anglican Order of Service – although generally (space permitting) we have also included references to other forms of ceremony, both secular and religious. In addition, some of the chapter headings in the book are likewise taken from the Anglican liturgy. An Anglican wedding is still the preferred choice for the majority of first marriages in the United Kingdom, but more than this, the wording of the vows are so familiar to most people that they seem to have become a part of almost everyone's image of and concepts about marriage – whether realistic or not. They therefore seemed appropriate as ways of looking at the various topics covered in these chapters. We are well aware that we are writing within a multicultural society, and we trust that atheists, agnostics and people of differing religious beliefs will feel equally accommodated.

PART I

DECIDING TO GET MARRIED

1

Love is a decision

'SO why *did* you two decide to get married?'
'She turns me on so much. I want to be next to her every second of the day. She's my dream woman.'

'I want a home of my own – and someone to provide for me.'

'He gives me a sense of security; I feel safer when he's around.'

'All my friends are doing it and I want to get away from home. My parents still think of me as a child!'

'We've been together for nearly two years. I think it's about time I made a commitment.'

'We have the same tastes, the same way of looking at things, the same sense of humour. She makes me laugh.'

'I couldn't do any better. I'm tired of waiting for Mr Right.'

'I want a baby soon, so much. I know he'll be a good father.'

'I want to make her mine – for ever. I don't want anyone else around her.'

'For the first time in my life, I feel really needed, as if I really matter. She's someone I can take care of, someone of my very own.'

'He asked me!'

'We had to decide one way or another: to get married or split up. We decided to get married.'

'Big car, good career prospects, lots of money. . .he's got everything I've always wanted in a husband!'

'I fancy regular sex.'

'We went out together when we were at school – he was my first boyfriend. We both played the field for a bit after school, but I've never really met up with anyone else I liked as much. Now I'm 21. . .I think we've waited long enough.'

'I'm coming up to 30. I always planned I would get married then – it's a good time to start a family. She's everything I'm looking for in a wife and she'll be an excellent mother.'

'I just couldn't bear to be without him. Don't ask me why, I just couldn't.'

'She really understands me. We shared a similar past, and she really knows what I've been through.'

3

'He/she will be my
financial support
homemaker
protector
status symbol
comforter
sensual and available lover
parent of my unborn children
friend and companion through my life. . .for ever and ever, for richer
for poorer, for better or worse, in sickness and in health, till death us
do part. . .'

People marry for a thousand different reasons. Some are sensible and
clearsighted, a few deeply mercenary; others are idealistic or impractical
to the point of reckless folly. But if you are like 90 per cent of the women
who were asked the same question by a 1982 MORI poll, you will have
one single answer:
               'Well, we love each other, of course.'
Of course, people get married because they love each other. Love, as
everybody knows, makes the world go round, and love is the key to
growth, fulfilment and happiness. Love gives its mysterious and radiant
blessings to lovers, to weddings and to marriages everywhere, and the
world would be a sadder and quieter place without it.
     But supposing we return to those couples who have told us that they
are marrying because they love each other, and ask them what, exactly,
do they mean by this? Perhaps they could not give a very clear answer.
Could you? So before we proceed any further, perhaps we should take
a closer look at. . .

This thing called love

The Greeks have four different words for love. The kind that they called
eros, romantic love or 'being in love', is the kind that the couples above
are mostly talking about, and it is essentially different from other kinds
of loving.
     Romantic love draws men and women to each other. It is an elemental
force which dominates their feelings about themselves, each other and
the world. In our mass-produced, mass-media world, love makes people
feel free, spontaneous, creative, important and unique. It gives them the
courage to make far-reaching commitments. When they have reached the
point of talking about marriage, romantic love is central in determining
the important decisions which they must now make about the rest of their
lives together. Without the certainty and the trust in the future which
love imparts, few perhaps would take the leap out into the abyss – into
marriage.

Being in love is not just a feeling. It is an entire state of mind with its own corresponding set of ideas, attitudes, expectations and beliefs. However, the experience of being in love, so familiar to most of us, is hard to describe or explain. June, a woman celebrating her third wedding anniversary, described it this way: 'There was this incredible excitement and energy which made everything sparkle and come to life. At the same time, everything else around you seems less important while you're so incredibly, intensely aware of the person you are in love with. Yet, at the same time,' she added thoughtfully, 'I wonder if I really knew my husband *at all* before I married him.'

As June observed, the state of being in love is not governed to any significant extent by our everyday sense of *outer* reality. In the state of mind of the lover, everyday, outer reality becomes overtaken and overwhelmed by a sense of *inner* reality with its own peculiar logic. This can make us far more intuitive and vulnerable, more in touch with those unconscious feelings and needs which we are normally required to repress and to 'grow out of' as we pay the price of living in civilized society. Yet it also makes us more irrational and headstrong, more self-deluding and more willing to believe that what we would like be true is – occasionally, despite all evidence to the contrary – actually true.

The pull of the unconscious

In some ways, the state of being in love is akin to the earliest, most primitive bonding between mother and baby – a profoundly trusting and sometimes overwhelming relationship. Love creates an intense physical and emotional union in which the boundaries which usually separate two people seem to dissolve. A baby in its total dependence is most vulnerable to the extremes of intensified emotion: in the arms of its mother, it is blissfully satisfied, but in its mother's absence, it is prey to the depths of rage, loneliness and despair.

When we are in love, we regress, or return, to our baby selves. At this earliest stage, the part of the person which perceives and deals with the real world (sometimes called the ego) is scarcely developed, and the self is ruled by the most unconscious primitive instincts and feelings. Logical, sensible criteria for choosing a mate may be overridden by needs that are far stronger and more urgent. . .and because there is no apparent explanation for this kind of compulsive selection, we call it 'chemistry' or 'falling in love'.

> *'I fancy my husband like mad. The chemistry between us is tremendous. It has livened up what could have been a boring marriage – you've got to accept that there are long periods of tedium in marriage. Of course, it's not everything. But as we have such a good time in*

*bed, I reckon that we have a good chance of making it work long
term.'*

Love, sexual passion, chemistry – call it what you will, it can make the
difference between a marriage which is alive and a marriage which, while
it may seem sensible, worthwhile and to have everything going for it, is
dead on its feet. I'd rather have anything but that, you might think. Yet
at the same time, unless it is tempered by a calmer sense of respect and
liking, sexual chemistry can be quite dangerous.

Mary is a woman in her mid-20s who comes from a family in which
self-expression was frowned on and where displays of physical affection
were few and far between. Mary has had a troubled emotional history
of falling for men who did not seem very interested in her – but now
everything seems different. She has met Mark, a research student, whom
she 'knew' at first sight was the one for her. This time, her feelings appear
to be reciprocated. Mark and Mary have fallen deeply in love with each
other.

Mark is physically the same tall, dark, saturnine type as Mary's father,
and the resemblance is more than skin deep; he, too, seems the strong,
coping kind. Quiet and reserved men have always held attraction for
Mary. They challenge her – perhaps *she* will be the one who will find the
way to their hearts? Nowadays Mary thinks of herself as an emotionally
open person – but actually men like Mark attract her because, however
'open' *she* may appear to be, there is no danger of real emotional intimacy
with such men. And intimacy is what Mary, underneath, is deeply afraid
of.

While ostensibly in control of his life, Mark, beneath the calm, strong
façade, is, of course, as afraid of his own feelings as Mary is. Sent away
to boarding school at 12, himself the child of a rocky, angry marriage,
he has buried his feelings to such an extent that he has completely lost
touch with them.

The inner similarity of Mark and Mary, mirroring each to the other,
initially draws them together. But then things begin to go wrong. The
human need for loving intimacy is a very strong one, and after not very
long, the relationship falls apart under threat from the inner loneliness
they are both repressing. The unhappiness that Mary felt as a child
surges up in massive resentment and neediness – 'Take care of me! Love
me! Cuddle me! Make me feel valued and good!' – which she nevertheless
finds difficult to express through a combination of inner inhibition and
the fear of losing Mark should she appear too demanding. Mark, for his
part, is appalled.

Mark's and Mary's relationship disintegrates in a series of arguments
over the rights and wrongs of Mark being too wrapped up in his very
demanding work. Mary becomes ever more needy, Mark ever more
repressed and self-contained. The similarities which attracted each to
the other now drive them apart – unable to express and to cope with

their own emotional needs, how can they possibly cope with each other's?

Are you being pulled by your unconscious into marriage? Getting married would clearly have been the wrong choice for Mark and Mary, as fortunately they realized. The apparent fitting together of their personalities was a fitting of neurotic behaviour patterns. Without the huge amount of awareness and effort which would have been needed by both to break the destructive patterns set up in their childhoods, they could have all too easily dwindled into those not-too-uncommon stereotypes: the emotionally withdrawn husband who only comes alive at work, and the frustrated, nagging wife who blames her husband's deficiencies for everything that is wrong with her life.

Coming home again

When people talk about meeting their prospective partners, they often use such phrases as 'I felt as if I'd known him all my life' or 'I was totally at home with her from the start.' These expressions are very revealing. The lover speaking these words has indeed returned home – 'home' being the first home, the parental home. The parental relationship is our first model for marriage and, however counterbalanced by subsequent experiences, it will always remain a powerful influence.

Some people are, like Mary, attracted to a partner who reminds them of one of their parents because the relationship feels so curiously, so comfortably familiar. In Mary's case, the attraction had some very negative aspects. However, the happier and more secure your early home life, the stronger will be your internal model for loving intimacy and mutual respect within marriage, and the better your unconscious is likely to serve you in its selection of a mate for you. As a result, this fitting of unconscious patterns can sometimes be very positive, giving couples an instinctive passionate rapport with each other's feelings and needs, particularly if the relationship is also grounded in clearsighted respect and liking for each other. The psychoanalyst Ethel Spector Pearson, in her book *Love and Fateful Encounters*, has said that, through falling in love, the self is exposed to new risks and enlarged possibilities: 'Love seeks to undo many disappointments of early life. . .successful love both reinvokes the past and moves us out of it.'

When we choose partners who closely resemble the major figures of our childhood or echo some aspect of our families, we can create a second chance for ourselves – a chance to heal the emotional wounds of childhood through re-experiencing similar situations differently now, with the maturity of an adult rather than the helpless confusion of a child. In learning to live with our adult partners the right way, we have the opportunity to rewrite the scripts we have learned from our parents and, this time, write in a happy ending. And marriage, which in so many ways replicates those first family relationships, is ideally suited for such rewriting – a theme which will be further explored again later in this book.

All for love and the world well lost?

The tradition of romantic love is so central to our own culture and to our notions of a proper basis for married life that it is hard to imagine that things could be otherwise – and still work.

However, in the Indian subcontinent, for example, marriages are still generally arranged on the basis of many factors – caste, class or tribe, family connections, relative prosperity, his earning prospects, her childbearing potential – of which the partners' feelings towards each other are only one (though nowadays, in enlightened circles, often an important one). The partners themselves are generally content to defer to their parents' greater experience in the selection of a mate. Romantic excitement, unless reinforced by different and more rational reasons for the marriage, is considered by all as a poor base for a lifelong commitment.

And perhaps they may have a point. Shaheen Bilgrami, a schoolgirl from a professional family of Indian extraction, certainly thinks so:

> 'The idea of romantic love is a delusion. Unstructured and spontaneous, it displaces a person from the real world into a world of fancy. . .the illusory world is deceptive and going back to reality is painful. Romantic love is a frivolous excuse for love, put forward generally by those who are 'in love with love itself'. The step into such a relationship is a step away from firm moral laws such as truth and honesty.'
> [The Independent, 11 December 1988]

The stability of arranged matches, which puts the Western world's marriage breakup rate to shame, gives one pause for thought. And it is not unusual for enduring love to develop within these matches (thereby neatly reversing Western cultural patterns and expectations).

Autres temps, autres moeurs – when all is said and done, we live in the world in which we live. In Western society, the individual and his or her feelings, desires and needs are valued in a way that no other society has been able to value them before. This is one of our greatest achievements, and it is symbolized by the primacy we give to romantic love – in all its impetuous, individualistic, rebellious, arrogant glory.

Let us not deny that love has – and should have – a primary place in marriage. But as the divorce rate spirals ever higher to previously unthinkable levels – one couple in every three in the UK and one in every two in the US (the average length of a British marriage is now just under ten years, less in America) – leaving in its wake impoverishment, bitterness, loneliness and the suffering of children, is it not time to stop for a moment and take stock, *particularly* if you yourself are on the point of deciding to marry?

> *'We won't end up in the divorce courts. It's something that happens to other people. We're sure of what we're doing.'*

On the positive side, you are probably right – you won't get divorced. (The good news! Two out of three marriages in the UK do not end in divorce!) There is, furthermore, a great deal that a couple can do to improve their chances of creating a long and happy life together.

'Create' is the key word here. There is no such thing as a marriage considered separately from the people who inhabit it. Together, a man and a woman *create* their marriage. They do this over months and over years, do it from the second they first set eyes on each other, through its daily routines, its pleasures and pains and its capacity to fulfil their separate needs and desires. And they create it together. Divorces, too, are created, also over a period of years – they are not like road accidents, when hapless victims who are crossing the wrong street at the wrong time are simply knocked over.

The human capacity to create is very powerful. However, the creation of a relationship on an entirely conscious, planned level can be dull and sterile, while the totally unconscious creation of a relationship may be anarchic, governed by childhood emotional patterns and, as we saw in the case of Mark and Mary, damaging to the best interests of the person as a whole. The best creative work in relationships comes when there is some kind of positive dynamic connection between the unconscious and the conscious. When you say 'I will' in the marriage vows, you are consciously setting in motion your desires, hidden and apparent, *willing* yourself to bring all your talents to the fore in making your marriage work.

When the couples with whom we opened this chapter say that they are marrying because they are in love, they may mean that they are blinded and infatuated by passion, and in this case, only luck and a great deal of subsequent hard work may stop them joining the divorce statistics. On the other hand, if they are genuinely ready to give themselves in marriage, they may speak the same words and actually be saying something else as well. Namely, that while they are in love with each other and while this is a deep and significant force which is enriching their lives, they have reached the decision to marry through consideration of some important questions. Our prevailing ideology of romantic love means that these issues are unlikely to be stated in so many words, yet they are often implicit in a marriage choice and likely to govern the ultimate success or failure of the marriage. The most important ones are posed below. How does your choice of partner measure up against them?

1. Have you each freely chosen to marry the other?

It seems obvious, except presumably to those who undertake them, that marriages that occur on the rebound, because of pregnancy, to escape from an unhappy home or from fear of being alone are unlikely to succeed if they have nothing else going for them. Into a similar category fall marriages undertaken from unexamined motives which defy all sensible criteria (*see above*).

2. Do you each feel ready to make a serious and abiding commitment?

Marriages are meant to last for ever, yet they come with no lifetime guarantee. (If they did, the life assurance company who offered it would have gone into liquidation years ago!) Most people who contract marriages want and expect them to last for ever, yet who can actually imagine 'for ever', any more than it is possible to imagine infinity? Not so very long ago, shorter life expectancy (especially for childbearing women) meant that the average marriage might only last 10 years or, with luck, 20. Nowadays a couple marrying in their 20s may be looking forward to another 60 years of life. *Sixty years together?* The imagination goes numb.

Nobody can foretell the future. This is the very reason why commitment, and lifelong commitment in particular, is so powerful and so risky. The marriage vows are very specific: they are for life. When you exchange your vows, you are each, in effect, saying that 'No matter what life throws at me, I will. . .' The ability to make binding commitments often increases with maturity as a person becomes more certain of his or her own identity and less swayed by external events – hence the poor prognosis for teenage weddings (in fact, the proportion of women marrying under the age of 20 dropped from 27 per cent in 1971 to 10 per cent in 1986).

Trying to plan the future is made tougher by knowing that it is not only for your own personal benefit that you will be trying to create a marriage that will endure. Most people who marry have children and, in doing so, become dependent on each other in a very real way. Children thrive in a stable, secure, loving environment, and the breakdown of a marriage may affect them badly.

This person you are planning to marry may well change – in 10 or 20 years' time, s/he might not be the person you chose to marry. Women, in particular, may change dramatically after marriage, perhaps in their 30s or 40s starting to flourish at a time when their husbands may want to settle for a quiet life, putting all their energy and creativity into their careers. A wife of over 17 years put it this way: 'I've really come to respect my husband, despite the difficulties we've been through, mostly because he's adapted so well. The person he married was quite different from me as I am now.'

So many of the reasons which drove our grandparents to marry – the moral sanctions and the financial need – have now disappeared. Today, cohabitation has little, if any, stigma. Marriage – procreative, faithful and, above all, permanent – is a very exact and rigorous contract to enter into. Thoughtful doubt indicates a sense of reality, not indecisiveness. If your doubts are great, a period of waiting, or the negotiation of a different, private contract between the two of you, may be the best choice, and you may be wise to reconsider or at least postpone having children for the time being. Marriage is not right for everybody. Why not hold on until you are quite sure that it – with this person – is really right for you?

3. Are you and your partner friends as well as lovers?

Or, to put it more prosaically, are you compatible? Sometimes compatibility means similarities – of taste, of emotional response or a sense of humour. Sometimes it is a question of complementing each other, as when one partner sees in the other qualities of steadiness of purpose perhaps or a generous idealism that he or she admires and would like to incorporate into his or her own life. (But beware: we have already considered how an unconscious fit of hidden needs can unleash strong feelings which can rock the psyche for good or ill.)

In friendship, flexibility and a degree of mutuality are important. The wife of a Hollywood film star once said: 'George and I are so compatible. We both love George.' This is the kind of compatibility that most wives now feel they can do without. Real friends in marriage are not the kind of people who see it as a heaven-sent opportunity to exploit and selfishly manipulate each other. Rather, they have the best interests of their partners at heart, encouraging and supporting each other's development and fulfilment. And they enjoy each other's company. They have a good time together.

4. Have you been able to establish genuine communication on important issues, and are you confident of your ability to maintain it?

When you and your partner start to talk about getting married, you have put yourselves on the line. You feel vulnerable. You may be afraid that if you reveal yourself, your needs, hopes and fears too unguardedly, your partner may be disappointed. Alternatively, you may wonder if he or she will really come up to *your* expectations.

To gain, you must be prepared to take risks. As a couple, you are starting to work out the entire framework of your marriage and you now have the opportunity to make sure that it is based on openness, responsibility and trust rather than on their gruesome opposites.

Sometimes people shudder at the word *communication*. But communication does not mean becoming judgemental and critical. Too often, it is the nice things that we forget to say to our nearest and dearest – one way or another, the nastiest ones have a habit of wriggling their way out.

Around the time they decide to marry, couples have an enormous amount of good will and intend to make their relationships work. Open communication at this point may serve to illuminate and even resolve an issue which, left unresolved, might become a severe sticking point when the marriage is more advanced and each more set in his or her own ways.

'What is the secret of a successful marriage?' we asked a marriage guidance counsellor of 30 years' experience.

'Communication,' she replied, 'communication, flexibility and the ability to express emotion.'

5. Have you given sensible consideration to the practical consequences of sharing a life together?

The transition from being a private, emotionally involved couple to being a couple contemplating marriage is a great one. Perhaps for the first time, financial, legal and practical considerations loom large between you. As well as making your plans for the wedding and, if you are not yet living together, for setting up home, you will be well advised to sit down together and think about married life later on. (The chart on pp. 14 – 19 will give you some idea of how the law will treat you differently.)

Most business relationships do not begin in a flurry of white lace and orange blossom. Nevertheless, a business relationship is what you are now contemplating. Your business, like any other, will involve the purchase and maintenance of considerable capital assets (particularly if you plan to be homeowners), the creation and allocation of income, the deployment of labour in keeping the enterprise both profitable and well run, and the supervision and management of junior members (also called children). To ensure that the family business will keep running smoothly in the future, now is the time to ask yourselves some questions:

- Do you have similar ideas about what would be a satisfactory standard of living?
- Will you pool all your resources or should the one who is earning most have most say in spending?
- Do you believe a wife should always support her husband's career moves, or only if they do not conflict with her own?
- Do you believe that a husband should always support his wife's career moves, or only if they do not conflict with his own?
- What kind of balance do you want to strike between spending your free time together and maintaining separate interests?
- Who is going to take on the all-consuming task of looking after your children once they arrive?

Perhaps you both have vague expectations that all these matters will work themselves out if they are left alone. They will, indeed – but unless you pay them close attention at this point, the way they work out may well not be as you wanted or intended. You may both have quite clear and certain ideas about the future – but unless you have talked through them in detail, how can you be sure that your ideas coincide? (One way of finding out is to draw up a marital contract. See pages 89–95 for details.) A famous *New Yorker* cartoon shows a couple kneeling at the altar. Each has a separate thought bubble depicting him or herself lolling blissfully in bed in the morning with the other partner smilingly bringing them breakfast. It is likely that this couple came down to earth with a bump before their marriage had even a chance of success!

Living together as a couple before you get married has much to recommend it even if, for religious or other reasons, you choose not to have sex together. It is a time when romantic passion can be tested against domestic mundanity – dirty socks and the weekly haul to and from the supermarket – and also against your mutual adaptability and respect for each other, qualities which will be required in good measure to sustain your marriage through the years to come. There is no statistical evidence to show that couples who cohabit first are less likely to suffer marriage breakdown as and when they do get married. Indeed, there is a slight bias in the opposite direction – according to the psychologists Michael Argyle and Monika Henderson, one study suggests that the breakup rate might be 36 per cent as opposed to 26 per cent for non-cohabitees. However, as they acknowledge, this may be less a reflection on the value of cohabitation as such than on the kind of people who are likely to cohabit – they seem to be less traditionally minded and to give marriage itself a less central place in their lives. It should also be said that our interviewees who had cohabited prior to marriage were all firmly convinced of the value of having done so. They felt that, in the transition period before the marriage proper, it provided valuable opportunities for exploring and testing out the relationship to its enduring benefit.

The choice to love, if it be a choice, may have one foot planted firmly in the deep and shifting sands of the unconscious. But it is no less love if the other foot is placed on the sane, firm ground of mutual respect and understanding and foresight. Love is an emotion. But love is also a decision.

Married vs unmarried

Comparing how the law treats married people and people who choose to remain unmarried can be an interesting exercise. Sometimes the laws are different when you might expect them to be the same; other times, the converse applies. Set out below is a chart offering such a comparison. The law in some areas is complex and we only have the space to provide a summary. In addition, although the information that follows was correct at the time of going to press, the law is undergoing fundamental and revolutionary change. Accordingly, you should check with a solicitor or Citizens' Advice Bureau for guidance on any specific issues. Finally, here, as elsewhere in the book, the law applies only to England and Wales; it may differ in Scotland and Northern Ireland.

Married

STATISTICS
In 1987 in the UK there were 351,781 marriages and 151,007 divorces.

NAME (*see* pp. 96–100)
On marriage, a wife chooses whether or not to take her husband's surname (most do). She can automatically do this, but there is no law compelling her.

BEGINNING OF RELATIONSHIP
Partners must marry according to the strict requirements of the law (*see* pp.49–52).

ENDING OF RELATIONSHIP
To end the relationship, the couple must go through divorce and obtain a decree absolute. There is only one ground for divorce: the 'irretrievable breakdown' of marriage. This has to be proven by one of five 'facts' – broadly, adultery, unreasonable behaviour, 2 years' desertion, 2 years' separation with both partners consenting to the divorce, 5 years' without the consent of both.

No divorce is allowed in the first year of marriage.
Note: Recommendations have been made to change the basis of divorce: watch out for changes.

Unmarried

About 3% of all women in Britain are estimated to be cohabiting: 8% of all single females; 18% of single females in their late 20s; and 20% of divorced women. Such evidence as exists about cohabitation breakdown suggests that the overall permanence of cohabitation is rather low, especially among students.

The woman can use her partner's surname: for many purposes, proof (e.g. a deed) may be required. It can be socially embarrassing if surnames differ.

The beginning of cohabitation may not be clearly defined. There is no legal recognition of a 'common law marriage' (unlike Scotland, where couples can be viewed legally as being 'married by custom and repute').

No formal ending is necessary. (Some couples have experienced this lack of ritual to be a loss.)

SEX WITHIN RELATIONSHIP

Husband and wife have a reciprocal 'duty' to have sex with one another. Celibacy within marriage can form the basis of a divorce petition.

No 'duty' on cohabitees to sleep with one another.

Contraception: some doctors and clinics may require the husband's consent before undertaking permanent sterilization or carrying out an abortion.

No obligation on the man to take any decisions about contraception, abortion or sterilization.

In the past, it was a legal impossibility for a husband to rape his wife. A recent Scottish case admitted the possibility of 'marital rape', but only if the spouses had separated; however, it is still highly unlikely that charges would be laid against the husband.

Man can be charged with the rape of a woman he is living with.

VIOLENCE

A husband or wife (and/or children) can be legally protected by court injunction from being molested or battered by a violent spouse.

A cohabitee has also the right to obtain a court injunction preventing violence from the other partner.

MAINTENANCE

During marriage, a husband has a duty to maintain (provide for) his wife. On separation or divorce, a wife can claim maintenance from her husband (and him from her).

There is no duty on cohabitees to maintain one another. However, parents are legally bound to maintain their children, and to this end, affiliation proceedings (to establish fatherhood) can be brought.

CHILDREN

A child born to parents who are married, or who later marry during the child's minority, is 'legitimate'.

A child born to parents who are living together is, in law, 'illegitimate'.

Note: The Family Law Reform Act 1987 has sought to standardize the treatment of 'legitimate' and 'illegitimate' children.

Either parent can register the child's birth. The husband is presumed to be the child's father in the absence of proof to the contrary.

Only the mother or the parents jointly can register the child's birth. There is no assumption that the man is the father of the child.

Both married parents have a shared duty to care for and support (maintain) their children, whether married or divorced.

The mother has the sole responsibility to care for the child, unless a custody order is made.

Custody, etc.
On divorce, *before the Children Act 1989* comes into force (late 1991), 'custody' (i.e. the parental rights and responsibilities towards children) of the children must be determined: this can be shared ('joint') or vested in one parent ('sole'). The child's primary carer will usually have an order for 'care and control'. 'Access' will usually be awarded to the other parent.

After the Children Act, parents, whether married or divorced, both have 'parental responsibility' towards their children, which can never change. If necessary, orders for 'residence' or 'contact', etc. can be made.

After the Children Act becomes effective, 'parental responsibility' will initially be the mother's alone, unless she and the father complete a special form and send this to the court. 'Residence' and 'contact', etc. orders will only be made if required.

Adoption
Married couples can adopt children as long as certain criteria (age, financial status, etc.) are fulfilled.

Most adoption authorities require applicants to be married (unless there are unusual circumstances e.g. 'hard to place' children).

Parent *caring* for minor child can claim Child Benefit.

Child Benefit
Every child's parent, no matter whether married or otherwise, is entitled to claim Child Benefit during the child's dependent minority (one claim per child.)

Single-Parent Allowance
This represents the difference between a (one claim per child.) single person's tax-free allowance and what was (until April 1990) the married man's allowance. It cannot be claimed by married parents while they live together. If they divorce, the primary carer will be able to claim.

Cohabitees can claim single parent allowance: since April 1988, the allowance is restricted to one per family.

Tax allowances for children
A married (or divorced) parent cannot claim tax relief for supporting his/her children.

Cohabitees cannot claim tax relief for child maintenance. A single parent (not cohabiting) can get a

After separation, some tax relief is available on maintenance payments (if made to an ex-spouse for the benefit of the children).

THE HOME

Both spouses have the right to remain in the matrimonial home while the marriage continues.

Privately owned home

Other things being equal, no problem in obtaining a mortgage in joint names.

Mortgage interest relief is limited to £30,000 on any one property.

Married couples can only claim one principal private residence exemption from Capital Gains Tax (CGT).

Whether or not the matrimonial home is in joint names, a wife has the right to claim a share of its value (as has the husband) either under the Married Women's Property Act 1882 (during the marriage) or in divorce proceedings if the marriage is over.

The building society must accept repayments from a spouse.

Rented home

No problems in renting a flat or house together, nor in obtaining a joint tenancy from a local authority.

On death, the surviving spouse of a statutory or protected tenant or secure council tenant can take over the tenancy.

tax allowance for looking after a dependant.

Unless there is contrary agreement, a cohabitee has no automatic right to stay in a home owned by the other, even if that has been the family home, unless s/he can establish a 'beneficial ownership' (see a solicitor).

In the past, some building societies and banks had restrictions on mortgages to cohabitees. You may still find your personal circumstances being checked more thoroughly.

After August 1988, same limitation as for married couples, but cohabitees can, in theory, choose two separate places as their principal private residences and obtain mortgage interest relief of up to £30,000 on each.

Cohabiting couples can claim principal private residence CGT exemption on two properties.

On splitting up, a 'non-owning' partner has far fewer rights to claim a share of the value of the home: usually, actual contributions must have been made to the purchase of the property, for structural improvements or to mortgage repayments (of the capital).

There is no requirement for building societies to accept repayments from a non-owning partner.

A few landlords do not like to rent property to unmarried couples.

Some local authorities prefer not to grant tenancies to unmarrieds. A cohabitee may be able to get a protected tenancy transferred to his/her name if the couple were living together as a family for several

years. However, only if a tenancy
is in joint names will there be real
security.

ASSETS

Property purchased from joint
accounts or bought together will
be owned jointly and equally. A
wedding gift is viewed as being
'owned' by the spouse whose
family or friends purchased it.
An engagement ring belongs to
the engaged woman, unless her
prospective husband says anything
to the contrary when he gives her
the ring!

Unless there is any contrary
intention, property bought from
joint accounts will be joint assets.
Not so for other assets: these will
usually belong to whichever partner
paid for them.

Any housekeeping allowance savings
belong equally to wife and husband.

Any housekeeping savings belong to
the partner paying the allowance.

DEBTS

A husband and wife are not liable
automatically for each other's debts,
unless these arose as house/flat
outgoings. In this case, a husband
about to be divorced is normally
liable for those incurred in his name
until the decree absolute.

Cohabitees are not liable for each
other's sole debts.

TAX

As of April 1990, for the first time
ever, married women are not
discriminated against in their tax
affairs. Each spouse is responsible
separately for their own tax affairs;
each is taxed separately; no longer
will the Inland Revenue only deal
direct with the husband alone.

Cohabitees are taxed separately.
Each is responsible for his or
her own tax affairs.

Instead of the husband automatically receiving a married man's
allowance, a married couple are
together entitled to a married
couple's extra tax-free allowance.
This will usually be set against the
husband's income. Each is entitled
to the equivalent of a single person's
tax-free allowance.

Each cohabitee is entitled to a single
person's tax-free allowance in his or
her own right.

Husbands and wives are not liable
to Capital Gains Tax (CGT) on gifts
made to each other.

There is no exemption for cohabitees
against CGT on gifts to each other.

INSURANCE

A husband and wife can each insure
each other's lives.

People living together can only
insure the other's life if they have a

financial interest in the other – e.g. if they are business partners.

PENSIONS
A wife can be entitled to a state pension by reason of her spouse's National Insurance contributions.

Each cohabitee's entitlement to a state pension depends on his or her own contributions.

Occupational pension schemes give benefits to a surviving spouse. A widow will continue to receive a pension.

An increasing (but still limited) number of schemes will allow cohabitees to receive benefits. A pension does not go to the surviving partner.

BENEFITS
A wife cannot claim Income Support in her own right; her husband has to claim on the couple's behalf.

Generally, the benefits payable to a married couple reflect the maxim that two can live more cheaply than one; together they will receive less than two separate individuals.

Cohabitees living together cannot each claim a single person's amount of benefit.

SEX DISCRIMINATION
The Sex Discrimination Acts make it illegal for a husband or wife to be discriminated against by the fact of their marriage.

There is no legal protection from discrimination against people who are living together.

ON DEATH
If a husband or wife dies without leaving a will, the surviving spouse receives an amount from the estate under the rules relating to intestacy (see p 126 ff).

There is no entitlement for a surviving cohabitee under the laws of intestacy.

If a will has been made, but leaves nothing for the surviving spouse, that spouse can make a claim under the Inheritance (Provision for Family and Dependants) Act 1975 against the estate.

If a will fails to make any provision for the surviving cohabitee, s/he can only claim if s/he has been supported by the deceased. Such a claim would be made under the same 1975 Act.

A wife can get widow's benefits on her husband's death.

A surviving female cohabitee is not able to claim widow's benefits.

A spouse can sue the person responsible for the deceased spouse's death under the Fatal Accidents Act.

There is no right for a cohabitee to sue under the Fatal Accidents Act.

2

Will you marry me? Formal engagements and other arrangements

I 'D been away by myself in Scotland for a week. When I came back, Richard was rather distant. Then he went out one night and came back very late – a bit drunk – with a bunch of red roses. He got down before me on both knees and said: "Will you marry me?. . .It's the thing I've wanted most in my whole life." I remember thinking – Oh God, this is it, then! It was so important, I didn't want to spoil it. I said, yes, of course I would. And then he produced champagne.

I think it was important to both of us that he took the initiative: I felt that unless *he* asked *me*, there would be less commitment on his part. Richard told me later that he'd needed to have a few drinks. He knew inside that I'd say yes – but a part of him had still been afraid I wouldn't.

We decided we couldn't tell anyone until we'd told my parents. I thought my father might be upset if Richard didn't do it properly and ask his permission. In the end, we decided we'd tell him first and ask for his blessing.

We arranged a meeting of both families at a local winebar. I shepherded everyone else in and Richard asked my father if he could have a word. They set off together in the direction of the local cricket pitch, through the pouring rain. My father apparently started talking about different things. . .he didn't seem to think it at all odd that Richard would want to walk round and round a cricket pitch in the pouring rain, listening to him. Eventually Richard managed to tell him. He was delighted and insisted on rushing straight back and breaking the news to everyone else.

The above is Helen's account of her engagement. Jane's was rather less formal.

We'd been living together for about six months and had just bought a place together. We had both been becoming certain that we wanted to spend our lives together and have a family. . .I've really only the vaguest recollection of deciding to get married. It was gradual and very mutual I liked that.

Once we'd decided to go ahead, though, it was quite a big thing to tell the parents. Rick said he'd do it. And he did have this notion (which I must say I found slightly antediluvian) that he needed to speak to my father first. Anyway, he phoned my parents, who live in the North, and spoke to him, and it was all fine.

Today, formal engagements have rather gone out of style, although the tradition of a formal betrothal ceremony, perhaps involving an exchange of rings and a religious blessing, sometimes the signing of a contract between the couple's respective families, is still important in many cultures where the attitudes of religion and society to betrothed couples having sexual relations or even living together may be much relaxed.

Indeed, it was once customary in some peasant societies (in which the production of children was the whole point of the marriage and crucial to the future well-being or even survival of the extended family itself) that a couple proposing to marry should be formally betrothed; then they would live together in a sexual relationship until a child was conceived, whereupon they would marry. This pragmatic custom meant that, should no conception take place, the couple's relationship could be dissolved with a minimum of fuss and the two could each try their luck elsewhere. (Or at least the man could – in practice, the woman would probably have to shoulder the entire stigma of failing to conceive as well as now being, so to speak, used goods.)

Among the propertied classes, betrothal was naturally considered a contract for the settlement of assets. The Church of England abolished its own form of betrothal ceremony some while ago, yet until comparatively recently, the law permitted the jilted to claim damages from their faithless partners in an action for breach of contractual promise. The aggrieved party would invariably be a woman, reflecting the idea that, in the breaking off of the engagement she had lost her meal ticket for life, not to mention her spotless reputation – a loss supposedly quantifiable in financial terms. Numerous cases are mentioned in old legal textbooks, raising to mind less the maxim 'Hell hath no fury greater than a woman scorned' than the pitiable sadness of spurned lovers anxious to prove themselves morally in the right.

Such times are, happily, long gone. Today, what matters most for a modern couple is to find some way for themselves to mark off a trial period – whether by way of a formal engagement or simply by living together 'as man and wife' for a certain time – during which the decision to marry will usually be made at some point. *Social Trends* reported that, in 1984, 18 per cent of British couples lived together before marriage, and by 1988 that had increased dramatically to one in two. Among the couples we spoke to, nearly all had lived together before their wedding and the deciding factor in getting married was often the wish to conceive a child, sometimes even an actual pregnancy. The Family Planning Information Service say that the cohabitation trend is still commonest among younger, better-off and better-educated couples, who tend to be the trendsetters in social habits. 'In Britain as yet,' they conclude, 'cohabitation seems to be more a prelude than a real alternative to marriage.'

Having taken the plunge and decided to get married, is there any value in actually declaring a transition period *within* the transition period of living together as a couple and going for all the trappings of a formal engagement?

If the thought of doing it all by the book appeals to you, the following are the main items you will need to consider.

Formal engagements

Making the announcement

Every day the newspapers carry anouncements in their 'Court and Social' sections about forthcoming marriages, the wording of which has changed little across the centuries:

Forthcoming Marriage

Mr R. Montague and Miss J. Capulet
The engagement is announced between Romeo, eldest son
of Lord and Lady Montague of Verona, Italy, and Juliet,
daughter of Lord and Lady Capulet also of Verona, Italy.

The wording of the announcement follows strict protocol, which can be gleaned from the pages of any wedding etiquette book, and can be duly adapted to cover every conceivable variation on the status of the newly engaged couple and their respective families. An engagement announcement, whether by post or newspaper insert or both, serves the purpose of enlightening those farflung relatives and family friends who might have no other way of finding out. It contributes towards providing a sense of social definition to that pre-wedding stage which can otherwise feel so odd and uncertain.

Approaching the bride's father

Such customs as this generally have less significance in our relatively informal era. Few potential bridegrooms are likely ever to have to face the gruelling inquisition of the unfortunate Jack Worthing in Oscar Wilde's *The Importance of Being Earnest*, who is forced to reveal in the course of his interview with his fiancée's mother that, as a baby, he was discovered abandoned in a handbag at the cloakroom in Victoria Station:

> GWENDOLEN: *I am engaged to Mr Worthing, Mamma.*
> LADY BRACKNELL: *Pardon me, you are not engaged to anyone. When you do become engaged to someone I, or your father, should his health permit him, will inform you of the fact. An engagement should come on a young girl as a surprise, pleasant or unpleasant as the case may be. It is hardly a matter that she could be allowed to arrange for herself. . . You can hardly imagine that I and Lord Bracknell would dream of allowing our only daughter – a girl brought up with the utmost care – to marry into a cloakroom and form an alliance with a parcel. Good morning, Mr Worthing!*

Today, the interview with your fiancée's father, if one does take place, is more likely to resemble a request for his blessing than an interrogation as to your provenance and your prospects. In any case, the latter is a throwback to earlier notions of a father having absolute control over the disposal of his unmarried daughter's money, until such time as the prospective husband might take the job over. But either way, an approach by the groom-to-be to his prospective father-in-law is a diplomatic move which may well please the latter and get the relationship off to a good start.

The engagement celebration

Sometimes the engagement party may itself be the moment when the couple 'get engaged' (presumably having consulted each other previously) and there may be a cake and champagne, even speeches. More usually today, though, an engagement party will not be regulated by the protocol and the inevitable expense involved in a formal wedding 'do'; you are free to have what you want, perhaps inviting friends with whom you wish to celebrate your wedding but for whom there will not be room on the day itself if the wedding is to be primarily a family affair.

In Greek Orthodox Cyprus, however, the betrothal ceremony is given almost as much weight as the wedding itself. We spoke to one London-based beauty counsellor, who has Greek-Cypriot origins:

> '*My husband's and my families both come from the same very small area in Cyprus, although we met at a party in London. After he proposed to me, we made preparations for the betrothal ceremony in Cyprus in January, just after New Year. The ceremony was beautiful – it felt as if we were getting a blessing for our relationship while we made ready*

for the later wedding. I felt really in touch with the whole of my family, too – it felt like a coming together.'

The engagement ring

An engagement ring is traditionally made of diamonds representing, amusingly enough, innocence. It is worn on the same finger as the wedding ring, even after marriage.

Once an engagement ring is placed on a fiancée's finger, the ring in future will usually belong to her, even if the wedding is subsequently called off. The only way to avoid this, for all you men wishing to preserve your assets, is to make it clear at the moment of giving that your gift is conditional. Thus, your proposal will have to run along the lines of: 'Darling, will you marry me? Here is a token of my love (but I want it back if you don't go through with the wedding).' Not particularly spontaneous, nor romantic, but that is the way of the law.

3

Just the two of you

LEAVING aside now the minor characters and the relatives and others who will only have bit parts to play in the unfolding drama of your marriage, we now turn to the most important people of all; you and your future spouse.

After the initial flush and exhilaration of announcing that the wedding will take place, arrangements for that momentous occasion seem to take precedence and you and your changing relationship can start drifting into the background, overshadowed by it all. . . But wait! Whose wedding is it anyway? Let us turn the spotlight back on just the two of you.

The waiting time

The period between the announcement of your marriage and the wedding itself can be something of a no man's land. In a sense, it can only really be defined in terms of what it isn't: it is neither the single life that has gone before nor the married life that is about to start. As such, it can be a rather uncomfortable place in which to be. The impatient may long for it to come quickly to an end: the sooner it is all over, the better. For the more cautious and pessimistic among us, the drawing near of the wedding day may inspire feelings of dread and fear: better the day never arrive at all. Most people will find themselves see-sawing between these two extremes, one minute wanting this waiting time to end, the next wishing it never would.

Yet this time that the two of you have together now is a special one. Whether you have been living together for some time, living apart or are still at home with your parents, whether you go for all the trappings of a formal engagement or don't bother, this is still a time when, for better or for worse, the foundation stones of your marriage are being laid. And as such, it is not always as easy, or as cosy, as you might have expected it to be. . .

Why are we arguing so much?

In the final fraught months as the wedding advances, you may experience, from time to time, an apparent breakdown of communications and a breakout of hostilities between the two of you. This can come as rather a shock. Here you are, having decided to spend the rest of your lives together, the pressure is on, your wedding day approaches ever faster – surely (a voice in your ear tells you) you should be like the contented couple you thought you once were. After all, you're getting *married* to each other, aren't you? But despite this and all your best intentions to the contrary, all you sometimes seem able to do is grumble, bicker, snap or snarl at each other.

At this stage, you can feel pulled apart by a conflicting and contradictory set of emotions. You may feel that your negativity threatens your relationship but be too uncomfortable to admit it, even to your partner. Consequently, you may end up thinking that you must be unique in this way. Not so!

As one woman told us:

> *'I felt somehow it was shameful. I was finally marrying a man I was very much in love with, yet the actuality of it was that, for much of the time, we fought so much I couldn't stand him. He was, it seemed to me, being jealous about quite irrational and trivial incidents, yet denied he was jealous and claimed I was at fault. In my turn, I was becoming obsessive about details over the wedding at one point, then making superhuman efforts to improve my career the next. We seemed to fight every day, almost without fail, for eight weeks. I was getting ready to call the whole thing off, but instead decided to make one last-ditch attempt to "save" the relationship (I thought in very dramatic terms then) by arranging for us both to go off for the weekend to Cornwall. Even then it wasn't that much fun, but it took the heat out of the situation and gradually things started to get better.'*

And from another woman:

> *'In the past, it seemed we'd always been fairly easy about accepting each other the way we were. My memory of that autumn before we got married is of getting quite stuck in ghastly convoluted arguments that got nowhere. I think, in retrospect, I was trying to make Peter different, I suppose trying to use power over him to make him change in quite fundamental ways that I thought would suit me. Of course, he just dug his heels in and we got nowhere. It was an awful time. Then, after the dreadful deed was done and we were finally married, the same problems which had seemed so intractable before just lost their charge.'*

Why can it sometimes be so hard to be a couple together in the lead-up to the wedding?

The stress factor

Tense, nervous, headaches?

Many couples feel themselves drained of all energy as the wedding approaches – nothing like the media advertisements of the stereotypically happy couple. Sometimes this feeling may burst out into irritability or anger – and who more fitting to be the butt of your bad temper than your nearest and dearest intended? But before you start worrying about what deep-seated problems may be lurking in the undergrowth of your relationship, take a moment to step back and to put things into perspective. If you take a look at the stress chart printed on page 28, you may gain a few clues as to why this is happening (if it is happening) to you.

The stress chart shows how different life events ('social readjustments') produce different amounts of stress. Strangely, scientists have found that *all* and *any* changes affect levels of stress – not just the ones popularly perceived as 'bad' changes. On the chart, the death of a spouse is rated as the greatest stress-producing event at 100 units. Marriage, however, also clocks up 50 and that, combined with other likely changes occurring around the time of the wedding, causes the total number of stress units to mount alarmingly.

Let us take a couple, Fred and Julie, who got married (50 units) in the New Year just after Christmas (12). They spent their honeymoon skiing (13 for a holiday). They had had a number of arguments with Julie's parents when planning the wedding (29) – particularly about the number of guests – but by the time of the wedding, there was a reconciliation. As a result, Julie's and Fred's families had a number of smaller celebrations: 'It's *so* nice now all the family are back in touch' (15 for the change in number of family get-togethers). On the honeymoon, Julie broke an ankle (53 – yes, this did happen!).

When they returned from the slopes, Fred moved into Julie's flat (20 for a change of residence plus another 31 for the mortgage of £45,000) and also switched jobs as he'd moved down to London from Manchester (36). He also had to adjust – seriously now, before it had just been a joke – to Julie's eating habits as she's vegetarian (15), and on the honeymoon, he'd finally managed to give up smoking (hurray! but another 24). He found this hard to maintain once he was back home, and his restless tossing and turning at night made it difficult for Julie to sleep (16). To try and tire himself out so that he slept better, he took up swimming on a regular basis (19), Julie hobbling along to keep him company.

Now this couple had already stacked up a staggering 333 stress points just in the first few months of their marriage. Now if they decide to have a child, Julie gets pregnant (40) and then stays at home to look after the baby (26), their tally of stress units for the first year or so will be sent shooting off the graph to almost 400 – four times the amount of stress

Stress chart

Life event	Stress value
Death of spouse	100
Divorce	73
Marital separation	65
Prison term	63
Death of close family member	63
Personal injury or illness	53
Marriage	50
Fired from work	47
Marital reconciliation	45
Retirement	45
Change in health of family member	44
Pregnancy	40
Sex difficulties	39
Gain of new family member	39
Business readjustment	39
Change in financial state	38
Death of close friend	37
Change to different line of work	36
Change in number of arguments with spouse	35
Mortgage over £40,000 (estimate for UK now)	31
Foreclosure of mortgage or loan	30
Change in responsibilities at work	29
Son or daughter leaving home	29
Trouble with in-laws	29
Outstanding personal achievement	28
Wife begins or stops work	28
Begin or end school/college	26
Change in living conditions	25
Revision of personal habits	24
Trouble with boss	23
Change in work hours or conditions	20
Change in residence	20
Change in schools	20
Change in recreation	19
Change in church activities	19
Change in social activities	18
Mortgage or loan or less than £40,000 (estimate for UK now)	17
Change in sleeping habits	16
Change in number of family get-togethers	15
Change in eating habits	15
Holiday	13
Christmas	12
Minor violations of the law	11

This table is reproduced, with adjustments, from Thomas H. Holmes and Richard H. Rahe's social readjustment rating scale, *Journal of Psychosomatic Research*, Vol. 11 (Pergamon Press, 1967).

that, according to this method of measurement, a widow or widower suffers when losing a spouse.

This is not to say that all couples experience stress in the same way. We all react differently, and, indeed, we all need some stress in our lives to keep the adrenalin going and to keep working well. But do you still wonder why you were feeling so tired? You should congratulate yourselves on how well you are surviving so far!

The death of fantasy marriage

Another reason why the period of adjustment before the wedding may be so difficult is that you may be witnessing the death throes of your idealized picture of marriage. As children, many of us create a fantasy about our future marriage and our future partner. However hard it may be to recall it now, most children will play-act about what their future husband – or wife (men are not immune to this either) – will be like. Experience and age *may* temper idealization, but conversely, the longer you delay getting married, the more you may idealize your dream man or woman (otherwise, why didn't we marry our last partner?). Justifying to yourself that you are saving yourself for that perfect match, for Mr or Ms Right, the fantasy may become ever more divorced from reality and ever harder to fulfil in the real world:

> . . .*He will be tall and dark/blond, and will have an excellent sense of humour/will be moody with a sardonic expression. He will be in touch with my thoughts and feelings at a profound level. He will enjoy bluegrass/Fifties rock 'n' roll/classical music. We shall be always in harmony with each other: he will complement everything about me. He will be a romantic and gentle lover. . .*
> . . .*She will be petite/tall and willowy, loving and warm, with a great sense of humour and a true understanding of cricket/football/computers. She will be very beautiful so that other men will envy me. She will always cheer me up, be a good cook and will keep the house effortlessly tidy – home will always be welcoming. She will be fantastic in bed. . .*

How hard it is then, once we have chosen our partner, to compare fantasy with the usual imperfect (if lovable) mass of humanity before us. More likely than not, he or she will fall rather short of the wonderful image we have formed in our minds. The catalogue of faults seems never ending. For one thing, he doesn't change his socks often enough (and he always farts!). She is far too untidy, and do you detect a certain likeness to Ena Sharples now that she doesn't bother wearing her make-up all the time? Once the initial flush of love has worn off, we start to see our fiancés with clearer eyes – and let's face it, none of us is perfect.

Especially if we have grown up in a not very happy environment, we tend to develop a secret or not so secret ambition to create a new form of relationship, one which is completely different from that of our parents. We won't make the same mistakes as they did; our relationships will be fulfilling, loving and nurturing, not cramping, unhappy and repressive. Marriage does indeed offer a precious opportunity for a fresh start of one's own; yet as we have seen, we very often choose precisely those partners who most resemble our parents – perhaps in an unconscious attempt to heal our family relationships and make it all right this time. We may think that we have chosen our Mr or Ms Right according to logical precepts, but what do we find when we wake up? That our prize from the treasure trove is the spitting image of Daddy or Mummy or a combination of the two – precisely what we didn't want in the first place!

We become angry with our partners just because they don't conform to our secret hopes and dreams. Just because we seem to have been given the booby prize when we expected (at the very least) to come first, we hit out in frustration and impotent anger (fuelled from we know not what source). In turn (for they are going through the same process themselves), our partners feel outraged that we are not as perfect (nor as accepting of them) as *they* once hoped and expected. Consequently, the attacks fly back and forth.

A time of testing

William J. Lederer and Eugene Burdick's 1959 novel *The Ugly American* is set in a Far Eastern war zone. An American priest is looking for a native whom he can trust to be steadfast against the Communists, someone who is 'surely and beyond mistake a dependable man'. To this end, he puts his driver U Tien through a number of tests, all of which the man passes. The priest still does not feel absolutely certain of U Tien's loyalty, however, and so he finally does what he knows is a cruel thing. He goes one day to a bazaar and loudly, apparently carelessly, spreads it around that he is looking for an ammunition pouch with which to arm the driver.

As the priest expects, the Communists come that night to U Tien's room and beat him up, looking for the gun which they are sure he must have. The next day, U Tien reports for work bewildered and angry, saying to the priest, 'You have not been wise in what you have said, sir.' But despite the betrayal, he *has* returned. The priest is now sure he can trust the man: 'This is the end of a time of testing. Now we know one another.'

A couple who agree to marry each other are thereby agreeing to place an enormous amount of trust in each other. It can feel as if your life, or at least a large degree of your hopes of future happiness, lies in your partner's hands. You know your partner will stay with you when you are at your best. Can you trust him or her to stick by you when you are at your very, very worst? Unconsciously, your mind may resolve that there is only one way to find out.

A man who has now been happily married for some time looked back on the rather rocky period before his wedding day:

'In retrospect, I'm now very aware that when we're on the verge of making major decisions – getting married, moving house, conceiving a child – in the playing-around period before we commit, things tend to be stickier and that's when we fight. In marriage, you're so tied to each other. . .it can be easy to see what you're giving up, yet the path you will walk down together is still intangible. It's a real surrendering to the unknown. I think that's when we still sometimes feel we need to test each other out.'

The battle for supremacy

Remember what we were saying about this being the time to lay the cornerstones for your new relationship? Well, even if you haven't been conscious of it, the process has already begun, for one of the first things that has to get sorted out in any relationship is: who is the most powerful?

In our families, we knew how the dynamics worked – either Father or Mother had the upper hand (in comparatively few families do we find equality between the partners and a genuinely democratic power arrangement). But who will be the dominant one in this partnership? The gauntlet is thrown down, the battle is on. And you find yourselves ranged on totally opposing sides to each other as you begin the power struggle on which life itself may sometimes seem to depend.

Love has been defined as a refusal to see relationships in terms of power; yet sooner or later in almost every relationship comes the moment when you discover that your own and your partner's views about some issue are in stark contrast. Not only that, but you each are absolutely certain that your own view is right. Rather than make any effort to understand and to accept his or her point of view, or simply to agree to differ, you try to force your version of reality on your partner – who retaliates by doing the same to you.

It's more than a matter of getting your own way – be honest, what you are really after is the unqualified admission from your partner that your way is *right* and the *only way*. The battle for imaginative dominance within the relationship has begun. It can only be ended, or at least put in perspective, by that willingness not to live your relationship as if it were a power struggle; the willingness to be open to each other, to stay emotionally vulnerable, to love and to allow love to grow within the relationship.

Working it through together

Your struggles to become a couple, however painful they may seem, are a necessary part of the construction of a genuine relationship. To suppress hostility and anger, whether out of lack of courage or for the apparently best of reasons – 'I don't want to hurt her,' 'I'm trying to put the relationship before my own needs,' 'He just wouldn't understand' – is only to stockpile trouble for the future. It is important to fight those crucial battles in order to create mutually acceptable boundaries and guidelines for your lives together. The more cleanly and honestly you are both able to express yourselves and, even more crucially, to learn to understand each other's point of view while not surrendering your own true feelings, the more your confrontations are likely to move your relationships on.

Then you may start to become more aligned together and more contented with your lot and your choice of life mate. Contentment, pleasure in each other's company and satisfaction at the real achievements within the relationship breed a will to give generously of one's best to sustain it.

While the days before your wedding will almost certainly be a testing time, they can also be fulfilling, exciting and even surprisingly tranquil. Here are some matters to consider with a view to making the waiting time a little easier on both of you:

The need to make many joint decisions

This will inevitably assert itself in the weeks and months leading up to the wedding. Perhaps for the first time you will be buying a home together: where? for how much? what kind of place will you be looking for? You will also need to pool your financial arrangements, start making budgets and allocate priorities. Not least looms the wedding itself with all the decisions, both major and trivial, involved with it, not to mention having to cope with each other's families. Joint decisions will have to be reached.

It all adds up to a difficult time, especially if, as a couple, you have previously managed to run fairly separate lives under the time-honoured precept of live and let live. The question of how a couple copes with pressure has been the making and breaking of many a marriage. You have an opportunity to assess your strengths and weaknesses as a couple in learning to handle it yourselves – and to proceed from there.

Letting go of idealizations about the wedding

Wedding preparations are enormously demanding in themselves. Combined with your individual work schedules (which, of course, carry on regardless), arranging stag/hen nights, planning the honeymoon and making preparations for your own new home, you can feel completely overwhelmed and at sea. As plans for the wedding start to take hold, you may feel as if you are on a roller coaster that never seems to stop. Matters which seemed trivial from your lofty pre-wedding stance start to assume colossal importance – for instance, your once best friend has forgotten to reply to the wedding invitation and your world falls apart.

Remember, however, that you (and the combined force(s) of your mother(s) if appropriate) can only do your best. Let go of some of the endless details. Your wedding will be wonderful anyway – it does not have to be perfect. Trust that you do not have to exercise an iron grip on everything to make the day work; allow for certain imperfections and some things going wrong – little hiccups are almost bound to happen anyway, and will in any event only contribute to your happy memories of the day, once it is a thing of the past.

Above all, do not become obsessed with your wedding at the expense of your relationship, for this will give you a great sense of anticlimax once the day draws to a close, as it inevitably will. Remember that your wedding will last for a day. Your marriage, you hope, will last for a lifetime.

Creating space to be together. . .

It is midnight. Two weeks to go until your wedding and you have just fallen into a pleasant and (you feel) well-deserved night's sleep. The phone rings. Your mother (for it is she) wants to check over some final details of the seating plan. . .

Even if you yourselves want to distance yourselves from the morass of detail that goes towards organizing a wedding, others may be determined to involve you ever further even against your firmly expressed will, or to involve you in ever more social gatherings. Be firm. Only respond to invitations – or even answer the telephone – if you want to. The world will not come to an end if you don't. Your fast-approaching wedding will be taking up much of your emotional energy and that of your partner. You may find, if you do go out, that you end up resenting your hosts because they will be talking about other matters, once preliminary talk about your wedding has been politely negotiated. Even if the two of you don't want to talk any more about the wedding, you may well prefer to spend time with each other rather than have to think up small talk with other people.

Most important of all, you need time and space for each other at the moment.

. . .and apart

As well as being drawn increasingly to their partners, many brides and grooms discover that they want to spend time on their own as individuals, to start to accustom themselves to their new status as married people and to get in touch with their own feelings away from all the pressures of others' needs and expectations. And sometimes, this being a time when you sense how the focuses and primary allegiances of your life are shifting, you may want to spend time with old friends with whom you share a part of your past or present.

It is important to respect both your own and your partner's needs here. The need for time on your own or with others is not a betrayal of each other; on the contrary, the more you are able to combine the ability to be separate with the ability to be genuinely intimate with each other, the better it bodes for the future of your marriage.

And what about premarital counselling?

Apart from the obligatory hour or so with the vicar if you are planning a church wedding (*see* Chapter 5), your gut reaction may be that you can manage your relationship yourselves without any help, however well-meaning, from a complete stranger. But pause a moment.

Good premarital counselling will not tell you what you should do or what your marriage ought to be like. It usually takes the shape of several sessions in small groups, in which there are exercises and discussions to increase your understanding of each other, and especially of points of possible future conflict. Forewarned is forearmed. Maybe your disagreements, no matter how hard you try, tend to all go the same way, resulting perhaps in angry deadlock or sulky withdrawal by one or both of you. Or perhaps there is one special topic – perhaps money management, perhaps jealousy about past relationships – which acts as a red rag to a bull for one or both of you, making adult communication impossible on this matter alone. Either way, the very fact that the counsellor *is* a complete stranger may put him or her in a better position to advise you than others who may be more involved in your life and even have their own axe to grind.

Experienced counsellors stress the solvability of the vast majority of emotional conflicts, *as long as* they are caught at a time when the good will of both individuals to resolve tensions is still strong, before attitudes harden and despair sets in, perhaps some years into the marriage. For this reason, premarital counselling may be helpful even for the most idyllically happy couple. (*See* Appendix 2 for organizations where premarital counselling can be obtained.)

'The aim is always more and more communication between the couple,' says Margaret Grimer, a marriage counsellor with the Catholic Marriage Advisory Council. At its best, premarital counselling can help a couple not to fear disagreement but to see it as a growth point, an opportunity for the limits and constricts which exist within even the best relationship to be pushed out and for the potential which exists within your relationship to fulfil more completely the needs and desires which you both have.

4

Whose wedding is it anyway? Coping with the family

*Therefore shall a man leave his father and his mother and shall
cleave unto his wife: and they shall be one flesh.*

Genesis 1:24

S O you have decided to get married. It was a decision made within
the privacy of your intimate relationship. Shyly, you make the
appropriate announcement to your families. Their reactions make you
feel pleased, proud and alarmed in approximately equal measures (after
all, you *had* been living together for two years – you didn't think it would
be such a big deal). You watch from the sidelines in mounting panic as the
intimate celebration you had envisaged evolves at the hands of your loving
parents into a limousine-champagne-marquee splurge for 300 guests (*their*
300 guests). . .

Of course, not every couple marrying today experiences the same
overboard reaction from their nearest and dearest. Some don't have
families; some, with iron will, keep their families out of the whole thing.
Some are just plain lucky. But it is not unusual for parents, even those
with good intentions, to cause real problems for their starry-eyed offspring,
casting a shadow by expressing disapproval or seemingly wanting to hog
the whole show themselves.

Parents' reservations can be obvious. One of Penny Mansfield and Jean
Collard's interviewees in their book *The Beginning of the Rest of your Life*
reported just that:

> '*At first when my mum and dad knew that we were getting very serious, they
> didn't like it. They had known that I had all these ideas about university
> . . .and somehow thought that Mick was stopping me from doing that, no
> matter how I explained it to my dad. And also I think he looked on me
> as his little girl and nobody else's and it was very hard. So we had a
> bit of a rough time. . .*'

Or their feelings can actually be disguised. Parental responses such as 'You could do better' or 'You're throwing your life away' or perhaps worst of all 'Well, we're not going to say anything, we don't want to interfere. . .' are upsetting, no matter how emotionally self-sufficient and independent from your mother and father you may feel yourself to be. The problems thrown up by over-enthusiastic, interfering parents may seem less demanding by comparison, but both types can create enormous tensions in the finely balanced and vulnerable lives of the couple waiting to marry.

Whatever your family's reaction, now may be the time when you realize that, love them or hate them, your family *does* matter to you. And your marriage will change your relationship with them at a profound level.

When we get married, men and women undergo a change of status and, with this, comes the need to break free from the parental family. Sometimes this separation is symbolic, formalizing a *fait accompli* many years old. But for those still living in the parental home up to the wedding day – and these comprise two-thirds of the men and three-quarters of the women in the Mansfield and Collard survey – the separation is an actual, very immediate one. In all cases, it is irrevocable: a wedding marks the moment of transition when the kids (even 39-year-olds!) finally grow up – the relationship between parent and dependent child becomes a relationship between adults, who also happen to be parent and son or parent and daughter.

Introducing a prospective son- or daughter-in-law, a comparative stranger, into the privacy of the original family can cause great anxiety on each side. Will he fit in with our ways? What has he told her about us? Will she like us? Will they like me? What will they think of my clothes/political views/work/social background? What if we don't get on?

And on top of all this, for the bride and her family especially, there are all the tensions connected with organizing the wedding itself. This chapter is concerned with these changes and their effects on the families involved.

Coping with the family

Almost every couple we spoke to whose parents were involved with their wedding experienced friction. There was the bride whose parents 'were generally very supportive. Mind you, I think that was because I gave way to them on everything. . .*everything* – except the cake. I really had my heart set on a round cake, and did I get it? Huh!' At the other extreme, we came across a dramatic example, where a couple who, unable to cope any longer with the ever-more-complicated and interfering plans of their (particularly the bride-to-be's) loving parents ('We're only doing it for you, dear'), packed their bags two weeks before the planned nuptial extravaganza, and crept off to a Register

Office ceremony with only two close friends in attendance as witnesses. Comments the wife:

> *'My parents were furious. I only hope one day that they'll understand. But I just couldn't stand the pressure any longer. My parents had arranged for the wedding just after my exam finals. I was so tired – it was all out of control – I felt as if I was going mad. We did still want to get married. But not their way: our way. So we ran away from the whole spectacle and only rang to tell my parents after we'd done it.'*

In these two stories and a million others, the people who were getting married are saying that it was *their* day – not their parents'. For the couple about to be married, it is an exciting but stressful time and they expect their parents to be there behind them, to offer support and help when support and help are needed and to keep out of the way when they are not. The fact that their parents do not seem sensitive to their offspring's requirements can be a cause of irritation or, at the other end of the scale, real bitterness and hurt. Why are they acting like this?

Understanding your parents' behaviour

In certain primitive tribes, the parents negotiate an appropriate marriage for their child. Once this has been finalized, there is a series of long and drawn-out rituals, involving the entire family on each side, which may last for months, even years. The new husband may pay a bride-wealth to his new parents-in-law, a symbolic compensation for the loss of their daughter. Or, like Jacob in the Old Testament, he may offer himself to work for them for a certain period of time.

Some wedding ceremonies culminate in the ritual of bride-capture, in which the 'kidnapping' of the new wife, as if by force, is enacted by the new husband and his family. This is accompanied by displays of wailing, gnashing of teeth and intense mourning from the bride's relatives.

So these parents are able to act out their ambivalent feelings about the wedding: their desire to prevent it, even as they are arranging it; their feelings of anger towards a man, a stranger, who is taking away, as if by right, the woman who has been at the protected centre of the family since she was born into it; and the sense of loss and separation that lies for them as parents at the heart of the joyous celebration of a new marriage.

The parents living in the primitive peasant societies which developed these rituals might wonder at our rather more perfunctory attitudes. Where, they might inquire, are 20th-century Western parents given the opportunity to express and come to terms with *their* feelings of loss? Where, indeed?

A ritual for separation

As a couple, you are right at the centre of the ritual of the wedding. You may be experiencing it primarily as a celebration of new beginnings, which indeed it is. In life, however, gain is usually counterbalanced by loss. The loss may in part be a sense of roads not taken ('What would I have done if I *hadn't* decided to get married now?'). Your wedding is also the clearest moment given to you to bid goodbye to the child you once were; to the time when your parents were the most important people in the world to you; and to the familiarity and security of the family home. You will never again return to it as a child. By marrying, you signify that you have replaced it with an adult home of your own creating.

These thoughts and the feelings they evoke may be in your minds as you approach the wedding day. For your family, who do not have the prospect of a new life ahead on which to focus their attention, the feelings of loss may be very much stronger. For them, the ritual of the wedding may have a special significance in enabling them to contain and manage these feelings and to let you go (whether you are man or woman), to 'give you away'.

Some religions – Judaism and Hinduism, for example – recognize this by allocating to all four of the parents a central role in the ceremony. Secular and Christian weddings do not. There is no formal role in the Register Office wedding for either the bride's or groom's parents. A Christian wedding acknowledges the significance of only one of the four: the father of the bride who, in a traditional wedding, walks down the aisle with his daughter, gives her away and subsequently leads the speeches at the reception. He is in an especially favoured position, and his role supports him in coming to terms with the change.

The mother of the bride, however, is offered no such dignifying ritual for easing the separation as she watches her husband walk down the aisle displaying their child on his arm for all to admire. She may have devoted far more of her energies to the preparations, and indeed far more of her life to bringing up the child who is now leaving for ever. No matter. For her, there is no public acknowledgement of her achievement, or of her loss. Instead, her inability to let go is mocked in a thousand mother-in-law jokes, while she is relegated to fussing on the sidelines about hats and cakes. Small wonder that, with all the emotional energy she is forced to contain, arguments over trivial issues have a tendency to blow up and dominate the whole proceedings.

The mother and father of the groom have even lesser roles to play. While bridegrooms' parents more and more frequently relieve the financial burden on their son and future daughter-in-law, there is no room to recognise their generosity – in this or other ways – by any greater role or higher profile at a traditional wedding. They are almost invisible. Yet the pain, particularly for the opposite-sex parent – the mother of the groom – may be particularly acute. The adage 'You're not losing a son but gaining a daughter' may sound coldly hollow to the mother when she knows he contacted her rarely enough even before he found this fascinating creature to marry. She fears she will be left out in the cold, relegated to the odd phone call and Christmas card.

Stress in the family

The stress chart on page 28 showed the relative stress levels which are attached to certain events in a person's life. We have already seen how the wedding creates particular stresses for the couple themselves: getting married scores 50 points out of a possible 100 – only 23 fewer than getting divorced. But on top of this, from the parents' viewpoint, a child leaving home tots up another 29 points. You will also be able to see that other events around the time of the wedding clock up more – a change in financial state (38) and a change in the number of family get-togethers (15), to name but a couple.

Therefore, both children and parents, from their different perspectives, face a stress-loaded time. The tug-of-war which so often develops over wedding preparations is really a symbol of the stress, both anxious and pleasurable, which *both* generations are undergoing.

Confronting the issues

Most of this book is about the issues which you as a couple facing marriage together are likely to encounter. Here are four issues which a child's marriage may lead their *parents* to confront:

1. An awareness of the passage of time and their own mortality
We rarely have the opportunity to consider how far we have moved on in our own lives. Great transition points – life events – are monumental markers to indicate to us how far we have travelled. As we encounter them, we have the chance, whether we like it or not, to look backwards and forwards on our lives like an observer.

For parents, a child's marriage is one of the last major life events which they will experience. One bride's father commented: 'I knew after this that the next thing to look forward to would be retirement, being put out to grass. And after that, well the big E. Other people were going on with their lives; mine seemed to be coming to an end.'

The difficulties are exacerbated by our particular cultural values. Once upon a time, old age was venerated, deferred to, honoured; but nowadays we have a youth culture, in which everyone wants to look young, old people are patronized and excluded from important aspects of life, and the facts of ageing and death are denied in a thousand ways. Few in their right mind can feel happy about getting old.

The parents of marrying children are usually in middle age (perhaps in their 40s or 50s). They may be feeling at the height of their powers, but this can only make the first inklings of mortality harder to deal with. It is a rare person who is not affected by the thought of how time has passed in their own life, and what the future may hold for them.

2. Making comparisons with the new couple

A sense of any lost opportunities in their own lives may, for many parents, be starkly brought into focus by their child's marriage. Couples attending the wedding of another in whatever capacity will often speak of how vividly the occasion brought back memories of their own wedding and the vows they exchanged. The almost tangible presence of these memories can give a special emotional resonance to the wedding in process, which is both moving and momentous.

Yet at the same time, even for the parents whose marriages have been so far happy and fulfilled, the contrast with the young couple, at the romantic beginning of *their* lives together, before any mistakes have been made, can be difficult to handle. Feelings of disappointment or envy may be aroused in parental breasts as they see their joyful children starting out on the adventure of marriage. For the single parent who has seen the promise of his or her marriage evaporate in divorce or death or struggled alone right from the start to raise a child, or for the couple who have stayed together but in an unhappy marriage, the contrast may be painful indeed.

Women are generally held to have more of their personal identity invested in the success of their own marriages. Thus for mothers, these feelings may be particularly strong. They may be expressed by coolness towards or even rejection of the bridal couple; alternatively, the mother may set herself up as a kind of rival to the bride, as one interviewee's experience showed:

> 'I decided to go against tradition and wore a pink dress on my wedding day. However, I was rather taken aback when my mother then decided to wear white – and quite a lacy sort of outfit. I wondered whether she was wanting to take over my role. My worries increased when she started behaving like a prima donna before the wedding. She even said afterwards that it had been the happiest day of her life!'

Such feelings may be difficult to cope with or even admit to oneself – what kind of a parent resents a child's own happiness or tries to compete on a child's wedding day? Yet, for many parents whose own marital experiences have proved less than fulfilling, the time of their child's wedding may provoke an unexpected attack of resentment, or a subliminal desire to re-create and better their own wedding day.

3. Accepting a child's sexuality

Nowadays, the vast majority of marrying couples have had a sexual relationship before their wedding, often for many years beforehand. That does not mean that most parents acknowledge this interesting fact.

Indeed, a great many prefer not to, even if it is, so to speak, shoved right under their noses. How awful is it to imagine your parents having sex? About as awful as it is to imagine your child doing the same.

In the prehistoric past, the male head of a tribe might claim all nubile females for himself by right, including even his own close female relatives. This led to fighting between the males of the tribe and also inbreeding – thus undermining the chances of the tribe's survival. As a result, the taboo against incest developed. A young female was required instead to make a new connection *outside* the tribe. This connection, dignified by ritual, was called marriage. We see a vestige of this taboo in the requirement in the Christian marriage ceremony for the father to participate in the marriage, waiving his rights, as it were, by handing his daughter over to the young pretender at the altar. Thus, marriage outside the family evolved from the general acceptance of the taboo against incest. . .and yet the desires forbidden by the taboo have not necessarily disappeared.

None the less, there is no getting away from the fact that weddings are all about sex – 'the joy of bodily union' as the Anglican Order of Service (of all things) puts it. So the child really has found a lover. Perhaps the lover is the spitting image of Mummy or Daddy; nevertheless the break has been made. The parent has no such rescuer and must struggle simultaneously with discomfort (the thought of their child doing 'it'), jealousy (at their child's choice of mate) and guilt (about having these feelings at all).

4. Sweet relief. . .and a little guilt?

Children are no longer, as they once were, economic assets. They are incredibly expensive – notably in terms of money – but also in terms of time, energy and parental anxiety. These drains on parental resources reach a crescendo in the preparations for a wedding. Yet at the same time, the end is at last in sight.

Thus, for many parents, sadness at the thought of the loss of the daughter/son may be tempered by relief and even some excitement at the thought of regaining their own lives again, particularly if the relationship between the parents is a fundamentally happy and supportive one. Advertisers and marketing people, the chroniclers of our time, are starting to recognize that such 'empty nesters' are relatively well off – in terms of both leisure time and buying power. Without the demands of their live-in children, they can rediscover the pleasures of comparative freedom and peace. Parents may secretly be planning to have a good time and live things up a little.

Can this be acknowledged? There may be considerable guilt at *wanting* to get rid of the child, so to speak. It is ironic that parents may overcompensate for these feelings by an excess of meddling, thus bringing down on their own heads the wrath of their offspring: 'They just can't bear to let me go!'

And the moral of all this. . .

. . .is that strong feelings which are not expressed tend to surface in silly, endless, repeated arguments about insignificant details which are made to stand for *real* communication.

- A mother engineers a dramatic row with her cousin's family on the eve of the wedding and demands they be barred from the ceremony. She is envious of the attention her daughter is getting and would like some herself. She does not think she will get any unless she forces the issue, and is secretly angry.
- A father dictates to his daughter the form of service, number of guests and choice of photographer. He is indirectly telling her that he wants the best for her, but in the heat of the moment, love gets fearfully mixed up with his need to control. Once she leaves his domain, will there be any love left for him, will there be respect? He does not know and is secretly afraid.
- A week before the wedding, an older unmarried sister refuses point blank to be the bridesmaid for her younger sister (which she had agreed to do with alacrity several months earlier). The arguments and conflicts thus provoked leave her vulnerable sibling upset and exhausted right up to eve of her wedding – at which point, the reluctant bridesmaid changes her mind and magnanimously agrees to fulfil her role. She does not want to have to play second fiddle and is secretly envious.
- A mother and father are locked in battle with the marrying couple about the number of friends of their own they wish to invite to the reception. They cannot see why the groom and bride are being so difficult. After all, they, the parents, are paying for the damned thing; it's *their* day as well! They argue and moan about their child having taken everything for granted from birth onwards, today being no exception. Privately or not so privately, they grumble about their offspring's selfishness and secretly resent having to pay for anything at all.

Anger. . .fear. . .envy. . .resentment. . .the stuff of which family get-togethers are made! Everybody can see both sides of a problem in which they are not personally involved – but when you're in the thick of it, objective perception seems to vanish out the window. The family feelings described above are neither unreasonable nor unfeeling; indeed, they can come out of an excess of caring, not a lack of it. They are perfectly natural. So are the feelings of the bride and groom who want the day to be an unclouded celebration of themselves, their mutual love and their resolution to spend the rest of their lives together.

One way or another, everyone has a great deal invested in making the wedding a successful and happy event, a final achievement of two sets of parents and a first for the newly fledged family. Beyond the ritual framework, the management of the wedding preparations and the wedding itself is up to you and, of course, your families. What will work for one family will not always work for another, but dealing with yours in as up-front a way as possible may help you avoid some common causes of friction and even turn this period round from something to be got through with gritted teeth into a valuable and fruitful experience.

The answer: communication

While you can't force anyone to bring their feelings into the open if they don't want to, what you can do is to withdraw, take a deep breath and, with a little good will, try to *imagine* what they may be feeling. Pretend for a while you are standing in that apparently horrible other's shoes – how do things appear from the other side of the fence?

The more in touch you are with your own feelings, the more comfortable you are likely to feel around your family. Sometimes what makes families so difficult to cope with is the fact that one member projects on to others those emotions or thoughts he cannot feel comfortable with in him or herself. Thus the daughter who becomes angry with her mother's endless fussing may be uneasy and anxious herself, wanting the wedding to be perfect and feeling she has to control every detail herself or it will all go wrong. These anxieties are projected on to her mother where they could be attacked. Once the daughter realizes what she is feeling and accepts that iron control of every detail is not, in fact, going to make the day more successful or happier (in fact, quite the reverse), she can relax and become more tolerant of her mother's nervous fussing. Her mother then magically becomes less anxious and fusses less.

However, blaming or criticizing someone is not the same as communicating a feeling! If the daughter above says, 'I can't stand your endless fussing! It's driving me up the wall!' this would have been truthful after a fashion. But she will still be attacking her mother rather than taking responsibility for her own feelings. In the circumstances, it would be more truthful to say: 'I'm feeling strung out and tense. I feel really anxious that everything should be sorted out properly and I'm afraid I'm pretty touchy as a result.' This is not a threatening or an attacking statement, and it is more likely to enable her mother to respond to her daughter's real needs rather than to retaliate.

Really, what it all boils down to is, first, minimizing opportunities for discord by intelligent management and, second, facilitating the creation of an atmosphere in which everyone's feelings can be expressed and accepted. This may not sound easy, but with commitment and due consideration, it is not too difficult. Remember that, during this period, you are laying down the framework of your future relationship with your parents as much as you are with your husband- or wife-to-be.

A wedding, among other things, represents public acceptance, approval and solemnization of the mature sexuality of the marrying man and woman and of their right to have sexual relations with each other which are private and at the same time supported and sustained by society at large. This makes it a momentous change in the parent/child relationship, which may be experienced by both sides as a great relief once the wedding itself has been successfully negotiated. For the first time since the stability of childhood was replaced by the turbulence of adolescence, both parents and son or daughter can find a new role within which to face each other, a new way of relating which feels comfortable and stable.

PART II

THE WEDDING

C LOSE your eyes for a moment and imagine a wedding. What image first comes to mind? Perhaps a variation of the following? The bride dressed in white, carrying a fragrant bouquet, radiantly shimmering under a floating veil. The groom (for he always seems to appear second) standing by her side, apprehensive (he still has his speech to make) yet proud. Best man and chief bridesmaid getting acquainted; littlest bridesmaid making a break for it but scooped up into the arms of her watchful mother. The bride's and groom's mothers fluttering around in feathers and silks, occasionally wiping a tear from the corners of their eyes, gossiping happily. Fathers standing close by, hands clasped behind backs, saying a lot less. A gaggle of guests decked out in the colours of the rainbow – old and new relatives and close friends – with a benevolently smiling vicar plumply presiding over all. The sun shines, a photographer endeavours to catch these moments for posterity. The prospect of the first reception drink beckons as welcome relief after the heat of the church and cars draw up to whisk the main players away towards that refreshment.

Is this the real picture or not?

The perhaps surprising fact is that this image does represent the most common experience of marriage in England and Wales. Although we have become a secular society and only 7 per cent of the population go to church regularly, the majority of couples (69 per cent overall) still choose to marry in church. Good news for the vicars: there are about 350,000 marriages every year. But is a religious or church wedding* going to be what you want?

Once you decide to get married, the whole experience can feel like being

*Throughout this book, 'church' will, where possible, be used as a generic term to encompass places of worship of all recognized religions and creeds, within which weddings may be solemnized according to the laws of this country. But although religious practices vary widely, in view of the fact that an Anglican wedding is the preferred choice of most of those who do marry in church in this country, when we have needed to be specific, we have usually written about Anglican practices.

on a runaway train, its speed getting faster and faster as the wedding
day approaches (for most couples, the pace becomes so quick that their
wedding passes in a blur). But for now, you probably have a bit of breathing
space – time to decide about creating your own individual style of wedding.

When it comes to deciding on your wedding arrangements, including
whether or not to marry in church, no one should dictate to you what they
think is right. What will be right for you is whatever *you* want. A wedding
is your once-in-a-lifetime (fingers crossed) opportunity to stage your own
show, so it's up to you to stage the show which will suit you best, bearing in
mind any limitations of cost and creed. Some people will have made their
minds up years ago and, at the age of two, set their hearts on a no-holds-
barred church wedding. Others may have equally deep-rooted feelings
about never marrying in church: being without religious convictions, they
think it would be hypocritical, and anyway are embarrassed by the display
of a religious ceremony. Yet others may be inhibited in their choice because
they are ineligible for the kind of religious service which they would like –
for example, if one of them is divorced or if the couple are from different
religious backgrounds.

We shall be looking in this section at the creation of your own style of
wedding, from the ceremony itself, on to the reception and the honeymoon.
When looking at the wedding, we shall be examining the technicalities
of getting married as well as contrasting what sorts of 'service' you may
expect to receive from churches and Register Offices respectively, as well as
considering the practical arrangements which go into making a successful
wedding. We shall also be looking at something completely different:
the do-it-yourself wedding, known as the 'ceremony of vows', a radical
departure from the traditional wedding format.

However, to start off, we shall be looking at the legal requirements of
getting married – after all, if you're going to do it, you might as well do it
right!

5

Legal requirements

Forms of marriage

IN England and Wales, a legal marriage can *only* take place by means of *either* (a) a civil ceremony in accordance with statutory requirements *or* (b) a ceremony performed in accordance with the rites of the Church of England or the rites of another recognized religious denomination.

Status of the parties

The bride and groom:
- must be, respectively, female and male.
- must both be over the age of 16. Between the ages of 16 and 18, consent to marry must first be obtained from the minor's parents (or guardian).
- must both be unmarried. If one partner is divorced, a decree absolute must be obtained in advance.
- must freely consent to the marriage. A marriage contracted under duress is not valid (no shotgun weddings!), and both parties must also be of sufficiently sound mind to understand the nature of a marriage contract.

Particular religious groups may have more stringent requirements, but under the general law, you may not marry your mother, adoptive mother, former adoptive mother, father, adoptive or former adoptive father, daughter, adoptive or former adoptive daughter, son, adoptive or former adoptive son, father's mother, father's father, mother's mother, mother's father, son's daughter, son's son, daughter's daughter, daughter's son, sister or adoptive sister, brother or adoptive brother, wife's mother, husband's father, wife's daughter, husband's son, father's wife, mother's husband, son's wife, daughter's husband, father's father's wife, father's mother's husband, mother's father's wife, mother's mother's husband,

wife's father's mother, husband's father's father, wife's mother's mother,
husband's mother's father, wife's son's daughter, husband's son's son,
wife's daughter's daughter, husband's daughter's son, son's son's wife,
son's daughter's husband, daughter's son's wife, daughter's daughter's
husband, father's sister, father's brother, mother's sister, mother's
brother, brother's daughter, brother's son, sister's daughter, sister's
son. (And try saying all that backwards after you've had a bit to
drink!)

Venue

At present, the only venues recognized by the law for the solemnization of
marriages are churches, Register Offices and places ordained by certain
religions which are so recognized within the law (usually specific places
of worship such as synagogues and mosques).

Currently, the only exception to this rule is a marriage permitted by
special licence (*see below*) to take place somewhere else, which will usually
only be granted under special circumstances. A government Green Paper
has recently proposed plans to widen the choice of venues on offer for
civil marriages. We will be looking at these briefly in the section below
on Register Office weddings.

An old law also states that the wedding must take place in a public, not
private, place: thus the doors of the church or any other venue cannot be
locked.

Times

Generally speaking, a marriage must take place between 8.00 am and
6.00 pm during the day. However, special exceptions are made for
Jewish and Quaker ceremonies and those contracted by special licence
or a licence issued by the Registrar General. (This rule on time and
the one relating to a public venue were evidently introduced in the 18th
century, in an endeavour to halt the increasing number of young, rich and
naïve heiresses being married in the dead of the night to unscrupulous
cads aiming to make off with their newlywed wives' fortunes – in
those dark days, the property of a wife became her husband's upon
marriage.)

Licences and formalities

A marriage may only be contracted once the following formalities have
been complied with:

In the case of Anglican church weddings

- *Banns may be called* in accordance with the requirements of the Book of Common Prayer. Publication of banns requires giving the priest some advance notice of the wedding. The banns are published by being read aloud in church on three successive Sundays preceding the marriage – it is expected that at least one of the couple should be in attendance to hear the banns being read out on at least one of these Sundays. The ceremony must take place within three months after publication of the banns.

  The banns will be read not only at the church where the wedding will take place but also in the parishes where either member of the couple reside if these are different. There is no residential qualification for marriage within a particular parish, although if you are not a parishioner, the clergyman may exercise his discretion not to marry you. He may not refuse to marry anyone who does live within the parish on the grounds that they are not a practising member of the faith, although a special (very limited) conscience clause permits him within his discretion to refuse to marry couples where neither has been baptised.

- *Or a Common Licence may be granted by a Bishop.* A marriage by common licence can take place much quicker: only one clear day's notice is needed before the licence to marry is issued. One party must swear an affidavit to the effect that there is no legal reason why the marriage cannot properly take place, that the other party consents to the wedding and that the man and woman, or both, have lived for at least 15 days prior to the application within the area served by the church that is to be used for the ceremony.

- *Or a Superintendent Registrar's Certificate may be issued* permitting marriage in accordance with the rites of the Church of England. (This is unusual for Anglican weddings as, normally, you would apply for this from your vicar.) The same assurances as for a Common Licence must be given but by 'solemn declaration', not affidavit. The notice must be displayed for three weeks in the Registrar's Office; then, if there has been no objection, a certificate enabling the marriage to take place in the district will be granted.

- *Or a Special Licence may be issued,* but only by the Archbishop of Canterbury. This allows a marriage to take place anywhere, at any time. They may only be granted for special and urgent reasons – for example, if a person who wishes to marry is too ill to leave his or her hospital bed. Only about 250 Special Licences are granted each year.

  (For further requirements of an Anglican church wedding, especially those pertaining to remarriages, see the section on church weddings on pp. 53–64.)

In the case of all other weddings (including those taking place at Register Offices and within the Catholic, Jewish, Muslim, Quaker and other recognized faiths)

One of you must attend in person to enter what is known as a 'Notice of Marriage' in the district where the Register Office is situated. The marriage will then be arranged in one of three ways:

- *By a Superintendent Registrar's Certificate.* Prior to giving notice, both the man and the woman must have lived for seven days in the area 'controlled' by the Superintendent Registrar (i.e. in his/her district). In this case, only one member of the couple needs to attend before the Registrar. If both live in different areas, they will each need to go to their own separate Registrars and they must each have lived in their respective areas for the last seven days.

    If the Registrar is satisfied with the information given, he or she will make the necessary entries in the notice book and arrange the wedding for at least 21 days later.

- *Or by Superintendent Registrar's Certificate and Licence.* A procedure similar to that for a Certificate is followed but the residential qualifications are different. Only one of the couple needs to give notice, provided that one of them has lived for at least 15 days in that district. However, the person not appearing must be within the borders of England and Wales or have his or her usual abode in Britain when the notice is given. One clear day after entering the notice (Sunday, Christmas Day and Good Friday excluded), the Superintendent Registrar will issue the licence for the marriage, which is valid for three months.

- *Or by Registrar General's Licence.* This applies only in very unusual cases. The Registrar General's Licence was introduced in 1970 and is reserved for special and urgent cases (e.g. where there is severe illness) where it would be impossible for the marriage to take place in a Register Office or other registered building. There is no residence qualification or waiting period required.

For all weddings

Before the service, any necessary certificates or licences are to be handed to the registering official. For a marriage to be solemnized, there must be two adult witnesses to the wedding, in addition to the necessary officials, and they must sign their names on the Register. These witnesses may be complete strangers to the marrying couple.

6

The Anglican church wedding

C HURCHES in Britain comprise some of the most beautiful buildings in the world – from the massive splendour of St Paul's Cathedral to the quaint and ancient charm of a quiet country church. Hardly suprising then that many couples choose to stage that very special day of their wedding – one of the most important of their lives – in such a setting.

> 'It was important to me to get married in church, even though I wouldn't call myself a practising Christian. But I do sort of believe in God and I wanted our day to start us off really well. The church – Mike's parents were married there, too – is so pretty. I couldn't believe how lovely it was when I first saw it. And the vicar was great. It just felt so right.'

More prosaically, the decision whether or not to marry in church may depend on a number of questions. The most common ones are:

- are we entitled to marry in church?
- will the ritual of a religious ceremony suit us?
- will the vows be right for us?

Let's look at each of these questions in turn.

Are we entitled to marry in church?

The notion of a wedding is today so tied up with that of the Church that it may come as something of a shock to discover that the Church was not always the primary performer of weddings. In fact, it was not until the 14th century in this country that the Church overcame opposition, replaced customary law and, through the ecclesiastical courts, gained full control over matters relating to marriage. In effect, the Church at that time hijacked the marriage service, which prior to then had by and large consisted of the couple giving simple secular promises to be husband and wife. However, having fought so hard for this powerful position, the Church lost it not very long after. In 1857, with the Matrimonial Causes Act, the Church finally had to relinquish its primacy over marriage, which was thereafter governed by the laws of the State. None the less, nowadays, the role of the Church remains central to marriage. It is still the place where the majority of us get married, and the special status of the Church of England is reflected in the legal requirements for a church wedding (*see above*).

The first step towards having a religious marriage ceremony will be to contact the vicar of the church where you would like to be married. You could perhaps go along to a few services to get the feel of the church if you have not been before. The usual procedure is for the two of you to make an appointment with the vicar, when he will take down the relevant personal information and then will tell you if there are any difficulties about marrying in church. As well as the standard sort of personal information (names, ages, addresses, occupations, fathers' full names and occupations), he may ask you if you have been confirmed and perhaps for your confirmation certificates if he does not know you. At this appointment, he will also tell you about fees and any arrangements for counselling and the rehearsal as well as about the wedding service itself. You can also talk to him about other matters such as the music at the ceremony, including your choice of hymns, and flowers for the church.

Because the Church is still the main body authorized to conduct marriages, every vicar is legally required to marry any couple living within his parish who asks him to, as long as both are legally free to marry and neither of them has been married before and is now divorced. In these circumstances, there is only one proviso, what is known as the 'conscience clause': if neither the prospective bride nor prospective groom has been baptized, the clergyman can refuse to marry the couple. In practice, however, very few vicars have ever exercised the conscience clause, and so if it is a first marriage for both of you and you live in the parish, you should have no problems in getting married in your local church.

> '*I was a bit worried about telling our vicar that we lived together – I thought he would disapprove. But when we had to give him our address when we went to see him to ask about getting married, he didn't seem to mind at all. Later on, he even told me that he thought it was a good thing for people to live together before they got married!*'

Some other clergymen may have less liberal views, but remember that whether you live together or not really has no bearing on his responsibilities: if you comply with the requirements, he should marry you.

The special case of second marriages

According to the strict letter of the law, a clergyman is not obliged to marry someone whose previous marriage has ended in divorce. (Widows and widowers are an entirely different matter; there are no such restrictions at all upon their remarriage.)

Legally, there is nothing to stop a vicar from marrying a divorced couple, but he doesn't have to. According to Section 8 (2) of the Matrimonial Causes Act 1965: 'No clergyman of the Church of England shall be compelled to solemnize the marriage of any person whose former marriage has been dissolved and whose former spouse is still living, or to permit the marriage of such a person to be solemnized in the church or chapel of which he is a minister.' So much for the law, but what about the Church's present day attitudes to marriage and divorce?

To try to gain some insight into the Anglican Church's current practice, we spoke to a vicar whose parish is in a leafy London suburb. These were his, not untypical views:

> 'The Church's teaching is that marriage is for once and for all. It is perhaps unique in that it does not allow any exceptions by way of annulment. Unlike the Romans [Catholics] or even the Orthodox churches [Greek and Russian], the Church does not allow second marriages, although by law the clergy are entitled to conduct second marriages.
>
> 'The issue has come up before the Synod [the Church of England's ruling body] on two occasions in the past 25 years or so. It's true that the Church is under great pressure to change its rigid position. Various ideas have been mooted. . .but instead the whole burden has been placed back in the hands of the clergy – in my view, an intolerable burden. Each member of the clergy has to exercise his individual conscience as to whether or not to remarry divorcees. People in different parishes will find priests with different views. It's recognized as a muddle.'

And his own views and conscience?

> 'I accept the teaching that marriage is indissoluble. I have much compassion and sympathy for people who have made mistakes, and if the circumstances are right, I will give a blessing for members of my congregation who remarry after a civil ceremony. But within my personal conscience, I do not feel I can marry such people.'

Not all clergymen take the same view, however. It is possible, if difficult, to 'shop around' and find a vicar who is willing to marry you a second time around – according to the *Sunday Times* (5 November 1989), 7000 couples do remarry in church every year. You could try asking your friends and members of your family whether they know of any flexible clergy who would

consider such a request. But even if you do find someone, you might have
to demonstrate some kind of link with the church of such a vicar.

What about the rules of other churches on second marriages?

The requirements of different churches vary widely. The Roman Catholic
Church, for example, does not recognize divorce at all, although it will
remarry a person whose previous marriage has been annulled.

The rules of the various Nonconformist churches (for instance, the
Methodist Church) tend to be less strict and rigid and could well provide
a viable alternative for a couple whose hearts are set on a church wedding.
There is no embargo on second marriages in the Methodist Church, nor are
the ministers likely to prove problematic about residence qualifications or
even to require you to be a member of their church. You can try contacting
your nearest Methodist church for further information.

Do you need to believe in Christianity to be married in a church?

This is really a matter for your own conscience. The Church of England
(or Wales) is a national church and, as explained above, will usually accept
anyone for marriage. You are most unlikely to be quizzed by your chosen
clergyman as to the extent to which you accept the tenets of the faith,
although you should be prepared for some religious instruction in your
pre-wedding counselling (*see below*).

As far as Christian teaching on weddings is concerned, this is what can
be gleaned from the New Testament, based mainly on the answers which
Christ gave to religious leaders when they were questioning Him about
His views:

- God planned marriage when he created man and woman.
- God's plan is for the union of one man with one woman.
- Husband and wife are to put each other first.
- Husband and wife become one person.
- Marriage is a calling and a gift from God.

Some discover a renewed interest in their faiths following on from their
weddings; others pay a form of lip service and then are relieved to be able
to slip away from the church as soon as possible. However, many find the
extra spiritual dimension of a church service very moving and special, no
matter what their preconceptions were.

*'It really meant something to me to say the vows in the presence of God.
I could feel Him during the service – though I'd never felt anything like
it before. I don't know whether our marriage will last, but the saying of*

*the vows and the whole church service were really special – I'd think again
before breaking any of them.'*

Will the ritual of a religious ceremony suit us?

The *Oxford English Dictionary* defines a rite or ritual as a 'form of procedure
required or usual in a religious or solemn occasion'. In a sense, all weddings
are rituals, solemn occasions formally marking a major transition in a
person's life. Yet a Register Office marriage, while it may be moving in its
very simplicity for the couple involved, is an altogether more matter-of-fact
and less ceremonial affair than a church wedding.

Genuine ritual tends to have a spiritual or religious dimension to it, and
it is this which may lead many couples, who may not be regular churchgoers
or indeed not even think of themselves as believers, to seek out a church
wedding, even while they wonder at themselves for so doing. Why should
this be so? What is the need that is seeking expression which may be fulfilled
by the ancient rituals and ceremonies of a church wedding?

A person's life is marked by certain moments of transition, when one
phase gives way to another. All over the world – in Surrey, Somalia and
Sarajevo – human lives share a remarkably similar pattern:

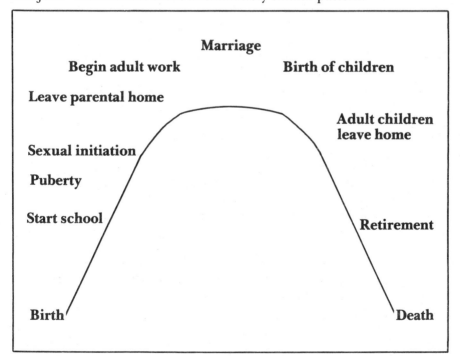

The details and the order may vary widely, of course, depending on
individual circumstances and decisions. Yet the arc depicted above (not

to scale!), even with variations, still forms the pattern of life for most of the people of our world, as it did for our ancestors. Such is human destiny.

These times of transition may be thrilling or painful; inevitably, they are highly stressful for all concerned. To manage and contain them, the human race developed rituals, or rites of passage. Through ritual, a heavy emotional weight can be structured and shared with others. Comfort may be drawn from the awareness of a common human destiny dignified by tradition and perhaps from some mysterious sense of the workings of God, fate or some higher spiritual power.

It is easy to feel yourself drifting through life, feeling, if you ever have time to stop and think about it, that your growth and change are getting little outward recognition. Through the enactment of ritual, we create signposts to mark our transformation from one stage to another. These signposts are important for others because they help them to see us with new eyes, and they are important for us because they enable us to leave behind outgrown ways of being and behaving and make a fresh start. Ritual can endow an occasion with structure, solemnity and meaning, playing a vital role as each of our own individual stories unfolds through life.

Today we live in an age when religious ritual, along with organized religion itself, has become, for many, old fashioned and out of touch. As a result, we are probably freer and are more aware of our own individuality; but the downside is that, as individuals, we have to carry more personal stress while we are less fortified by faith and a sense of spiritual purpose and share less with the wider community. The church wedding, on the other hand, is the great ritual survivor, as well as one of our most culturally enriching traditions.

At its worst, a church ceremony can be a meaningless, if pretty, charade. One bride, who had no particular religious beliefs and whose wedding was entirely organized by her parents, had this to say of her church wedding:

> 'The church was public. It felt like a movie which someone else had written, produced and directed, not something really happening to me. I just felt like an actress: all I had to do was to turn up on time and speak my lines. All I got to choose was my own dress.'

(Revealingly, this woman was later divorced and chose to solemnize her next significant relationship in a Ceremony of Vows instead of a formal and legally binding marriage.)

At its best, however, a church wedding means taking part in a ritual which gives the sense of being involved in something much bigger than oneself, something not easily expressed in words but nevertheless very important.

The desire which non-religious couples often have to marry in a place of worship is not hypocritical or frivolous. The thundering organ, the ancient smells of incense and candlewax, the sightless, serene effigies of plaster and stone, the dark and silent spaces of the church hallowed by generations of our forbears who have wept, prayed, sought sanctuary and made thanksgiving within its walls – our yearning for the individual events of our lives to connect with these symbols and somehow to draw from them a sense of meaning and dignity is no less true or real for its defiance of ordinary logic.

Are the vows right for us?

This is a serious and important question which it is easy to sidestep as the roller-coaster of the wedding starts to accelerate. Unlike a home-made Ceremony of Vows in which a couple are free to write their own vows or a Register Office wedding in which the couple simply promise to take each other as man and wife (*see later for details of both*), the promises which most religions demand that couples make to each other and to God are detailed, demanding and absolute in their nature. It is well worthwhile looking at the vows that you will be making before you actually have to say them in church; at the very least, you will know your lines better.

The following are some of the most significant promises which a couple marrying in an Anglican church and using the Anglican Alternative Service Book 1980 will be required to make:

> '*X, will you take Y, to be your wife (husband)? Will you love her (him), comfort her (him), honour and protect her (him), and forsaking all others be true to her (him) as long as you both shall live?*'
> '*I will.*'

Here the fidelity and permanent nature of the relationship is stressed, and also the quality of the relationship. You promise to love, to comfort honour and protect your partner in the expectation of being able to keep that promise. Love is thus conceptualized as a decision, an act of will and not just as a feeling.

The use of the word 'will' is significant. You are not just agreeing to marry your partner, but *willing* that you shall be married in a promise that is intended to be binding upon you both in the present and in the future.

> '*I, X, take you, Y, to be my wife (husband), to have and to hold from this day forward; for better for worse, for richer for poorer, in sickness and in health, to love and to cherish,* * *till death us do part.*'

A marriage will be most tested when times are difficult. The couple here vow to be steadfast to one another, no matter how adverse the circumstances. The obligation begins upon the day of the wedding and

---

*In an optional variation, the groom here promises 'to love, cherish and worship' and the bride 'to love, cherish and obey'.

can only be ended by the death of one of the partners.

In the Book of Common Prayer 1662 version, the bride *must* promise to obey and to serve her husband. Within the more modern ceremony, it is optional, and whether to include it is usually left to the couple to decide. For more on the question of obedience, see below.

> *I give you this ring as a sign of our marriage.'*

In the wedding ceremonies of many different religions, the joining together of husband and wife is expressed by the giving of a ring symbolizing unending love – as a perfect circle it is unbroken and, in a sense, infinite.

Today, rings are often exchanged, but traditionally, the ring has been given only by the groom to the bride. It has been well observed that a ring is one of the most ancient symbols of the female; thus when the bride stretches out her finger and it is enclosed in the groom's ring, the groom thereby gives his new wife his own femininity to hold, as she gives him her masculinity, expressed by her outstretched finger. Thus the act becomes a symbolic mirror-opposite of the act of sexual union.

> *'With my body I honour you, all that I am I give to you, and all that I have I share with you.'*

The physical nature of the love between the couple is expressed in a beautiful phrase which emphasizes that this physical loving is to be grounded in respect and honour of the partner's person. The couple also agree never to withhold from each other – a simple, unqualified promise which does not discriminate between material or emotional withholding.

Many couples report feeling something really special when they repeat their vows to one another. For one of us, Helen, this was the most important part of the service: I didn't want to get into a Royal kind of mess about Richard's names and so on and I wanted us to be comfortable with the vows before we got to church. So we practised saying them to one another – even though it was rather embarrassing at the time. When we then said them to one another in church, it was extraordinarily moving. Everyone else – including the vicar (although he was giving us the lines and saying, "Say after me") – disappeared into the background. It was just Richard and me, saying these beautiful words, and looking deep into each other's eyes. People came up to us with tears in their eyes after the ceremony saying how lovely it was and how sincere we were – I think it was special for them, too.

In our stiff-upper-lip British culture, it is not always easy to show your feelings and be moved by great emotion, but if you and your partner can leapfrog your inhibitions and really *feel* the vows as well as say them, the ceremony can take on a special significance.

And as for keeping those vows – well, who knows? The past statistics are far from encouraging, but then commitment becomes harder the longer it is tested. Perhaps one solution would be to create another ceremony on an important anniversary – as did this couple:

> *'On our tenth wedding anniversary, Christopher told me he would pick me up at lunchtime after he'd popped in to work (it was a Saturday) and he'd take me out somewhere really special. The kids kept giggling – but I didn't take any notice. I thought we were going to a restaurant. Imagine my surprise when Chris took me to our local church – and we got married all over again – with our daughters in attendance. It was lovely – I cried my eyes out.'*

The promise to obey

The question of whether or not to agree to obey should be a matter for the couple to work out between themselves – so thought one of us, Jane, and her husband-to-be when they turned up for what they expected to be a fairly perfunctory eve-of-wedding counselling session. However we were taken aback when the vicar informed us: 'All the women I have ever married in my church promised to obey and that is an end to it.' Unfortunately, as we lived outside the boundaries of his parish, he was technically able to refuse to marry us; and I had had my heart set since childhood on marrying in the small Norman church over which he now presided – my parents and my grandparents had both been married there and my grandparents now lay in a grave in the churchyard. It seemed as if an impasse had been reached, and only a month before the wedding was scheduled to take place.

Father X said couples had to find some way of resolving serious arguments. He said, without a trace of irony, that we were obviously strong-willed people so it was most important to find a clear way of sorting out differences – could we think of a better one? When pushed, he said that I would only have to obey if Rick were worshipping me, i.e. putting my interests first when he gave me the order! We couldn't agree: I saw the wording of the promise to obey as unqualified and I wasn't prepared to make it.

The story did have a happy ending. Father X eventually agreed that we might follow our own consciences, adding rather sniffily: "At least you're prepared to sit down and think about what the vows really mean – most of the couples who come in here just do exactly what I tell them. . ." Regrettably, however, my own small step into modern times did not help other brides marrying in that small Yorkshire town: Father X still insists that every woman he marries has to promise to obey!

Jane and Rick's story makes a general point. Had we taken the line of least resistance in the interests of not rocking the wedding boat and acquiesced in making promises which we were not making in their hearts, they felt that we would have been betraying or at least compromising something fundamental about our relationship. 'Our wedding vows were

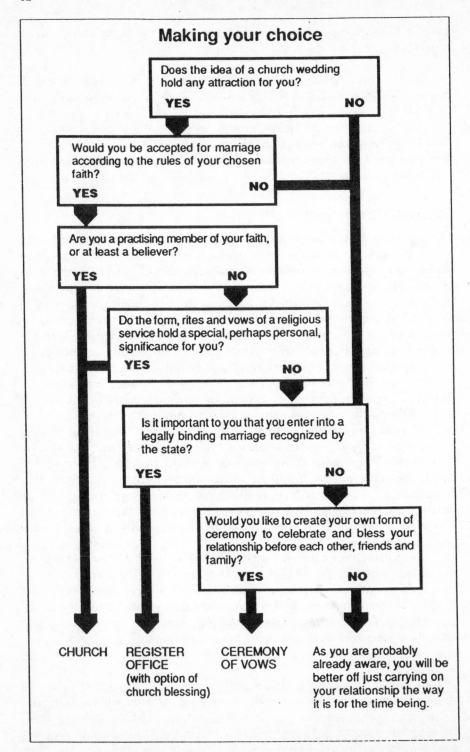

Making your choice

Does the idea of a church wedding hold any attraction for you?

YES   **NO**

Would you be accepted for marriage according to the rules of your chosen faith?

YES   **NO**

Are you a practising member of your faith, or at least a believer?

YES   **NO**

Do the form, rites and vows of a religious service hold a special, perhaps personal, significance for you?

YES   **NO**

Is it important to you that you enter into a legally binding marriage recognized by the state?

YES   **NO**

Would you like to create your own form of ceremony to celebrate and bless your relationship before each other, friends and family?

YES   **NO**

CHURCH   REGISTER OFFICE (with option of church blessing)   CEREMONY OF VOWS   As you are probably already aware, you will be better off just carrying on your relationship the way it is for the time being.

the only vows we ever intended to make. They were serious, and they had to be real.'

What can you expect from a Church of England wedding?

We have already touched on what a Church of England vicar might expect from you, but what about the other way round? What might *you* expect to receive if you marry in church?

Counselling

The amount of counselling that you might be offered by your clergyman varies according to the cut of his cloth. Some will arrange group sessions (attended by a few other couples also marrying in the same church) over a period of several weeks; others will hold individual counselling sessions. Some vicars will bravely tackle 'hot' subjects such as sex and money; others steer well clear. Our vicar again:

> '*Most clergymen will want to do some form of counselling; it would be irresponsible in the case of most couples to make them do without. Some will give four to five hours before the wedding, spread out, say, once a week for a few weeks. I follow the pattern that I was trained to do when I was ordained – one counselling session the week before the couple marry. . .*
>
> '*I don't actually counsel on practical matters between the couple – I don't feel I have any cause to. My attitude is that, by the time a couple come to me, they've made up their own minds. I give them the benefit of the doubt, allow them their own integrity and freedom to make their own decisions.*'

And what subjects might be covered?

> '*I'll talk about the importance and seriousness of marriage, but not about the emotional and sexual relationship. The thing I feel is of most importance is to stress the fact of its being a Christian marriage: it's not just a contract, but there's a third dimension, that of God. I will talk about the mystery of the marriage as the Church understands it. It can be very difficult if a couple have no awareness of faith or of religion. But each couple is special and unique.*'

The rehearsal

Again, if you marry in church, like as not you will be offered a form of rehearsal for the real thing. This will usually take place either a week before or sometimes on the eve of the wedding itself, which can be a good antidote to pre-nuptial nerves.

The rehearsal may range from a highly choreographed walk-through involving all members of the bridal party to an informal chat combined with a short homily from the vicar, to which only the starring couple themselves are invited. Your vicar should tell you in advance how many people he will want there.

At the rehearsal itself, the vicar may give you tips on how to turn from the altar without falling flat on your face (the best method is to do a long slow wheel around, particularly if you have a long train), as well as the more standard advice about who should carry the rings (the best man), where he wants the bride's father to stand and so on. Don't be afraid to use the opportunity to ask questions and to settle your mind on any matters that are still worrying you.

7

Other religions

O F course, not all couples having a religious ceremony will marry in an Anglican church. We are now a polyglot society and marriages of a rich variety will be performed all over Britain in any one year. Here we look at several different types of wedding: a Roman Catholic wedding; a Jewish wedding; an Eastern-style wedding (of the Ismaeli Muslims, which combines elements of the Islamic and Hindu traditions); and a Quaker wedding, one of the Nonconformist forms of ceremony.

A Roman Catholic wedding

For Catholics, a wedding is one of the seven sacraments central to Church ritual – a sacrament being defined in the *Catechism* as 'the outer sign of inner grace'. The wedding ceremony is unique among the sacraments in that husband and wife, in union with the priest (who is there to witness and bless their joining together), are specifically empowered to administer the sacrament to each other through the act of giving and receiving their marriage promises.

The priest we spoke to has a multi-racial inner city parish in north-east London. He emphasized the indissolubility of the wedding vows as long as they were intended by both parties at the moment of marriage. These vows, he said, were made not to the priest but directly to God, and he added firmly: 'If you don't believe that, you shouldn't be in the Church. If you do believe, then you're making your promises to God the creator. They cannot be broken.' For this reason, individual Catholic parishes are likely to have comparatively rigorous programmes for engaged couples, consisting of several lessons of instruction. Sometimes couples may be referred on by the priest to the Catholic Marriage Advisory Council (*see* Appendix 2) to partake in one of their pre-nuptial programmes. Our priest said he insisted (and this is by no means untypical) that there be a waiting period of at least six months between the time when the engagement is announced and when the wedding may take place. Unlike his Anglican brethren, a Catholic priest is entitled to refuse to marry a couple of his own parish whom he does not consider to be fully prepared.

In recent years (since the Second Vatican Council) the rules for Catholics marrying outside the faith have been considerably relaxed. In many circumstances, a dispensation may be granted permitting a Catholic marrying a non-Catholic to be wed within the church of their partner's religion. It is emphasized, though, that the dispensation must be applied for *before* the ceremony – it cannot work retrospectively. If a couple elect to marry within the Catholic Church, the non-Catholic partner no longer has to promise to allow any children to be brought up within the faith. Instead, the Catholic partner simply has to promise that they will so be brought up to the best of his/her ability.

The Catholic wedding itself is not, initially, dissimilar to an Anglican one. It begins with the usual prayers and responses and the Liturgy of the Word (i.e. Bible readings and psalms), moving on to a sermon and then to the marriage rite itself. The priest then asks the bride and groom the following questions:

- Are you ready freely and without reservation to give yourselves to each other in marriage?
- Are you ready to love and honour each other as man and wife for the rest of your lives?
- Are you ready to accept children lovingly from God and bring them up according to the law of Christ and His Church?

Each partner must answer 'I am' to each of the questions and must solemnly declare that s/he knows of no lawful impediment to their marriage. Each agrees to take the other for their lawful husband/wife 'according to the rite of our Holy Mother the Church'. The couple then agree (in words almost identical to the Anglican rite) to take each other 'to have and to hold from this day forward, for better for worse, for richer for poorer, in sickness and in health, to love and to cherish till death us do part.' Rings are then blessed and exchanged.

Where a Catholic wedding *is* unique is that it very often (although not necessarily) forms part of a nuptial mass, when the wedding rite itself is followed immediately by the communion rite. The bread and wine are taken by the bride and groom and often by the wedding guests as well. The priest we spoke to commented, 'The mass is the central feature of our faith – what better way to start off the commitment of married life than by joining in it together?' In the communion liturgy, the priest offers the communion gifts on behalf of the couple and asks of God that 'the mystery of Christ's unselfish love, which we celebrate in this eucharist, increase their love for You and for each other'.

A nuptial mass is likely to work best when both wedding parties are of the faith. At a mixed marriage taking place in a Catholic church, one guest remarked that it seemed odd to see all the bride's family queuing up for communion while the groom's side remained firmly anchored in their seats. In such circumstances, a simple wedding ceremony may be preferred and will be perfectly acceptable. The service will then, of course, be rather shorter.

A Jewish wedding

Marriage, according to the annotated *Jewish Marriage Service*, is the 'ideal human state and the basic social institution, established by God at the time of Creation'. The present-day orthodox Jewish form of service is an amalgamation of two latter-day ceremonies: the betrothal (*erusin* or *kiddushin*), which establishes a legal bond between the parties; and then the marriage itself (*nissu'in*) which takes place under the *chuppah* (canopy), representing the new home the couple are about to build together. Only after the second ceremony would it be usual for the man and woman to live together as man and wife.

It is customary that the bride and groom do not see each other for at least a day before the wedding, and some couples also keep up the tradition of fasting on the day of the wedding until after the ceremony. The bride and groom are conducted to the *chuppah*, usually by their parents. In traditional ceremonies, the afternoon service is read prior to the marriage ceremony and the bride and groom may quietly add their confession of sins to start off the marriage on a clean slate.

The form of the traditional Jewish ceremony varies considerably from that of the Christian one. During the wedding service, the bride remains silent – her silence signifies her consent to the marriage. There is no joint exchange of vows, but the groom enters into a form of contract with his bride, the consideration for which is a nominal 200 silver *zuzim* (an old form of money). The contract is completed, signed, sealed and delivered and given to the new wife to keep. Presumably if her husband then later breaks any of its tenets, she can wave it above him to bring him back to heel!

The marriage contract in the traditional ceremony reads, in part:

> *Now (name of bridegroom). . ., son of (name of father). . ., said to this maiden. . .(name of bride): 'Be thou my wife according to the law of Moses and of Israel, and I will work for thee, honour, support and maintain thee in accordance with the custom of Jewish husbands who work for their wives, honour, support and maintain them in truth. And I hereby make for thee the settlement of virgins, 200 silver* zuzim, *which belongs to thee, according to the law of Moses and of Israel; and I will also give thee thy food, clothing and necessaries and live with thee as husband and wife according to universal custom.'*
>
> *And (name of bride). . ., this maiden, consented and became his wife. The wedding outfit that she brought to him from her father's house, in silver, gold, wearing apparel, house furniture and bedclothes all this (name of bridegroom). . .the said bridegroom accepted in the sum of 100*

silver pieces and (name of bridegroom). . ., the bridegroom, consented to
increase this amount from his own property with the sum of 100 silver pieces,
making in all 200 silver pieces. And thus said (name of bridegroom). . .,
the bridegroom:

'The responsibility of this marriage contract, of this wedding outfit,
and of this additional sum, I take upon myself and my heirs after me, so
that they shall be paid from the best part of my property and possession
that I have beneath the whole heaven, that which I now possess or may
hereafter acquire. All my property, real and personal, even the mantle on
my shoulders, shall be mortgaged to secure the payment of this marriage
contract, of the wedding outfit, and of the addition made thereto, during
my lifetime and after my death, from the present day and forever.'

(Name of bridegroom). . ., the bridegroom, has taken upon himself the
responsibility of this marriage contract, of the wedding outfit and the
addition made thereto, according to the restrictive usages of all marriage
contracts and the additions made thereto for the daughters of Israel, in
accordance with the institution of our sages of blessed memory. It is not
to be regarded as a mere form of promise with mental reservation, or as a
mere form of document. We have followed the legal formality of symbolical
delivery (kinyan) between (name of bridegroom). . ., the son of. . ., the
bridegroom, and (name of bride). . ., the daughter of. . ., this maiden,
and we have used an article legally suitable as an instrument whereby all
herein is duly and properly confirmed.

One Jewish bride said about her wedding:

'I loved the fact that the whole family were involved – my parents and my
husband's both standing with us under the chuppah, and all drinking from
the same cup and handing it the one to the other. It was beautiful that they
were all there to share with us those special moments. Then the moment when
the cup is specially broken: I believe that however many pieces it broke into
means that you will have that many happy years in your marriage. However,
the breaking of the cup has a deeper significance: it was supposedly started
by a rabbi who, on his marriage, wanted to remember his sadnesses in the
midst of his greatest happiness.

'The orthodox and the reform services can vary a lot – but they are all
beautiful.'

An Eastern wedding

Many Ismaeli Muslims left East Africa in the 1970s, fleeing to Britain,
the US and Canada. Their wedding customs derive from Hinduism
(many were Hindu converts), African customs and Islam, the latter
particularly for those who originally came from northern India and
Pakistan.

The marriage is set in train by a ceremony – the 'private sherbert' – at the bride's home, when the hopeful groom and his family arrive (with warning) bearing gifts of clothes, perhaps, and dried fruit, and are offered a special drink by the bride's mother. This pink drink is known as sherbert but, made with milk, ground nuts and vanilla, it is as different from the English conception as it is possible to be. A toast is drunk and the wedding planned.

The wedding itself, as in many Eastern cultures, is spread over several days. First, the couple have to obey the rules of the State and marry in a Register Office – but the rings exchanged here will be hastily taken off after the ceremony as the couple are not considered to be married until after the religious ceremony. The next event is again before the wedding proper, when the bride and groom are prepared by their families for their big day. The groom will be anointed by family and friends, and in return for this privilege, the anointers will offer gifts. The bride's hands and feet will be painted with intricate henna patterns and she, too, will be anointed in return for gifts. The groom and his family arrive in the evening, again with gifts of jewellery, clothes and delicacies. The trousseau bought by the bride's family will usually be on display. The whole event is very much a family affair with formal and frequent exchanges of gifts.

The following day, the day of the wedding, the bride and groom are made ready by their respective families, and the groom, traditionally, collects his bride to take her to the mosque. The religious ceremony is fairly short, again with no speaking parts for the bride or even the groom. (Perhaps this evolved as a way of overcoming wedding nerves. . .) In the presence of two witnesses – the best man and chief bridesmaid – the bridal couple will sign a document signifying their marriage. They then go on to a wedding feast organized by the groom; another feast will be arranged for the following day by the bride's family. This is, perhaps, a good way of beating the inevitable sense of anticlimax following on from the highs of the wedding.

A Quaker wedding

For over 200 years, the Quakers (or Society of Friends) have had their own special form of wedding service and their own Registering Officers (which means that you would not have to 'back up' a Quaker wedding by a Register Office ceremony, as usually is the case in the UK for most minority religious ceremonies).

The marriage service is always part of the normal worship meeting. This is a time of silence when any member may give a spoken message. At the beginning, a Friend will explain what a Quaker wedding is like and then the meeting will proceed.

At a fairly early point, the couple themselves, when they feel it is right to do so, will rise up, join hands and declare each in turn:

'Friends, I take this my friend [name] to be my wife [husband] promising, through divine assistance, to be unto her [him] a loving and faithful husband [wife] so long as we both on earth shall live.' They both then sign a certificate of marriage, two witnesses also sign and then the certificate is read aloud by the Registering Officer. Rings may be exchanged, but they are not a part of the actual ceremony. The meeting thereafter continues with silence, prayers and perhaps messages for the couple. The whole service is very simple, and, as a result, can be most moving.

8

The Register Office wedding

M ANY couples, even though they are wedded in a religious ceremony conducted according to their own beliefs (for example, Hindus and Muslims), will also have to participate in a Register Office marriage service in order to be properly married in the eyes of the State. Others have no choice about their choice of venue – a Register Office it has to be. For yet others, the formality of church proceedings, the *angst* of organizing a church wedding and the demanding nature of the vows required are too much. Particularly if people have no faith of their own, they can come to the view that it would be hypocritical suddenly to attend church on a whim, just because they (or one of them) prefer the 'look' of a marriage in church. If you are such a couple, you may feel that the simplicity of a Register Office wedding has many attractions.

You will not be offered any form of premarital counselling before a Register Office wedding. If you want any (and it is considered by many people to be a good idea), you will need to arrange your own (*see* p.34).

A Register Office wedding ceremony centres around a simple promise to be husband and wife to each other ratther than a full exchange of vows. If you decide to marry in a Register Office (not 'Regist*ry* Office' as it is so commonly but mistakenly known), the formalities are reduced to a minimum.

The Register Office marriage ceremony

A marriage conducted in a Register Office will be much shorter and simpler than even the plainest church ceremony. The following is taken from the *Marriage Appointment* leaflet (reproduced with permission) which will be issued to you when you make the appointment for your marriage. This leaflet confirms your appointment for the marriage and deals with certain logistical details. It goes on to say:

You will no doubt want to know what happens when you attend for your marriage. I hope the following explanation will be of help.

When you arrive at the Register Office on the day, the Registrar who is registering your marriage will see the two of you privately in the Marriage Room to check the particulars which will be entered on the marriage register: your full names and occupations, ages, your addresses, your fathers' names and occupations and whether either of you has been married before (the Registrar will want to see the original decree absolute if the latter is so). The fees will also be paid at this time.

Your guests will then be invited to join you in the Marriage Room, the two people who will be your witnesses sitting one on each side of you. If a ring or rings will be used, there will usually be a velvet cushion to place these on. The marriage ceremony will then take place, being conducted by a Superintendent Registrar, who in his introduction will remind you of the solemn and binding character of the marriage ceremony.

Each of you in turn will be asked to declare that you do not know of any lawful reason against your marriage and the Superintendent Registrar will ask you to repeat after him:

'I do solemnly declare that I do not know of any lawful impediment why I — [your full name] may not be joined in matrimony to — [the full name of your fiancé(e)].'

If a wedding ring is given, the bridegroom will then be asked to place it on his bride's finger. Similarly, if the bride wishes to give the bridegroom a ring, she will be asked to place it on his finger.

You will then join hands whilst each of you speak the words by which the contract of marriage is made, repeating after the Superintendent Registrar:

'I call upon these persons here present to witness that I——[Your full name] do take thee——[the full name of your fiancé(e)] to be my lawful wedded wife [or husband].'

The ceremony will end with the Superintendent Registrar declaring you to be husband and wife.

There follow logistical details requesting that the wedding party should attend ten minutes in advance of the wedding, and a further reminder that you will be required to provide two witnesses to the marriage (and, in cases where there is a language difficulty, that you should provide an interpreter).

What will a register office wedding be like?

Some Register Offices are like faded Hollywood palaces with sweeping marble staircases, red velvet curtains and huge echoing chambers. Others are sparkling-clean and modern. But in either sort, a sense of romance and poetry is probably something you will have to bring along with you.

Sometimes couples can be disappointed by the conveyor belt aspects of a Register Office, while others, who want the ceremony over quickly and with a minimum degree of fuss, are grateful for the relative brevity and informality.

Here is the experience of Hazel, who chose to be married in a Register Office and was sure in retrospect that she had made the right decision:

'We chose to marry in a Register Office as Joe is Jewish and I am Christian. Neither of us wanted or intends to change our beliefs so we thought it was only right to marry somewhere neutral.

'Having said that, our wedding at the Register Office was a very, very pleasant experience. Beforehand, as I am very aware of surroundings, I wanted to choose a place that was special. We explored the possibility of getting married in Kensington & Chelsea Register Office but found that we didn't comply with the residence requirements. Also, there, as it is such a popular place, I found you actually had to queue personally three months in advance of your chosen wedding day, which was when the Registrar opened the register, to be able to get the time that you wanted. People should know that you often do have to book well in advance.

'We decided to marry in Islington Register Office – our local one. We made an appointment for the wedding three months in advance – they operated the same system – and then went down to see the Superintendent Registrar a few days later. He was very nice. He showed us around the room where the ceremony would take place and where the guests would wait. He told us about a few practical details, like arranging for the guests to arrive ten minutes in advance and that he didn't allow photos being taken during the ceremony but would allow one video. He also, as I recall, spoke about the importance and seriousness of marriage. He took things nice and slowly and I never felt rushed.

'The Register Office itself was beautiful – sited in a 19th-century town hall. Quite splendid. The room for the ceremony was beautiful, too – very plush, with polished mahogany panelling. The only drawback was that there was only space for 30 guests, which could have been a problem though it wasn't for us. We just decided to invite 30 special guests to the wedding and then the rest to our later reception.

'On the day, when Joe and I arrived, we were taken to the Registrar's own offices and she checked formalities. We were actually to be married by a woman Registrar who had a black woman assistant – I liked this arrangement very much! Joe paid the fees, or what was outstanding, then. We were very well looked after.

'The guests were ushered into the Marriage Room from the waiting room. The Registrar then went in, followed by Joe and the best man, then me and my bridesmaid. I think there was music playing. The room looked lovely with all the flowers.

'The woman did it very well – I found it very moving – the pace that she took the ceremony at and the way she did it – it was all beautiful. Everyone

*was impressed – I had a lot of people coming up to me afterwards saying
how much they'd enjoyed it. The ceremony was quite short, but there was
lots of time for photographs. I never felt it was like a sausage machine,
though we did get married in February – I don't know how busy it would
be in June!*

*'The thing I was most impressed by was that it was very professional.
I suppose they specialize in weddings – it's the only ceremony they do –
and I felt that they'd made it into an art form.'*

A church blessing

If you get married in a Register Office because you are ineligible for a
church wedding, your local vicar may still be prepared to bless your union
in church – a compromise which many find acceptable. Alternatively
you could consider having your own subsequent Ceremony of Vows (see
chapter 9).

Civil weddings: the shape of things to come?

A government Green Paper has recently proposed plans to widen the
choice of venues on offer for civil marriages, although the original
suggestion that marriages be allowed to take place anywhere (including
in private homes) appears to have been scrapped. The present proposal,
according to a statement from Registrar General's Office, is 'that local
authorities should be able to offer a choice of buildings in which civil
marriages could take place. . .[which] could include stately homes or
hotels.'

As we go to press, the proposals are still under discussion and any
decisions look a long way off. There has been some criticism on the
grounds that, because the new facilities would only be available at a
cost, they would be creating a two-tier structure for civil weddings – one
version for the rich and one for the poor. Not surprisingly, the churches
have also been critical. You could check with your local Registrar to see
if any change is envisaged.

9

We did it our way: the Ceremony of Vows

A number of pioneers, as yet few in number, have turned their backs on the whole system and rejected outright the pomp and ceremony of a church wedding or even the formalized structure of a civil one. But rather than have no ritual within which to declare their relationship to the world, they have devised their very own form of vows ceremony – a sort of do-it-yourself wedding. These ceremonies are not wedding services in the usual sense – they do not comply with the legal requirements set out in Chapter 5 and will not 'marry' the couple in anything but their own minds. They may thus be appropriate for people who, for whatever reason, do not want to be married in the formal sense, yet wish publicly or privately, to exchange personal vows and to have their relationship solemnized and blessed in their own eyes and those of their friends and families.

Anna and Stewart were such a couple. With the birth of their first child imminent, they wanted to formalize their relationship in the presence of close friends and relatives in a way which they felt would be personally binding on them. They were both dismissive about legally binding marriages, especially religious ones. Stewart said: 'I never wanted a church wedding. Always a private one. I'm against the Church – it means nothing. And a Register Office seems cold. I want to make a public declaration of my feelings for Anna, and I want people to come away with something – a sense of joining and love.' Anna, whose first marriage had ended in divorce, told us: 'I felt I was much more on the line than I would have been in a traditional ceremony. Once I was pregnant, it was clear that this was a permanent relationship. I wanted a public commitment, to show other people. I was married in church before; it was my mother's day. It just wasn't real for me.'

They decided to hold their ceremony in their own Victorian house in north London, filled on the day with flowers, music and sunshine. They had worked hard beforehand getting the house, into which they had recently moved, completely renovated for the occasion – on the morning of the ceremony itself, they were up early, companionably

chopping vegetables for the buffet while welcoming the first guests. They
structured the ceremony by starting with some classical music and poetry
readings, going on to a formal blessing from Stewart's father. The vows
were then exchanged between the couple, who stood facing each other at
the front of the room before all the sitting guests. The ceremony ended with
the performance of a song that a friend, who was a professional singer, had
written especially for the occasion.

Anna and Stewart spent a long time before the ceremony preparing the
vows which they would make. Anna told us:

> 'They really took a long time to write. We each thought of what we wanted
> and then discussed it. We each wanted to find our own language, and yet to
> have our two sets of vows fit together. It was a difficult process but a really
> valuable one for both of us, I think, to consider what we were prepared to
> commit to and what we weren't.'

This is what they came up with:

> *HE: You will be my one and only lover.*
> *SHE: I choose you as my one and only lover.*
>
> *HE: I will give of myself in such a way that it enriches our relationship.*
> *SHE: I will give of myself always in such a way that enriches our
> relationship.*
>
> *HE: I promise to remember that you love me.*
> *SHE: I promise to always remember your love for me and to act through
> that knowledge.*
>
> *HE: I promise to give all my love to you and to tell you how much I love
> you and to acknowledge you for all that you are and do.*
> *SHE: I promise to always tell you how much I love you and appreciate
> you and to acknowledge you for the things that you do and are.*
>
> *HE: I promise to cherish and to take care of you and our child.*
> *SHE: I will love and cherish and care for you.*
>
> *HE: I will be there for you and our child.*
> *SHE: I will always be there for you and our child before all other
> commitments.*
>
> *HE: I will support your search for happiness and self-fulfilment.*
> *SHE: I will support you in your search for self-fulfilment and
> happiness.*
>
> *HE: I will work with you to create a home in which we and our own
> child will know love.*
> *SHE: I will work with you to create a home in which we and our child
> will be happy.*

HE: I promise to withhold none of myself in raising our child.
SHE: I promise to withhold none of myself in bringing up our child.

HE: I will nurture and encourage your well-being, spiritually, mentally and physically.
SHE: I will do what I can to nurture your physical, emotional and spiritual well-being.

HE: I am and always will be your friend.
SHE: I will always be your true friend and be open and honest with you.

HE: I will be truthful and loyal to you at all times.
SHE: I will not lie to you or ever betray you.

HE: I promise to share with you all that is mine.
SHE: I will share with you all that I have and own.

HE: I love and adore you, and this ring is a symbol of this love and commitment I now make to you for the rest of my life.
SHE: I love you and choose you. This ring is a symbol of my commitment to you now and always.

You will see that the vows that Anna and Stewart made were not identical.

For your own Ceremony of Vows you could get some ideas from the written wisdom of others; reading about other forms of ceremony used by different creeds and cultures and browsing through some love poetry may give you inspiration. Appointing a master or mistress of ceremonies to assist you on the day would help it run smoothly. The main advantage of this form of ceremony is the freedom it affords you. You could have the ceremony in a forest clearing, in your own home or in a hired hall; you need only invite your dearest and closest friends – or even no one at all. You could throw together a few quiches and salads or have a properly catered reception. In short, you can do whatever you like. . .

The legal position

Anna and Stewart chose to emphasize the emotional and spiritual aspects of their relationship in their vows, but there is no reason why you should not, either within the main ceremony or within a collateral document, make arrangements about more down-to-earth matters – for instance, the name the female partner will take, the financial, domestic and childcare arrangements the two of you will make. Many couples have subsequently rued the day that they did not sit down before their marriages and make proper agreements about how they would run their lives together – matters which are all too likely to crop up uncomfortably later on.

If you are particularly practically minded, you could also decide in advance how you will arrange your financial affairs in the sad event of a break up – for example, whether you intend to divide your assets equally. Such a document will operate primarily as a declaration of intent, and is not necessarily binding. Should it ever come to a legal battle, the courts have power to override any such document and make whatever provisions which they see as being in the best interests of the couple and, particularly, of any children of the relationship. (And in fact, even if you are legally married, the courts have exactly the same power to override any pre- or post-nuptial contract you may have entered into as a couple.) For more information on marriage contracts, see Chapter 11.

If later, after a Ceremony of Vows, you wish to be married in the legal sense, there is nothing in the world to stop you from going ahead. For a full comparison of the rights of married and unmarried couples, see the chart on pp. 14–19.

10

Creating your own style of wedding: the reception and all that

W HILE the decision as to where you will get married may be the most important one in terms of setting the tone for your wedding, organizing the practical arrangements can take up just as much – if not far more – of your time. And we start off with that old bogey – money.

The cost

Few can consider the question of where to get married in isolation from the other things that go to make up a wedding: the engagement (or whether to get engaged at all), the stag/hen nights, the reception venue, the honeymoon and, perhaps of overriding importance for a good number of people, the complete cost. Sometimes the budget available may be a dictating factor in the overall tone of the wedding.

Weddings have a tendency to come at a time when you have many demands on your finances as a couple. You may be moving together into a new home, with all the horrendous expense which that involves; possibly you will be saving towards the moment when you can reduce your work commitments to make way for a baby. In planning your wedding, finance is one area that you ignore at your peril. Even if your parents are bearing the brunt of the cost, it is still worth considering whether you want to go all out on a full traditional ceremony and reception or whether some of the money that this would have cost might, with your parents' agreement, be put towards the deposit on a home or even a fantastic honeymoon.

You should, therefore, carefully weigh up the pros and cons of having an expensive wedding: be sensible about your budget if you, in fact, have little money to spare. (This is a heartfelt, 'Do what I say, not what I do' from Helen, who spent her first married year deep in debt as a result

79

of splashing out on a big wedding!) If your funds are tight and your parents are unable to assist in any major way, it is, unless the wedding is of supreme importance to you, far better to save your money for the inevitable costs of setting up home together rather than blowing all your savings or a loan on an ephemeral day.

Splitting the cost

Traditionally, the cost of a wedding is borne by the bride's parents, the groom being responsible for (if he can afford it) certain specific items, such as the honeymoon, flowers for himself and the best man, the rings and any car-hiring charges. Nowadays, this is still often the case, but the financial arrangements can vary greatly, with the costs perhaps met by the wedding couple themselves, or shared between them and their parents, with the groom's parents contributing, say, towards the cost of the drinks at the reception. However these things are arranged, it is as well to sort out well in advance of the actual day who will bear the financial brunt of which items.

Once you have determined your budget and who will pay for what, you are in a position to decide how you want to arrange your own special day. Many weddings imaginatively organized on a tight budget have outshone the most lavish affairs. If you cannot afford and perhaps do not want a formal reception for 300, how about a picnic by a lake with contributions from friends and family alike, or a champagne celebration in the local fish-and-chip shop (warned in advance of course!)? With creativity, you can devise a very special and unique occasion without enormous funds.

Organizing the reception

Plan well in advance. Particularly if you are going to have a significant number of guests and want a proper wedding party, the very first thing you should do is to decide on your reception arrangements, and if you are going to want a reception venue, book that first of all. To quote one well-known London venue organizer: 'The days of spontaneous romance are over. Our Saturdays are now booked up 18 months in advance. I sometimes feel that people decide on their wedding date first and *then* go out and choose their marriage partner!'

Many of the glossy bridal magazines have helpful checklists, so to ensure that everything is done and on schedule, buy one of these. However, it should be said that many of the time scales are conservative and need to be adapted to your own special case. One of us, Jane, bought her wedding dress two weeks before her wedding, rather than the six months set aside in the checklist. But if you are going to have your wedding dress made, you *will* need at least six months.

A formal reception: to have it or not to have it

Opting for a wedding with all the trimmings – white dress, morning suits, huge reception, great big cake and so on – has much to recommend it, if you can stand the pace. One of the things that can recommend it (but which may be anathema to some) is the formal pattern of the wedding reception. You and the rest of the wedding party have to line up on arrival and greet the guests (try not to talk too long to those at the front of the queue as those at the rear will be dying to get inside and get a drink). Then there is the meal, cake cutting, speeches and toasts, a change of clothes for the newlyweds and off and away – all these will contribute to the structuring of your day.

Although some couples prefer to have a more informal celebration, the reception can end in formlessness if there is no one there or no old familiar pattern to tell people what to do and when. Most people like being given instructions and being orderly – chaos can soon result if they are left to do their own thing. If you do decide against the more formal wedding reception, keeping some of the highlights – for example the cake cutting – and appointing someone to be in charge to start everyone off eating and to tell people when the cake will be cut and so on is good people management.

The honeymoon

Don't expect too much of the honeymoon. You will probably both be too exhausted even to speak for the first day or two. It may be better to arrange to go away somewhere not too far away for the first few days (or at least the first night) to help you get your breath back, rather than jetting off immediately to a tropical island whose charms may diminish as you use up the remainder of your emotional energy stuck in a traffic jam on the way to the airport.

Honeymoons can have a malicious knack of turning into French (or Italian or wherever) farces. On her honeymoon in Italy, one of us (Helen) experienced two car breakdowns, getting stuck for five hours with an Italian car mechanic who felt his male pride hung on his ability to fix an unfixable Fiat Panda (pride eventually took a fall), thereafter ending up a hotel which had only just opened after being closed for several months (the water which spurted from the taps was bright orange!) Finally, her fledgling husband had his pocket picked in the streets of Rome, before a four-hour wait at the airport for the flight home iced this particular cake.

As Helen's mother might have said: 'It's all part of life's rich tapestry.' These things are sent to try us. If some of the same starts happening to you, remember it will at least give you something to dine out on when you get back home. Then again, your honeymoon may be fantastic and proceed without a hitch – it's wise just not to have too many expectations.

Getting away from it all

If you cannot bear the prospect of a full formal wedding, with the possibility that arguments between members of your family will detract from what is, after all, your day, you could consider taking advantage of the 'wedding packages' now on offer from some travel agents. At about £1500 per person, they do not come cheap, but for that price, you could be whisked away to some beautiful Caribbean island, have your wedding (including witnesses) all organized for you and then start straight off on your honeymoon *without* the added hassle of getting to the airport.

Doing it your way

As one option, we include the comments of one interviewee, who arranged her wedding at 48 hours' notice:

> '*My husband's family were scattered all over England – the only time that they all really meet is at Christmas. Three days before Christmas 1987, he proposed. We decided that, rather than wait, we'd just go right ahead and do it as fast as we could. We got a licence in 24 hours, married on Christmas Eve, had 20 guests (about two of whom I knew) and a Christmas cake that doubled as a wedding cake. It was glorious – the feeling of spontaneity and all the Christmas spirit. I wouldn't have had it any other way.*'

The above example illustrates the fact that you don't need to conform to a rigid ideal to make your marriage a success. You don't have to have a white dress if you don't want one – Helen got married in gold, with each of her seven attendants dressed in a different colour of the rainbow. Not all of you may share her exhibitionistic streak – but what is it you'd like to do? Live out your dreams. After all, this is *your* day.

A few tips for having a ball at your wedding (the things they don't tell you in the etiquette books)

* If any member of the main wedding party has a tendency to hit the bottle when under pressure, fix the time of the wedding early in the day, well before the pubs open. This can save a lot of tears later. Similarly (an old one this), arrange for any stag or hen nights to take place at least a week in advance. Potential grooms have

been known to be placed in a drunken stupor on the non-stop London-to-Edinburgh train . . .

- Haggle like mad about all costs; don't be afraid that it's not romantic. You can also get a lot of mileage out of telling people you are going to get married: hotels or inns (for the honeymoon) will often give you a free bottle of champagne or fresh flowers and will otherwise try to make your stay as pleasant as possible.
- For some reason, weddings seem to bring out the demon lover in some of us. Great for the bride and groom, but a little disconcerting if your old Uncle Alf makes a pass at the chief bridesmaid. While you can't stop this activity among your guests, you may want to plan your seating arrangements with care if you are going to have formal sit-down meal, to try to ensure that the right people end up going home with one another.
- Befriend your vicar, if you are having a church wedding. We all like to be liked, and a vicar can get quite upset if he thinks you are just taking advantage of him for the great day and have no intention of ever returning to church. Chat him up a little: he can make or break your day.
- Pick the right right-hand man and woman. Your best man or woman should preferably be sober (or at least with a good memory when under the influence), witty and a good speaker. Married best men (and women) have much to recommend them, having gone through all the *angst* before and thus being aware of what you are going through and what can go wrong. Bridesmaids should be sober as above, over the age of three (minimum) and the sort of person that looks after the bride as a No. 1 priority rather than using the opportunity to chat up the best man (particularly if he's married).
- Bossiness is a quality much to be admired in your stage managers (e.g. best man/woman, photographer, even the bride's mother). Arranging a wedding involves enormous feats of organization, and being laid back doesn't help at all.
- On the day of the wedding, keep taking the opportunity to step back, breathe and take it all in. The hours will fly by, and otherwise you may be left with only a blurred memory. Be as conscious as you can of what is happening (keeping alcohol consumption to a minimum can help!). And enjoy yourselves!

Common wedding superstitions

The wedding itself is the principal but not the only ritual which thrusts its way into the consciousness of marrying couples. There will be few brides who do not follow the old adage 'something old, something new, something borrowed, something blue.' You may deride superstitions as a load of old nonsense, but can you really afford to ignore them as the great day approaches?

About the date of the wedding. . .

Married in the month of roses, June,
Life will be one long honeymoon.

June is a popular month for weddings: with the triumph of hope over experience, people actually do expect fine sunny weather. And June derives its name from the goddess Juno, the protector of women and of marriage and the wife of Jupiter, the father of all the gods.

Marriage on your birthday is said to be unlucky *unless* the bride and groom share the same birthday (although the dates must be a year or two apart), in which case it is said to be particularly lucky!

About the bride. . .

Most of the wedding superstitions have the bride as their object. Perhaps their complexity and sheer number were designed to take her mind off the worries of the wedding; at least if she occupied herself with trying to abide by the superstitions, they would take her mind off other things. Here is a selection:

The dress

It is generally considered unlucky for the bride to make her own dress (even dressmakers will usually not make their own) and particularly unlucky to try on the full bridal outfit and accoutrements too soon (leave off a shoe, the old wives suggest).

As for its colour:

- White is a symbol of purity and of virtue.
- Green typifies youth, hope and happiness (although the bad fairy alludes to jealousy).
- Red is a sign of vigour, courage and great passion.
- Violet represents dignity, pride and high ideals.

An old veil is supposed to be luckier than a new one, particularly if it is a family heirloom.

On the way to the church

Lucky signs include:

- the bride being woken by birdsong, and finding a spider in the folds of her dress.
- The bride leaving home by the front door, with her right foot first.

- 'Happy the bride whom the sun shines on.' (This seems particularly unfair with our climate!) The Germans say the exact opposite, looking on each drop of rain as a blessing to the marriage.
- the bride seeing a lamb, a dove, a spider, a toad, a chimney sweep or a black cat en route to the church.
  Unlucky signs include:
- espying a funeral party or a pig crossing the road in front of the wedding car (but, on the bright side, the chance of catching sight of a suicidal pig hurtling around your average church must be fairly slim).
- the bride weeping before the wedding (she may, naturally, weep buckets afterwards).

About the groom

- He should not see his bride on the wedding day before the wedding itself, nor may he see the wedding dress beforehand.
- Under no circumstances should he turn back for anything once he has left for the ceremony, nor should he drop the wedding ring before putting it on his bride's finger.
- He should carry a small mascot in his pocket and pay the church fees with an odd sum of money (presumably the vicar will not object to a penny more rather than a penny less).
- After the honeymoon, he should carry his wife over the threshold of their home. (A few exercises in advance of the wedding would not go amiss: on a practical level, it must be bad luck to drop the bride!)

PART III

NUTS AND BOLTS

11

Marriage contracts

MARRIAGE is itself a form of contract – but the terms can often seem pretty hazy. The vows you make in church, if you opt for a religious ceremony, can provide a form of structure for your relationship, although many of the couples we interviewed perceived them more as ideals to aim for rather than principles which regulated their day-to-day existence. But whether you marry in church, or in a Register Office or whether you simply choose to live together, one thing all of us have in common is having to decide how we, as couples, will run our everyday lives.

Once upon a time, it was simple – Adam delved and Eve span. But now, like as not, as both men and women do a bit of metaphorical delving and spinning, together with a million and one other things, it's not so easy to determine how your relationship will operate. How will the children be brought up, what about sex, how will you work out financial contributions are all questions which are bound to come up, as well as the more mundane but none the less essential issues of how you deal with the housework and cooking, not to mention what you will do if the marriage runs into difficulties.

In marriage alliances of the latter part of the 20th century and in those of the 21st century, isn't it about time we evolved a new, perhaps more open way of organizing our lives together? One such way is to make up for yourselves and enter into a *marriage contract*. You can choose to enter into one at any time before or after the wedding, although as things change over time, you may need to adapt or update it from time to time. As one American lawyer said as she signed her prenuptial agreement: 'Nobody but a fool would make a contract for life . . .'

Why a marriage contract?

The attitudes we came across towards marriage contracts were fairly extreme. Some people simply hated the idea: 'No, I could never imagine doing that. I hate rules and regulations – it would take all the romance out of things, wouldn't it?' Others, with reservations, loved it:

89

'Well, it might help. I sometimes don't know where I stand. If we worked things out properly in advance, that could well make things a lot clearer. Maybe it would give us more security, too – knowing what will happen rather than just . . . I wouldn't mind giving it a go!'

The idea is certainly not a new one: in the old days, wealthy English families set up settlements for their daughters on marriage, to ensure that family capital could be kept tied up and out of the hands of potentially spendthrift husbands. And nowadays they are becoming increasingly common. In the United States, for example, marrying couples are encouraged to enter into marriage contracts – or 'agreements' – that set out each partner's responsibilities, which, says John Haines, an American family mediator, helps to give them 'a clear understanding as they embark on marriage'. In Europe, marriage contracts are very popular. In Switzerland, for instance, no woman with assets of her own would dream of entering marriage without the financial issues being neatly tidied up in black and white beforehand. And in orthodox Judaism, the form of marriage itself is symbolized by a contract (see p.67–8), which becomes the property of the wife so that she can shake it at her husband if he dare to disobey. Admittedly, the present-day value of 200 silver *zuzim* may be hard to negotiate on the open market, but it's the thought that counts.

And that's the nub of our need to look at the issues which are bound to come up in marriage – the thought. Too often, people marry in a daze and then wake up to find that their partners have views quite different from their own. This can make life difficult. Comments one wife of nearly ten years:

'I think I would have seriously rethought our marriage if I'd realized what my husband's attitudes were about childcare. I just never dreamed he'd see it was all down to me – I thought he'd play his part. Now it's maybe too late. But if, in the beginning, we'd have sat down together and worked out what our attitudes were, at least I'd have had the chance to negotiate – and to know what I was letting myself in for.'

Husbands may similarly be in for a nasty shock when they come down to earth and find that their wives have no intention of doing all their ironing and that they can't get a button sewn on even if they offer to fix the dripping tap. It all comes down to expectations. If these are too great and unrealistic, you're setting up problems for your future life together. But if you each know, after working out the issues with one another, what your expectations really are, then your marriage is being built on strong foundations.

Contracts will not, however, work automatically by themselves. They need the added ingredient of goodwill on both sides to make the marriage work smoothly. Don't underestimate the value of sitting down and talking to one another about the issues that are likely to come up or are already staring you straight in the eye. Even if you ultimately decide not to go ahead and devise a full, written marriage contract, discussing the possibility of having one can be a good focus for talking things through.

The legal status of marriage contracts

One drawback of marriage contracts is that they come with a legal health warning. Because marriage, as an institution, is regulated by the law, the courts preserve for themselves the right to examine the way in which married couples regulate their affairs. You can't state in a contract that it is a final, once-and-for-all agreement – the courts will always retain for themselves the final say, however much you may want to avoid this. So, even if you agree in your contract that, in the event of a breakup, all your property will be split according to what you each have earned, the courts will not necessarily see themselves as being bound by this. *In effect, your contract is highly unlikely to be legally enforceable.* The courts will not force one of you to take care of an equal share of the housework, even if that is what you have agreed in your contract.

A marriage contract is really a gentleman's (and gentlewoman's) agreement – a matter of honour between you and your partner. It may not have the full force of the law behind it, but it does give you the opportunity to commit yourselves to a way of living that will support and nurture you both – not one at the expense of the other. It can also be tailor-made to suit your own particular circumstances. Because you and your partner will decide for yourselves what sorts of issues you want to cover, it can be as broad or as narrow in scope as you like.

So what sorts of things could a marriage contract cover?

Although this is not an exhaustive list, a contract could contain provisions for the following:

Purpose   What aims do you have, jointly and/or individually, for the relationship and also for the contract?

Duration   Do you want to create a contract for life or for a certain fixed term? A marriage, like any relationship, is constantly evolving. You do not need to chisel in stone the terms by which your marriage will work throughout its lifetime. It is probably sensible to fix a limit at first – say, of 12 months – to see how things work out. Or you could have a contract that is valid until you have children and agree to renegotiate then as you wish.

Your work   What are your work priorities? Do you both want to work, and are you both able to? Whose career comes first, or are your careers equal?

Finances   Will you pool your earnings or keep your incomes separate? Do you intend to have savings? Will you divide up any savings or other assets you already have? How will you deal with any debts?

Property   What about properties either of you own in your own right? What about properties bought while you have been together? Are these owned jointly? What about properties in the future?

Your home   Do you want to live in the country or in a town? Do you prefer living in a modern or an old building? Who will be responsible for choosing the décor and furnishings or can you share this? Are you both willing to have people to stay?

Housework   How will this be divided? Who will clean, cook, wash up, do the washing and the ironing? How will this change if one of you is not earning?

Surnames   Will you, as a wife, take your husband's name or do you intend keeping your own name? What surname will your children have?

Sex   Do you both intend to be monogamous? Will you tell each other if you are not?

Children   Do you both want children? How soon? How many? Who will be responsible for caring for them?

Religion   Do you have any conflicts over religion? Will your children be brought up with any religious beliefs? If the two of you are of two different religions, which will the children be brought up in?

Wills   Have you both made wills? How do you wish to deal with your estates?

Personal behaviour/habits/hobbies   How will you eat together if one of you is vegetarian and the other not? If only one of you smokes, are you going to designate smoke-free zones in the home? If one wants to play sport one or more days a week, is this acceptable?

Problems   What will happen if the relationship goes wrong? Would you wish to attend counselling? If either of you breaks the agreement, how will you resolve that?

Many of the emotional issues that can be contained within the contents of a marriage contract are discussed in Part IV.

Marriage contracts: an example

The above list will give you an idea of the kinds of issues that could be covered in a marriage contract. Here is a fictitious form of contract (which does not exhaustively include each issue mentioned above) which you can adapt to suit your own particular circumstances.

**THIS AGREEMENT is made in England this—day of—19—
BETWEEN Fred Smith (Fred) and Mimi West Smith
(Mimi) both of 12 Acacia Avenue, Anytown.
BACKGROUND
Fred and Mimi wish to create a contract to govern their
mode of living together in order that they shall both
create a loving and satisfying union between them.
THEY HEREBY AGREE AS FOLLOWS:**

1 This Agreement will last for a period of three years from the date hereof.

2.1 Fred intends to continue working as a design consultant for the foreseeable future. He would like one day to set up his own company but wishes to gain at least a further five years' experience in employment. As his work may entail travel abroad, Fred may spend periods of up to three months abroad in any 12 calendar months for so long as no children have been born. If Mimi becomes pregnant, Fred agrees that he will use his best endeavours to agree with his employers that he will work within a radius of 50 miles of the Anytown area.

2.2 Mimi intends to continue working as a teacher until such time as she becomes pregnant. She wishes to remain at home for a period of at least six months following the birth of any child she may have, and thereafter would like to return as a supply teacher, working no more than three days per week during school terms until all her children reach school age. She and Fred agree that, no later than three months after the birth of their first child, they will discuss childcare and work arrangements further to explore whether they are both still in agreement with the plans set out herein.

3.1 Fred and Mimi intend to be faithful and committed to each other.

3.2 They both value a fulfilling sexual and mutually loving relationship highly. They agree to make time to spend with one another, spending at least one evening a week and one day at weekends together. An evening begins at 6.30 pm.

4.1 Fred and Mimi shall each pay into the joint account a sum not less than three-quarters of their respective earnings.

4.2 Any savings made by either or both shall be shared equally.

4.3 All payments relating to the mortgage, house outgoings, food, television, hire/purchase, pensions and insurance shall be paid from the joint account. Any other payments shall be met individually by Fred and Mimi.

4.4 In the event of the joint account exceeding the overdraft limit of £250, Fred and Mimi shall meet the shortfall in shares of 6:4 respectively.

4.5 In the event of Mimi becoming pregnant during the term of this Agreement, Fred and Mimi will renegotiate all of Clause 4, save for 4.6 below.

4.6 Fred and Mimi shall each insure the other's life in the sum of £75,000.

5 All property and assets whatsoever held by Fred and Mimi shall be viewed as joint assets, held in equal shares, save for Fred's golfclubs and Mimi's word processor, which belong to each of them individually.

6   Fred and Mimi shall live in Anytown for the foreseeable future, although they hereby agree to discuss further and keep under review Fred's wish to live in the Italian countryside.

7.1   Fred and Mimi intend to divide household tasks equally. They shall alternate on a weekly basis responsibility for (1) cooking, shopping and throwing away rubbish with (2) washing up, washing, cleaning and general household chores. They shall use their best endeavours to make this arrangement work.

7.2   This arrangement shall be reviewed after a period of six months. If it has not worked to the reasonable satisfaction of both of them, Fred and Mimi agree to explore the idea of employing a cleaner.

8.1   Fred and Mimi both wish and hope to have children, although they shall not attempt to have a child for a period of at least six months from the date hereof.

8.2   They both agree that having children is their first priority and that the needs of the children shall, wherever possible, be given first consideration.

8.3   In terms of childcare, they agree that Mimi will, in the first place, give up her job to care for the children. Fred shall fully contribute to and share in the care of their children.

8.4   Their child(ren) shall be brought up according to the tenets of the Church of England.

9.1   Mimi wishes to be known by her married name of Smith but will keep her maiden name of West as her middle name.

9.2   If Fred and Mimi have children, they shall each take Mimi's maiden name of West as their middle name (or as their last middle name).

10.1   If, in the opinion of at least one of them, the relationship undergoes serious problems, Fred and Mimi agree to attend marriage guidance counselling.

10.2   They further agree that neither of them shall commence divorce proceedings without first attending at least six marriage guidance or conciliation sessions.

11.1   If any of the terms of this Agreement are broken, Fred and Mimi shall, in the first instance, endeavour to resolve the breach between themselves. If they fail to reach agreement, then they shall refer their problem to a marriage guidance counsellor.

11.2   The terms of this Agreement shall not be varied save in writing and signed by both parties.

12   Fred and Mimi agree to review this Agreement at the end of its term.

SIGNED by Fred Smith and Mimi West Smith

In the presence of:

(This agreement is drafted so that a witness will also sign, having watched Fred and Mimi signing their own names to the document. However, it is not necessary to do this if you do not wish to have a third party be involved.)

Entering into a marriage contract is a bold step. To confront head-on and all at once the issues which come up from time to time in a relationship may prove to be too much. This at least was the attitude of couples who consulted Helen while she practised as a matrimonial lawyer. Although a number came to her to discuss the terms of a cohabitation contract (similar in form to a marriage contract), in the end none completed them. Some found the experience of discussing all these issues useful; others found it to be just too much. No married couples in her experience (admittedly a straw poll) were brave enough even to try, although a few did enter into trust deeds dealing with their property.

Remember: if you do wish to take this step, the agreement is not legally binding. If you are having difficulty in drafting the terms, it can be helpful to see a solicitor to ask for some advice.

12

The name game

S O what's in a name? Well, quite a lot. Marriage is essentially a public statement. To live with someone outside marriage is no longer considered to be morally reprehensible and it can be financially advantageous. But what marriage *does* still provide is a unique form of social recognition and blessing, a public dimension to your private union which may give your relationship an unexpectedly positive reinforcement as it continues to unfold. Marriage confers upon married folk a clear status within the family circle and within the eyes of the world at large. In this respect, life for *un*married adults can be problematic:

- A businesswoman in her mid-30s murmurs in vexation: 'I could be Prime Minister! If I wasn't married, it wouldn't make a jot of difference to my parents. I'd still be their little girl!' Men may ridicule the neutral feminist 'Ms' but how many of them would care to be known as 'Master' Jones until permitted by marriage (and by marriage alone) to shed, metaphorically speaking, their long socks and shorts and join the ranks of mature men by putting 'Mr' in front of their names? It is a distinction by which women are assessed every day of their lives.
- At a family reunion in the parental home, the unmarried 29-year-old son is instructed to abandon his live-in lover of seven years to shiver on the sitting-room couch while his married younger brother and wife bask together in a double bed under the warm glow of parental approval.
- The LWS factor. How on earth *do* you refer to him or her when you are 'living with someone'? 'Boyfriend' sounds adolescent, 'partner' sounds offputtingly brisk and business-like, 'lover' a little *too* descriptive. 'He-whom-I-live-with' is both ambiguous (could mean a lodger) and a trifle long, and while 'significant other' may be cool with Californians. . . All this can be solved at a stroke: 'This is my husband/wife' is clear, straightforward and sounds gratifyingly mature.

Such problems as these may sound trivial, yet what they express is a very real confusion, even unease, in placing the *un*married couple within a society which is still by and large, cemented together by the institution of marriage. These difficulties may, accordingly, be quite influential in breeding the desire to marry. Karen and Michael had met in London and lived together for many years. But Karen found visits to her parents' house in a small Welsh village increasingly difficult. She never felt able to take Michael back home with her:

> '*I can only think now that my parents may have thought – who is this person, using our daughter? They blanked him out completely. Though they never actually refused to have him down, it would have embarrassed them so much with everyone in the village gossiping and knowing I wasn't married. When we told them that we were getting married, they were delighted. Over the moon. . . Yes, I think my parents really were the driving force behind my marriage. . .*'

Marriage represents public acceptance, approval and solemnization of the sexual relationship between an adult man and woman. Once the wedding has been successfully negotiated, everyone – and particularly within the family circle – may feel enormous relief at the new roles clearly provided for them. Yet in the name game, for the woman at least, the resolution of one dilemma only brings on another. . .

A wife by any other name?

The decision as to whether or not to change your name on marriage can be one of great symbolic importance. For women, that is. Although exceptions existed in the past, notably when a male commoner married into the nobility, on the whole men have never been expected nor expected themselves to subsume their birth names into their partners' in the interests of family unity.

The custom that a woman changes her name to her husband's upon marriage is so deeply entrenched in our society that many people mistakenly assume it has the force of law behind it. Not so. The law about surnames is remarkably simple and clear cut. As long as there is no intention to defraud or mislead, you can change your surname as often as you like, simply by declaring your intention to do so. You can change your name today to Minnie Mouse or Starship Enterprise. Nobody can stop you. (Note, however, that this does not obviate the occasional need to be able to provide proof of your newly assumed identity. For this, a deed poll may be necessary – see below.)

Nevertheless, the debate about whether or not women should change their names still continues; and for many, it continues without a satisfactory ending. The following are the main alternatives, with their respective pros and cons.

Changing your name to your husband's

This is the conventional and still the preferred choice of the vast majority of new wives. It offers the great practical advantage that the arrival of children will present no complications: they will simply assume the existing family name.

One new wife, who eventually decided to change her name, agonized for some time at first: she wanted to share the same name as her husband but was loath to shed her maiden name. Her husband could not see what all the fuss was about: 'Until I suggested that he could change his surname to mine, instead. He went very pale: "But that's *my* name," he said!'

For another of our interviewees, the choice was not as difficult as it had at first appeared:

> *'Originally, I had viewed the decision to change my name from a feminist perspective and was determined not to give up something that was mine. I then realized that my options were still both men's names – my father's and my husband's! My mother's name (which was her father's name anyway!) didn't come into it. Eventually I abandoned what I thought had been strongly held beliefs, and took my husband's name: I like him a lot more than my father and I much prefer his surname.'*

There may be a special symbolic importance for a man in having his wife and children adopt his family name. A woman's parentage of her children can never be questioned; they issue from her body and are, indisputably, hers. A man can have no such absolute certainty. In the past, as today, his parentage is demonstrated to the world by his wife's acknowledgement of it, symbolized by her adoption of his name on behalf of both herself and her children. Sometimes it can matter deeply to a man that his wife be seen by others to share his name, as one of our women interviewees discovered, rather to her surprise: 'It was funny because our joint account had my single name on it, and when we were walking around Mothercare and buying some things, Nick got really embarrassed because I wasn't down there as his wife. So we got the name on the account changed. . .'

Keeping your maiden name

We present ourselves to the world by our names; we answer automatically if someone calls us by our name. The name by which we have been known since our birth becomes, in effect, a part of us. If we as women have started off upon our own careers and have achieved in our birthnames a measure of distinction, respectability, fame or fortune (however little this may seem in the eyes of the rest of the world), to leave our names behind can feel like losing a part of everything we have built up for ourselves in our pre-marriage lives.

For this reason and for others, some women choose to retain their existing names. It is a choice that makes a strong statement to the world that, within your relationship, you have both decided to keep your separate identities despite the fact you are married. This may seem right for some couples and may work particularly well in childless marriages or in the transition period before the arrival of children.

However, when a child arrives, whose name does it take? Usually, it seems, the husband's. At this point, a wife may feel uncomfortable about having a different name from the rest of her family, and quietly succumb. Some women find a workable solution by retaining their maiden names professionally and adopting their husband's surname in their homelife. This choice may require careful thinking through as well as organization: what about your passport? and your credit cards? have you got acceptable back-up identification for both names, as necessary? You may end up by feeling a bit schizophrenic; on the other hand, you may enjoy the freedom and separation of home and work identities indicated by your use of two separate names.

Hyphenating your names or adopting a new family name

When the writer E. F. Benson's Miss Mapp marries Major Benjy-boy Flint, she hyphenated her name with his because 'he had only an Army Pension and she was a woman of substance in every sense of the word and it was only proper.'

Snobbery apart, finding a new name to share – whether an amalgam of your existing names or something completely different – may be the right choice for some couples because of the degree of mutuality and shared compromise involved. The changing of both your names symbolizes the willingness of both of you to alter and adapt to a new married identity.

The device of adding together the bride and groom's surnames, however, even if aurally attractive (which many are not), only works for one generation. The offspring of such marriages will be left to dream up another way out if their new surnames are not to take up all the pages of their passports when they, in turn, marry.

A wife who changes her name to her husband's on marriage will be asked, at most, for a copy of her marriage certificate as proof of subsequent identity. If you do both choose to adopt a new name, a number of public bodies – for example the Passport Office – usually require some kind of formal proof. To this end, a solicitor can prepare a form of document – often called a deed poll – which acknowledges your different name and your intention to be known by it in future. The cost for this service is not high – usually in the region of about £50. So, if your own particular answer involves you both altering your names, it would be wise to go and see a solicitor so that you can have your choice formalized.

13

In prosperity and adversity

In an instant Will was close to her and had his arms round her, but she drew her head back and held his away gently that she might go on speaking, her large tear-filled eyes looking at his very simply while she said in a sobbing childlike way, 'We could live quite well on my own fortune – it is too much – seven hundred a-year – I want so little – no new clothes – and I will learn what everything costs.'

George Eliot, *Middlemarch*

A study of married couples in the United States reported in the newspaper *US Today* in May 1988 showed, perhaps startlingly, that a full 52 per cent of all marital arguments were about money. Money has taken the No. 1 hot spot in relationships between the sexes; no other subject is as guaranteed, on the surface at least, to produce so much emotion and potential conflict. And it may come as no great surprise to you to find that the topic of housework is not far behind as a source of discomfort and argument.

Caught in the escalating (and expensive) cycle of getting married, becoming a householder and then perhaps a parent, moving up the career ladder and surrounding yourself with all the usual accoutrements of success (i.e. what everyone else you know seems to take for granted), while at the same time having to negotiate between your different individual priorities and attitudes to money management – it is not surprising that money can move centre stage in marital quarrels.

Housework is, in some ways, the other side of the equation – or used to be, at least, in the days when the marriage deal was that he went out hunting every day and she stayed at home to take care of the cave and the children. Simpler times. But now when man needs to hunt no further than the nearest supermarket and man and woman frequently share the burden of producing an income to support the household, has that change been reflected in the way household tasks are shared out? The answer seems to be a resounding NO!

101

In the rest of Part III, we will be looking at various aspects of money management in marriage, and also the question of who does what in the home. But before getting down to this, an important question needs to be considered: namely, *is* it money – or, indeed, housework – in itself which can generate so much aggravation? Or is it what the whole equation of who earns, who spends and who cleans the toilet symbolizes: a question of who really has the power in the relationship?

In our society, some goods and services almost invariably have prices attached to them and therefore have a commercial value. Some other, very important ones do not – and the most notable are the many and varied domestic services provided by homemakers, usually women, for their own families. To support a household, money must be acquired in the outside world, but the relationship must also be cared for from within. Marriage thus exists at the cutting edge between the commercial and domestic realms.

In a thriving business, some workers must be deployed in manufacturing goods or offering services, going out into the world, making contacts and contracts, selling and trading. Other workers will be involved in forward planning, management and catering for the well-being of the company's personnel and ensuring that the business keeps on line towards its ultimate goals. Profits will be deployed into a level of reimbursement which keeps the workforce and management active and contentedly productive, to meet running expenses and, insofar as possible, to contribute to long-term investments.

A good company recognizes the value of its management structure and support personnel as much as it recognizes the value of its manufacturing and trading staff. Employees are deployed in the areas for which their talents and skills best befit them. Each department has its own contributions to make, without which the company would not survive. Each depends on the others to keep functioning and recognizes the others' worth. It is, of course, exactly the same in a good marriage. Or is it?

Money: a loaded subject

When a couple first marry, they may maintain, for a while at least, fairly separate financial arrangements – independent incomes, individual accounts and personal savings and debts. Yet even from the very earliest days, shared arrangements must also be made. By virtue of living together, even the most independent couple take on shared financial responsibilities – for mortgage repayments or rent, taxes and electricity, gas and grocery bills. In addition, there may be one or more cars to run, holidays to plan for and all kinds of further expenses. Unless you as a couple are exceptionally well-heeled, priorities need to be established. And unless your earnings and existing financial commitments are identical (an extremely unusual state of affairs), there is the vexed question of what proportion of each income should go towards joint expenses, and how what is left over might be apportioned for individual spending or saving.

And as the relationship develops, particularly if one of you stops or reduces work to start a family, inherent tensions may come to the fore. In few enough relationships are the salaries that are earned, and the work burdens that are taken on to earn them, more or less equal. We may today be starting to feel uncomfortable with the previously universally accepted idea that the one who earns or earns more (usually the husband) should have more prestige and the right to have more say in how the family's spending priorities are ordered – yet this state of affairs still applies in a majority of marriages.

When you first start a serious relationship, your partner's attitude to money (not to mention the delicate subject of his or her present wherewithal), *may* not enter too much into conscious consideration. Yet subliminally, have you not taken careful note of this aspect in building up your mental picture of your beloved, idealized or otherwise? For his or her relationship to money – how they get it, spend it and save it – not only places them in the public world, it also speaks volumes about why you are attracted to each other in the first place and foreshadows the patterns which may start unfolding once your relationship gets under way.

Duncan's parents were cautious and frugal in their attitudes to money, maintaining a far lower standard of living than their income could have allowed them. Duncan was attracted to his wife because, among other things, she is similarly careful. She makes Duncan feel safe and secure, but at the same time, *her* thriftiness makes him able to be more extravagant in what is to him, given his background, quite a rebellious way. He knows she is his brake, his safety net.

Joan has mixed attitudes about money. After her parents' marriage broke down messily, she was brought up by a rich maiden aunt, who regarded Joan's parents' Bohemian lifestyle with disdain. Joan at first chose men who were much older than she was and who were well off financially. However, the man she finally fell for is a struggling poet, who looks to her to provide their joint income. Through her experiences with him and their battles over money, she has been forced to examine what her priorities and values really are.

Whether, like Duncan, we ultimately opt for marriage partners with whom we can establish financial dynamics similar to the ones which reigned in our own families, or whether, like Joan, we apparently rebel and attempt to establish different ones, the chances are that, one way or another, we shall be setting up and re-enacting power struggles in some respects similar to the ones we saw rehearsed in our childhoods.

In Duncan's case, his wife's caution has set up a familiar and thus safe environment for her husband, while also freeing him to be more adventurous in his spending. Full of ambivalent feelings about his own family's thrift and the unnecessary sacrifices and struggles which he had hated even as a child, he can now vent his irritations on his wife – with his tacit agreement, she had assumed the monetary driving seat – while allowing *her* anxieties to have free rein in determining the financial arrangements they will make as a couple.

In her final choice of mate, Joan has, on the surface, rejected the values of her later childhood – i.e. that money is of great importance – and chosen a man whose values and lifestyle more reflect those of her own parents. Unconsciously, she is re-enacting the role she played as a tiny child, when seeing the chaos all around, she took control and tried as best she could to look after the family herself. In her conflicts over money with her husband, she veers between trying to control everything and despairingly giving up and demanding that her husband takes responsibility for their financial affairs (just as her aunt came to the rescue when her early family life collapsed).

Marriage can all too easily become a power struggle – about who has the right to make decisions, who is the most respected, who is dominant and who is subservient. The struggle is frequently played out in the money arena: Will her extravagance or his frugality prevail? Does the one who earns more have more say in spending? *Should* s/he have more say? Will the couple take on a bigger house/mortgage/work commitments or will they make shared time with each other and with the children a more important priority? Is unnecessary scrimping and saving causing resentment and tensions? And will the unexpected legacy from Auntie Maud be spent on a trip down the Nile or used to pay off the credit card bill?

The foundations of the division of power between a couple and the values which will dominate their marriage are laid down in its opening chapters. In a healthy relationship, a couple will be able to work out between themselves their priorities in making and spending money and will share an accurate assessment of their circumstances. Decisions can then be negotiated democratically and financial matters dealt with on a more or less matter-of-fact basis.

In an unhealthy relationship, too much power can reside in one partner to the detriment of the other, causing anger and resentment which are likely to flare up over issues unimportant in themselves – did she really need to buy that expensive free-range chicken? How could he have frittered away so much money at the card table without noticing? And because the couple rarely acknowledge the power struggle openly for what it is, because they rehearse the same battles about money over and over again in the same pseudo-reasonable fashion, they never have the chance to get to grips with what is really going on.

From an individual to a couple to a family: changing financial roles

In the spring days of a marriage or relationship, there may be not much to choose between the couple in terms of the respective earning power of each. Yet even in these halcyon early days, when love is young and two incomes flow smoothly into the couple's assorted bank accounts, there may be a very real difference between men's and women's perceptions of their own and each other's careers and relationships to money – differences which may become more noticeable as the years slip by and children arrive. For money and the getting of it still tend to have different places in the respective worlds of men and of women.

Women's money

We have moved a long way very quickly from the days when all an old-fashioned girl was looking for was an old-fashioned millionaire. Women once worked only if they had to (i.e. if their fathers or husbands could not provide), and wifedom and motherhood were perceived by almost everyone as a woman's true vocation. Today's woman has moved far from the world not only of her grandmother's but of her mother's generation. She has stepped out into the world of men, side by side with whom she now works and earns.

These rapid changes have meant confusion for little girls born since World War II. On the one hand, they saw their mothers generally confined to the home, devoting their lives to their menfolk and children. Money was man's domain, sometimes enviable, sometimes unattractive – always foreign. On the other, they heard the rumblings of feminism urging them to get out of the home and carve 'proper' careers for themselves. The traditional woman's work of running the home was derided; the important thing was to be independent – and that meant financially independent. The little girls' mothers whispered to them that they could do it: 'Go out and find yourself (as I never could)!' 'Enjoy a career of your own (I never had the chance)!'

The mothers saw their chance – they would find fulfilment vicariously, through their daughters' achievements. And the little girls learned the lesson. They marched firmly into the marketplace. They worked hard at their chosen careers and made their money, dutifully did their aerobic exercises, formed strong (if competitive) relationships with women friends and had sexual relationships with men. They had their own jobs, cars and one or two annual holidays abroad.

Yet for the married career woman without a 'wife' to take the strain, it has not all been unalloyed bliss. Welcome to the Monday morning rush hour and the corporate world! The increasing tendency of women to rely on the traditional male buffer of alcohol and cigarettes to cushion the blows and get them through the day is a clear sign that the strains are beginning to show. Comments Kate, a young mother who is starting up her own business from home and finding it hard work:

> *'I never seem to have a minute to myself. If ever I do take a moment out of the day to sit down and have a rest, all I can see is unironed washing or the fact that the bathroom cupboard needs another coat of paint. So I get up and it starts all over again. We're trying to have another baby, but since I fall asleep in the evening as soon as I go to bed or even sit down, Gavin isn't having much joy in getting me interested. I feel as if I'm juggling all the time – and what will happen if I drop a ball?'*

Once in the workplace, to keep their heads above water, women have had to be as committed as men – as well as remaining the traditional homemakers who must make life easy and pleasant for their husbands. The strain inherent in their frenetic lifestyle may become hard to cope with once the marriage is well and truly under way. And when the family household is enlarged by the arrival of Junior (who has not been designed to conform to the dictates of the eight-hour day), it's all change. . .

The wife who reduces or stops her paid work to have a baby may have very mixed feelings. Despite impressions to the contrary in the media (staffed to a man or woman by people who *have* arranged for someone else to look after their children, or else do not have any), she is still the norm – only 7 per cent of mothers of preschool children work full time. This is reflected in the career patterns and expectations of women. Even today, few women see ahead of them the long work-tunnel perceived by their men; instead they tend to anticipate a series of periods in work alternating with periods at home with their children.

On the positive side, a woman leaving paid work may feel relief from the constant pressures (and boredom) of being someone else's wage slave. She is less rushed, less torn in two; she does not suffer the guilt of the full-time career mother. She has enough time (and more inclination) to be able to look after her family, and as a result, they may all feel happier and more valued, too.

Joanna had spent ten years in the competitive business of advertising before marrying at the age of 30 and leaving work to have a baby:

> *'It was difficult leaving work at the end and I really expected to miss it when I was finally at home with the baby. But I'm surprised at how rewarding I find being a mother – being able to load up the push-chair and saunter off with her to the park on a fine spring morning to feed the ducks instead of jamming on to the Victoria Line tube with everyone else. . . It is difficult financially – not having an independent income any more, of course,*

but mainly just because there is so much less money generally coming into the family. Still, having more time compensates for a lot.'

Of course, not every woman finds the transition so surprisingly pleasant. On the negative side, a woman may sense her value and prestige in the eyes of the world taking a sharp drop, and may judge herself accordingly – the 'I'm only a housewife and mother, I'm afraid' syndrome. Feeling powerless, she feels guilty about spending 'his' money on anything for herself, or she becomes the mirror-opposite: a shopaholic who resents her husband's financial clout and fights back with her charge card. Or she may just miss the companionship and challenge of work, deciding sooner or later that the life of a non-earner is not for her.

Peter and Robin married after they had lived together for three years, primarily because they wanted to start a family. Peter's income was erratic – he worked from home as a car trader – but at times it could be very profitable. Robin's income – she worked at a job which she enjoyed very much, as a school secretary – was steady but comparatively low. After they had their first baby, Robin had planned to stay at home until the second one arrived, but soon found herself feeling fed up:

'I used to get so tired and bored all day when it was just me and the baby. I love him very much but not to the extent that I don't want to have any other kind of stimulation. I wanted to go back to work as soon as my maternity period was up, and I did so, even though the actual cash isn't that important. I just needed to talk to someone. But once the second one comes along, I suppose I shall have to give it all up.'

One of the difficulties for Robin was certainly her new and not so welcome reliance on Peter for cash.

'I always had my own money – I could do what I wanted with it. Now I have to get money out of the joint bank account. I suppose I don't mind too much about not having any privacy about money – not that he's at all difficult. It's just that I'd like something of my own.'

Women may have been told that they can have it all, but is it really possible to have a sense of equal value without equal earning power? And if equal earning power along with equal commitment to paid jobs is the answer, who will provide the extra hours in the day to care for the home and the children? And in the meantime, how are the menfolk coping?

Men's money

> *It is a truth universally acknowledged, that a single man in possession*
> *of a good fortune, must be in want of a wife.*

Jane Austen, Pride and Prejudice

Men seem to have been taking a primarily reactive role in the recent social changes affecting the family, responding as best they can to the radical demands of their women. Many men still seem to be reeling from the shock. And the shock can be most apparent in marriage, when men find they are not getting what they bargained for:

> *'I think I expected a certain amount of, well, services from my wife. I*
> *don't mean sex, but sort of doing the washing, getting my shirts ironed,*
> *having meals cooked. I mean I can cook, I think I'm a good cook, but I*
> *didn't expect to have to do it much. She hardly ever seems to be in, and*
> *even when she is in, she's tired. And as for ironing – well, I've given up*
> *even thinking she'll do it. I don't mind so much really – it's just that I*
> *never thought it would be this way.'*

Men still generally expect to take on the dual roles of a career and, ultimately, family provider. Jobs may change, change frequently even, yet a man's career tends to remain a constant identity-giving focus. A man who marries has 'responsibilities'; he knuckles under and accepts the harness willingly (or at least stoically) for life. The work-tunnel starts the moment he begins his first full-time job and will only come to an end on his retirement some 40+ years later.

When men were little boys, the bargain that was tacitly struck between the male and female sexes seemed clear: 'I'll provide the money and you'll look after me.' But, seemingly while men were not looking, the goal posts have been moved. How do men see themselves today in relationship to money? Their attitudes on the whole appear to have changed far less than women's.

The two most frequent role models that boys have to measure themselves against seem to be starkly different mirror-opposites. A boy saw his father cast in the role of *responsible provider*. As far back as the boy could remember, his father went out to work (where he seemed to spend an astonishingly long time), he brought in the pay packet and he supported the family. If Mum worked at all, it would only be later and then only part-time, after she has served out her son's Cocopops and juice, packed his satchel and waved him off to school. Her earnings (such as they were) were deemed pin money. Dad was the one on whom the family depended for its survival – and if this message were not plain enough, his mother would reinforce the importance of what went on outside the four walls of home. 'Don't disturb your father. Can't you see he's tired?' ordered Mum, washed out herself but uncomplaining. 'I can't make Sports Day, I've got an important meeting,' said Dad, importantly. The demands of the workplace relegated the family into second place.

The boy came to the conclusion that work at the office, or the factory, or wherever it was that so exhausted his father, could not be a bed of roses. However, while the boy was constantly assured of the need to get a good secure job, his father and his friends privately whispered to him about the pleasures that were in store before this life sentence of work started: 'Go travel the world – meet a few people – enjoy yourself – have a few laughs! Sow your wild oats!'

So the adolescent schoolboy was introduced to the second stereotype – the *careless spender* – and encouraged to give in to his burgeoning hedonistic desires, secure in the knowledge that Mum or Dad would pick up the pieces as required. It was all seen as part of the initiation to growing up. Whether he earned or received an allowance, he would blow his new-found cash on getting drunk or buying a motorcycle. He discovered girls, and spent his money with a view to getting them into bed. He found that the desire to have money to throw around can all too easily become confused with more intangible needs – the need for prestige in the eyes of your peers, the need to be seen as mature, sophisticated and sexually desirable.

Girls are not, of course, immune from using money this way, but in the teenage mating game, boys are as likely to be judged on their spending power, car and material sophistication as girls are on their prettiness, curves and general amenability. The deal does not necessarily change much as the years pass; the truth is that material wealth and power are regarded as sexually attractive qualities in men by many women. Once a man has settled down into the role of responsible provider, the alternative role of casual spender – bit of a lad? playboy? adulterer even? – may exercise a potent, forbidden charm.

And as the fantasy of attracting hordes of admiring women may be a part of what lures a man into the role of spender, so getting married (in male mythology) means he is caught/trapped by his woman and hitched up to the cart which he must thereafter drag through life in order to earn his (and the family's) crust. This theme is vividly explored in the 1962 film, *A Kind of Loving*, when our hero, Vic (played by Alan Bates), sees his hopes and ambitions dashed when the girl he is courting tells him she has fallen pregnant. Vic does the decent thing and marries her, and resigns himself to the work from which he has been longing to escape. But his new wife loses the baby, and this tragedy is compounded by the day-in, day-out strains of having to live with an intrusive mother-in-law. Vic's bitterness and resentment and his wife's failure to understand how his hopes have been dashed scar their marriage.

In all of the trauma of finding their way in the material world, men are taught that they cannot expect to be thrown a lifeline by their women. While it may be all very well for a woman to nurse a secret (or even not

so secret) ambition to 'marry well' (i.e. to marry someone stinking rich),
a man who looks for a wealthy wife will be derided as a fortune hunter or,
worse, a gigolo. Women may trade their thoroughbred good looks for the
security of a relationship with an ugly but wealthy man. Men who do the
same must be emasculated toy boys. So men must always be financially
independent; must stand alone.

Sometimes married men, working ever longer hours and seeing their
pay packets disappearing in an endless stream of mortgage payments,
grocery bills, housekeeping expenses and charge card arrears, may
feel resentful – recalling, however fleetingly, the days of their youth
(glamorized in retrospect) when they were free to enjoy the fruits of
their own labour and accountable to no one but themselves, in contrast
to their straitened circumstances of the present. . .

And baby makes three. . .

However a couple have coped about money when it was just the
two of them, the arrival of a child marks the next great revolution.
Children have an astonishing power to transform the lives of modern
couples and send them catapulting back into the roles of their
parents: she gives up her job to look after the child; he tries to
maximize his income to make up for the hole caused by the loss of
hers.

The American psychologist Guttman describes the birth of children
as the 'parental emergency'. In his view, the psychological male/female
differences arise mainly out of the battle to raise a child. After a baby is
born, men take up the masculine role (strong and responsible fathers)
and women the feminine (warm, nurturing mothers) rather like soldiers
taking up battle stations. He believes that it is only when the children
have grown up and left the home that parents are freed once again to
'be themselves' and play around more with the male and female parts
of their personalities.

In chapter 20, we will be considering in detail how the arrival of a child
may affect the pre-existing marriage relationship. Don't underestimate it
– but it must also be said that the more you have previously managed to
defuse the emotional charge surrounding the money/housework question
and the less you play power games with each other over the question
of who does what, then the more chance you have of making the great
transition a positive one.

Back to basics

As a couple, it will be that much harder to reach a financial consensus
if your personal priorities vary widely. Two people, even (or especially)
married ones, can rarely be relied on to reach complete agreement over

what is a necessary or even a comfortable standard of living and what sacrifices are justified in striving to reach it.

Nevertheless, a working basis which allows for individual differences should not be that difficult to reach. In this, as in all else, honesty, respect for each other's point of view and open communication will get you a long way – for money power games tend to become murkiest where the realities of a financial situation are least discussed:

- A high-earning wife secretly fears that her success is emasculating her husband. She feels guilty yet also enjoys using the power it gives her. He withdraws, becoming ever more passive and silently resentful in the relationship.
- A husband's demanding job allows him little time with his family. He feels marginalized in family life and uses his earning power to assert his authority. He conceals his salary and withholds 'his' money so that his partner has to ask for it in a way that embarrasses her. Robbed of the opportunity to budget sensibly, she feels as powerless as an infant. She retaliates by running up huge credit card bills in his name.
- A woman who believes the family is hard up refuses to become involved at all in the family finances, indicating boredom when her husband suggests they should look at things together. This enables her to ignore the fact that they are actually quite comfortably off. She therefore can go on saving and being miserly, making her own and everyone else's life cramped and miserable, in the complete emotional certainty of her own poverty – just as she has always done.
- A woman gets angry with her husband because 'he is not earning enough.' They acquiesce together in leaving her to balance the cheque book and make budgets. He 'doesn't have a head for figures' so he has to accept her version of reality (i.e. that he is not earning enough). But he feels bullied, and does little to improve the situation. Why should he when he never had to take responsibility for it in the first place?

These not-untypical scenarios show how hopelessly emotional issues can become clouded by financial ones – then both end up by becoming completely intractable. The million dollar question for each of the couples listed above, must be: What would they have to confront in their relationships if money itself were no longer a problem?

Money itself can all too easily become the arena within which other battles are fought – and because the real issues are not confronted directly, they stand little chance of being resolved. Who among us, with hand on heart and eyes shining brightly, can truthfully say that we have never, would *never* play murky power games with money? The temptation to do so is an omnipresent part of human nature. Yet it is not a temptation into which you will have to fall regardless.

For money matters can often be sorted out surprisingly easily if both partners are willing to look honestly at their financial situation together and to take shared responsibility for it. And there is no time like the present.

14

Money management

NOT everyone who gets married has their own individual financial affairs as perfectly under control as they might wish – so the prospect of dealing with *joint* budgets can seem particularly daunting. Yet it need not be.

The Three Golden Rules for money in marriage

1. Putting money into perspective

Important though money certainly is, you will surely run into trouble if you give it too much *emotional* importance in your relationship. The more you choose to invest money with emotional charge, the more likely is it that money (i.e. power) battles will intensify in your relationship – regardless of your actual financial circumstances. The opposite also holds true: if you can keep a sense of proportion, valuing money in its place but not letting it take the driving seat, you are making the best possible start in creating a safe, happy home and genuine freedom from financial stress.

2. Awareness and honesty

These two go hand in glove. Conscious awareness of your current money situation is a way of being honest with yourself – and a prerequisite of being honest with others.

If you are thinking about ignoring the need to balance your budget, sort out your tax or deal with a pressing debt, think again. You will only be piling up problems for the future: it is an inflexible law of physics that money problems will always come boomeranging back to you. If, however, you tackle them right at the start, they need never develop into problems at all.

The beauty of money – you might say, its saving grace – is the certain nature of pounds and pence. They are what they are – unlike people, they do not argue, deceive or pretend to be what they are not. So much in this month, so much out. Do the figures tally? How should a surplus be used? When will we be able to pay off this debt? Where can we make economies? How can we increase our total income? These are all highly practical questions. They require practical answers; and the more you are able to reach sensible, informed joint decisions, then the less risk there is of a murky power struggle wending its wearisome way onwards and downwards in your marriage.

Some couples take on board the notion of marriage as a business partnership:

> 'We try to have financial planning meetings every month. When we're broke, we plan very carefully as to who will be responsible for what – we've never had a joint account, so each of us gets responsibility for different outgoings. And when we're better off, we work out what both of us can save. As long as we stick to talking things through, we manage the family budget so much better.'

3. Budgeting

Staying with the idea of marriage as a business relationship, your management board will need to undertake some kind of budgeting procedure to keep your finances under control and make the most of your business prospects. There is no mystery to budgeting. It simply means calculating how much you will be spending on your outgoings for a fixed period and also (the more tricky bit!) working out how you will meet those outgoings.

If you have both been living in the same home for a while, the best way of discovering your outgoings will be to calculate all your outgoings in certain main categories (use the simple form of budget on p.115 as a guide), based on past experience. As long as you manage most of your money through bank accounts and have kept your statements (including credit card statements) and cheque book stubs for a reasonable period, your job will be easy. (If not, now is the time to start keeping proper records.)

We suggest that you start by working out the relevant sums spent under general categories (starting with the ones suggested in the sample budget and amending them as necessary as you go on) over the period of, say, the last six months or year. Then work out the monthly average in each category. Finally, add 5–10 per cent to cover likely price increases for the current year. If you calculate for a period of less than a year, you will also need to make seasonal adjustments in respect of fuel bills and so on. You now have your *average* monthly expenditure; each month your actual expenditure may go up or down, but if you have done your sums right, it will work out over the year.

If you have not lived together before or even if you have lived on your own beforehand, you may have little upon which to base your projected

Calculating your budget

MONTHLY INCOME   £
His earnings   _____
Her earnings   _____
Any freelance earnings (average)   _____
State benefits (including Child
   Benefit, Family Credit, etc.)   _____
Investment income   _____
Other   _____

TOTAL AVERAGE
MONTHLY INCOME   _____

MONTHLY EXPENDITURE   £
Mortgage/rent   _____
Poll tax/water rates   _____
Average monthly bills
  (gas, electricity, telephone,
  TV licence, insurance [house, contents,
  life], ground rent, etc.)   _____
Transport costs
  (season tickets, petrol, car
  service, insurance, tax, etc.) _____
Monthly groceries/housekeeping   _____
Personal spending (clothes,
  hobbies, etc.)
  his   _____
      hers   _____
      children's   _____
      total   _____
    Loan, HP, credit card repayments   _____
    Childminding   _____
    Holidays   _____
    Pension/savings plans   _____
    Presents, treats   _____
    Special planned purchases
     (taking a monthly average)   _____
    Tax/NI (if self-employed)   _____
    Other   _____

Add 10% cushion (if possible)   _____

TOTAL AVERAGE MONTHLY EXPENDITURE   _____

NET SURPLUS/DEBIT   _____

outgoings. No matter, you can find out as much as possible from family and friends and carry out some informed guesswork, again using the sample budget as a starting point. If you have never budgeted before, it may be as well to limit yourself to a maximum time limit of six months so that you can check on the accuracy of your figures at the end of that period. The winter months naturally tend to involve the heaviest home expenditure, with higher gas and electricity bills and Christmas spending draining many a family budget of any spare cash. Summer may also have its own particular financial burdens if you take your holidays then.

It is also wise (if you can possibly afford it) to put aside a sum for such unexpected thrills as increases in the mortgage rate, house repairs and car breakdown. You could, for example, set aside an additional 5 per cent of your total anticipated outgoings as a cushion. Not all couples can afford this safety margin, having extended themselves to the absolute limit to be able to buy their own first home, but if you can somehow make savings from elsewhere, your efforts will reward you with peace of mind. If this money is not needed, it can be carried forward or the optimistic can blow it on an end-of-financial-year getaway holiday.

Joint and separate accounts

The sample budget is set out on the basis that your earnings and other income will be pooled. The usual way of doing this is simply to conduct all financial operations from a joint account. The household funds can then be equitably administered on the basis of Karl Marx's old motto: 'From each according to his ability; to each according to his need.'

The advantages of operating this system are: (a) it is simple and involves only one account; (b) it ensures that there is complete openness between the couple; and (c) the partner who is earning less or not at all has automatic access to money without having to ask/remind/beg/threaten the other. On the other hand, no secrecy means no privacy, and it may also feel harder to make individual decisions about allocating funds to personal priorities. Sometimes the higher earner may feel resentful that their greater contribution to the common pot is just getting swallowed up. And unless each person sticks scrupulously to the budget or checks with the other before making any personal purchase, the account can easily become overdrawn.

> 'We both prefer not having joint accounts. That way, if I'm getting a bit out of control, he needn't know about it – though, of course, that only works so far. Having entirely separate accounts does mean harder work, in terms of planning, but I much prefer the feeling of separate responsibility.'

Like this couple, you may wish to keep your own separate accounts to ensure a degree of privacy from each other – useful, for example, if you want to buy your partner a present and don't want him or her to know the cost. The answer may be for each to have a separate account into which his/her income is paid on a monthly basis. Each then transfers to a third joint account a sum (usually proportionate to the actual income of each person) sufficient to meet the estimated shared monthly expenses of the household – and the rest is theirs to do what they want with. This more complicated system (a potential of three bank accounts to overdraw) will work best if you know there will be a reasonable amount left in the joint account after household expenses are met and also if you are both earning roughly equal amounts. If one partner is not earning anything, a further sum may need to be transferred from the earner's personal account to the non-earner's account for his/her personal use.

The Andrews' Solution for handling family finance

One way around the problems of dealing with the desire to remain independent while contributing as much as you both can to the family's finance was described to Helen by a former business partner of hers. In honour of Angus and his wife Lesley the technique is called the Andrews' Solution. Try it and see whether it will work for you.

The concept is simple, yet challenging. It is this: that each partner will always contribute equally to the joint account whatever his or her actual income, and that both partners' work will be equally recognized (whether or not one was spending time at home to look after the children or working full-time outside the home).

Having grasped the principle, the logistics are a little more complex and will work best given certain preconditions:

- both incomes are reasonably predictable.
- the combined incomes exceed outgoings.
- both partners each have a sole account and together have a joint account.

The first stage of the Andrews' Solution is to calculate how much will be needed to pay into the joint account to meet all joint expenses – this includes all payments on the house, any insurances and pension payments and all regular monthly payments, but not holidays, entertainment or leisure expenses. Husband and wife then divide this figure by two, to create two equal shares (making any necessary adjustments if the total is an odd number). They then ask their bank(s) to create standing orders for the amount of their share to be deducted from each of their sole accounts and deposited into the joint account.

The next stage is to add up all the income that both of them receive and again divide by two. They then work out who is receiving more than the other and make adjustments as necessary to ensure that each has the same amount paid into his/her own individual account each month, this being achieved by the higher earner arranging a further standing order. Hey presto! Immediate equality of monetary matters!

> *'The beauty of it is that, whatever either of us is earning, we both feel as if we are contributing jointly to the 'pot', and we both have our own money, so we do keep some privacy. The system took a lot of the frustration out of our financial dealings with each other – for example Lesley never had to ask me for money when she took a few years off to have and then look after the children. It's the perfect system for us – although I have to say that it only will work if you're prepared to put the effort in and prepare a proper budget in the first place.'*

As the system is not easy to understand in theory, we have set out below a worked example to give you an idea about how the Andrews' Solution would operate in practice.

An example of the Andrews' Solution in practice
The Owl and the Pussycat married in 1968. For the first year, the Pussycat earned more as a singer than the Owl did as a teacher. She earned £15,600 net (after deduction of tax and National Insurance), while the Owl earned £8400 net per annum. After working out a budget, they found that a total of £12,000 would be needed in their joint Owl & Pussycat account to pay their bills for the year.

1   First, they added up their total income: £15,600 + £8400 = £24,000.
2   Next, they worked out how each of them should get the same amount paid into their own sole accounts every month: £24,000 ÷ 12 ÷ 2 = £1000.
3   Next, they worked out the amount that each of them should pay into the joint account: £12,000 ÷ 12 ÷ 2 = £500. They each set up standing orders from their own separate accounts to the joint Owl & Pussycat account for £500.
4   Finally, they worked out how the Pussycat, as the highest earner, needed to adjust her income so that she was paying to the Owl the difference between his earnings (£700 per month) and their equally divided joint income (£1000 per month). So the Pussycat arranged for an extra standing order to pay the Owl £300 per month to ensure that they were both receiving and both paying out the same amount.

Later, the Owl and the Pussycat might need to make adjustments should the Pussycat decide to stay at home to raise their children, but the division will always be worked out on the same principle – equality.

Dealing with debt

A failure to ensure that you cut your outgoings according to the cloth of your income (or, alternatively, that you make enough money to cover your ongoing needs) will, as sure as debts are debts, create considerable problems for you. Once you are heavily in debt, it is not easy to extricate yourself, and the strains that debt puts on a relationship can be considerable. As Charles Dickens' Mr Micawber so succinctly put it:

> *Annual income twenty pounds, annual expenditure nineteen nineteen and six, result happiness. Annual income twenty pounds, annual expenditure twenty pounds ought and six, result misery.*

More often than not, debts arise when one or both partners blank out and overspend or take on new commitments without really being sure where the money to pay for them is going to come from. The situation can become far worse if this state of willed unconsciousness continues and overdue payments are ignored – stuffing unopened final tax demands and solicitors' letters to the back of your socks drawer is *not* recommended.

Sometimes debts may be concealed from a husband or wife, perhaps 'to spare them the worry' (or more likely to avoid recrimination). It can be a very nasty shock indeed when the other partner finds out, as he or she almost certainly will – another good reason for you *both* to make sure that you know what is going on financially, even if in practice the day-to-day management is left to one of you alone.

Broadly speaking, you are not responsible for debts that have been built up by any other person – even if that person is your spouse. Having said that, there are a number of exceptions which can almost seem to invalidate the rule.

The first is that you are both jointly and separately liable in full for debts built up on any joint accounts, or in respect of a joint mortgage or rent. You are also liable for your spouse's unpaid community charge (poll tax). Unpaid credit card debts will generally be the sole responsibility of the main signatory on the card, but if you do share a card, check the conditions of use.

All debts are potential timebombs if ignored, but the ones to be most concerned about are 'secured loans' – e.g. mortgages. If you do not keep up your repayments under a secured loan, your creditors may be able to sell your home over your heads – sometimes for considerably less than its marketplace value – and you will be homeless and blacklisted by credit companies.

If you face a situation where your spouse has mounting debts and the creditors are threatening to take possession proceedings against your home, you should consult a solicitor *at once* to see how you can be protected. One way is to apply to the court under what is called the Married Women's Property Act 1882 (which is equally applicable to both men and women) for the court to make a declaration as to which assets are yours and which your spouse's (although, if the debts have been run up against the two of you jointly, this step will not be open to you). If the property is in your spouse's sole name, your solicitor should be able to register a charge (called a Class F Land Charge or a Caution) which will prevent the property being dealt with without your knowledge or consent.

In any case, sticking your head in the sand in the face of mounting debts in the hope that they will go away is not the most positive attitude. Generally the best tactic to adopt is to take the initiative and come clean with your creditors. It is in their interests to negotiate, and most will: all they care about is getting their money, sooner or later, and the majority will only take out a court action when they feel there is no other option available to them.

You will then usually be able to work out a realistic schedule for repayment of debts over a period of time or negotiate another workable solution. For example, you may be able to consolidate your debts – that is, pay them all off together by taking out a new single loan at the best (lowest) rate of interest and with a repayment schedule that you know you can meet. This works particularly well if your existing debts are to credit card companies or other outfits that make their profits by charging people like you around 30 per cent interest per annum or more - small wonder such debts never seem to get paid off!

If things look really black (especially if you have fallen badly in arrears with secured loans), the ultimate solution may be to consider selling your present home and moving somewhere cheaper/smaller. Again, you will be in a far better position if you take the initiative instead of waiting until you are pushed into a course of action by a credit company armed with a court order.

Where to get help

You may feel that you would never have got into this mess in the first place if you weren't hopeless with money, and for this reason, you despair of ever getting out of it unaided, especially once panic has set in. But help is at hand.

Many Citizens' Advice Bureaux operate a money advice service. Counsellors will look at your special circumstances and advise you: sometimes they will even intercede with creditors and negotiate on your behalf. Neighbourhood law centres may also be able to help.

Tax Advice

Set out in Appendix 1, you will find a guide to dealing with your tax affairs – aimed primarily at married women who are now, for the first time, legally responsible for dealing with their own tax affairs.

15

Insurance, pensions and wills

O THER issues which are guaranteed turn-offs are your insurance and pension arrangements and your wills. This chapter has not been secretly written by an undercover insurance sales executive, so you will get no hard sell about the first two matters. It is more intended as an *aide mémoire* so that you can consider whether you and your family have adequate financial protection to weather the storms of matrimony ahead. As for making a will, it is easy to do, won't cost you a packet and leaves you with the security of knowing that you have ensured that your loved ones will be looked after as well as possible in the sad event of your popping off rather earlier than you planned.

Planning for the present

This really boils down to insurance. Insurance companies are in the business of protecting you financially against risk. House and home represent by far the highest concentration of possessions, and it is here that most insurance policies are focused. Although only 60 per cent of all UK home buildings (the bricks and mortar of flats and houses) are covered, three-quarters of British households have their contents insured (in times of rising burglary figures, this is hardly surprising). And there is a slowly increasing trend to insure against ill health and its treatment. So, what do you need?

Buildings insurance

If your house is already mortgaged, or if you live in a leasehold flat, it is likely that your mortgagee (the bank or building society) or the freeholder will already have arranged for buildings cover. This will meet the cost of rebuilding if your home sweet home burns down or disappears down a disused mine shaft. This cost will be less than the overall value of your property, but from time to time you should check that the cover is adequate (a surveyor can give you a figure if you are in doubt).

Contents insurance

This will cover you if all your belongings are stolen, or if they are destroyed by fire or another hazard. Being underinsured is a problem – a fact which people only become uncomfortably aware of when they have to make a claim. Particularly if you have received a bonanza of wedding gifts or some other windfall, make sure that your policy covers everything – not just those tatty old chairs you inherited from your grandmother. The premium rates will vary according to which part of the country you live in – an inner city area will have a far higher weighting than somewhere in the heart of the country. Also, read the small print before (rather than after) signing the policy, as the exclusion clauses may later preclude you from making a claim. A classic example is provided by the policies that insist upon window locks and special door locks – if you don't have them, you may not be able to claim after a burglary.

Car insurance

Enough said. Well, almost enough. You can have two types: third party and fully comprehensive.

Third party car insurance will not cover you for your loss if an accident you are involved in was your fault – so it's worthwhile paying the extra, if you can afford it and your car is in reasonable condition, for fully comprehensive. Shop around for different quotes. Some companies offer especially reduced premiums for women-only drivers or for careful drivers (the two are certainly not mutually exclusive), or even drivers belonging to particular professions, such as teachers.

Private medical insurance and health insurance

Although heavily advertised, private medical insurance is still taken out by only 6 per cent of the UK population, mostly paid for by employers who get generous discounts on block bookings. Private medical insurance has its drawbacks: it can be expensive, especially for the elderly or the chronically sick and usually will not cover you in emergencies, when you're abroad or when you're having a baby – in fact, the majority of occasions when you're most likely to need it. Also, the kind of care and treatment you get in some small private hospitals may definitely be substandard to what you might receive in an old NHS teaching hospital which looks a lot shabbier but is nevertheless all geared up for the job: when a poll was taken recently among hospital consultants working in both the private and public sectors, the great majority of them said that, where their *own* illnesses were concerned, they would greatly prefer to be treated on the NHS! And finally, for some, there is also the question of the ethics of queue-jumping.

These reservations aside, some people do get more peace of mind from having medical insurance – they appreciate the opportunity they feel it gives them for getting their ailments treated as quickly as they need to be and also the more individualized care they feel they receive as private patients.

Health insurance will pay you a fixed weekly or monthly income in the event of your becoming incapacitated by illness. It is aimed at those who rely wholly or heavily on self-employed income. Again, it has its drawbacks – there may be substantial exclusion clauses, and relief may be limited to cover only a certain period of time – so read the small print carefully. It also tends to be quite expensive.

Planning for the future

This can really be divided into two categories: life and retirement.

Life assurance

This comes in a variety of different flavours. The bargain basement type is *term assurance* which will cover you for a specified tax-free annual income over a certain period – say until your youngest child reaches 18. Similarly, *life-only cover* will guarantee your family a cash sum in the event of your death before a certain age as long as the premiums are kept up in the meantime. In both these cases, there's no money back if you fail to die within the life-cover period.

A pricier alternative which also operates as a kind of saving scheme (and so may be worth considering if you have some money to spare) is called a *with-profits* or *endowment policy*. This is often taken out in tandem with a mortgage (see p. 135) and will cover not only your death but, at the end of the cover period, should provide a lump sum together with accrued profits – the amount depending on how successfully your payments have been invested by the life assurance company in the intervening years.

Pensions

These come in even more varieties: there are the old traditional types, which basically operate like endowment schemes (*see above*), and the newer ones which are linked to unit trusts. These are almost universally recommended, but of course, stocks can go down as well as up. . .

Pensions are complex and you do need to get good advice before deciding which company to invest with. Suffice to say here that you may have a pension plan organized by your employer (an occupational pension scheme), or you may opt out of the system and do it yourself.

The government recently introduced the Personal Pension Plan (an adaptation of the old form of retirement annuities). You are eligible for one of these if you are:

- self-employed.
- an employee or director without the benefit of an occupational pension scheme.
- an employee with an occupational pension scheme but with non-pensionable earnings from other work.
- an employee and member of an occupational pension scheme but you wish to opt out from that scheme.

Benefits range from tax advantages (you can set the premiums off against your higher rates of tax) to flexibility with some of the better schemes – in some, for example, you can draw on the funds saved when you reach the age of 50 rather than having to wait for retirement age. The schemes are also portable, so that if you change your job, you can carry over your scheme to your new work.

You may well have already been bombarded with leaflets and telephone calls about making pension arrangements. It is certainly wise to start off a pension plan at an early age rather than waiting until the children come along (when you probably won't have any spare cash anyway). Remember, however, that the companies which have the most aggressive sales techniques may not be the best performers in the market. You can check with tables produced by, for example, the Consumers' Association and financial papers for performance levels of the company you are considering using for your pension arrangements. One of the highest performers pays no commission to brokers; as a result, it may be more rarely recommended. Check the small print of any policy before signing – and watch out in particular for penalties if you stop your contributions or if you die before retirement age.

Using a financial adviser

It is notoriously difficult to get sound and impartial financial advice. Advisers are often out to get the best deal – for themselves rather than for you – by recommending the policies with the highest commission: In-house advisers will, obviously, recommend their own 'products'.

First of all, arm yourself with as much information as you can get hold of, through a reputable organization such as the Consumers' Association. Draw up a list of what you think your requirements are – a pension, life assurance, investment savings? – before getting a financial adviser. Make sure that anyone you deal with is regulated by the Financial Services Act, and don't be shy of asking for further quotes if you're not happy with the initial advice.

Making a will

It's tempting to think 'Why bother?' when it comes to the question of making a will. Or 'Maybe I'll do it next month' (and then the month after, the month after that and so on). But if you're already thinking of buying a home, getting to grips with financial budgeting and the like, making a will is part and parcel of sensible overall financial management.

On marriage, any will that you have already made (unless made expressly 'in contemplation' of your marriage) will be automatically revoked (made invalid). If you don't already have a will or have done nothing about your prenuptial, now invalid, one, then your 'estate' – everything that you own – will be divided according to the laws of intestacy. Your surviving spouse will get your personal chattels (your own belongings), the first £125,000 of your assets plus interest at the rate of 7 per cent per annum from the date of your death to the time of distribution. The remainder of what you have owned (if there is any) will be divided into two equal parts, one for the surviving spouse and one for your parents.

If you die intestate and you have children, your surviving spouse will receive the personal chattels as before, a lump sum of £75,000 from the estate and interest calculated as before. Again, the remainder will be divided into two; one part to be invested for the surviving spouse, who will get the interest accruing (but not the capital, which will pass to the children on his or her death), the remaining part to be given to the children (once they become of age). If you're not married, all your property will pass by law to your family – which here doesn't mean your partner (although there are rights for your children to inherit and rights for dependants to claim against the estate, which a solicitor can explain to you in greater detail).

These inflexible rules may very well not suit your own particular circumstances. Although the figures look high, your spouse could easily find him or herself in a situation where your home has to be sold to allow for the division specified by law – at a time when s/he and the children most need the security of a stable home environment. The other advantages of making a will are that you can ensure (potentially considerable) tax savings after your death, as well as being able to determine exactly where you want your property and money to go according to your own particular wishes. It is far better to be safe than sorry: make a will either before the wedding (when it is said to be made 'in contemplation of your marriage') or as soon after the happy event as you can.

Providing for your family in the event of your or your partner's death

You need, first of all, to decide how you want to deal with your home. Many mortgagees insist upon your taking out either an endowment policy or a mortgage protection policy, which will mean that the mortgage will be paid off if you die. However, you still need to ensure that your wishes about ownership of the home are clearly set out in your will. Many people choose to leave their share to their spouse absolutely.

You can also make specific gifts of money to the children These will be held for them 'on trust', so that they can't touch it until they reach the age of 18, although you can specify a later qualifying age.

Special bequests

As well as ensuring that your family is taken care of, you can leave special items – for example, a favourite piece of jewellery or a painting – or a specific sum of money to individuals. You can also see that your favourite charity benefits if you have some money to spare. Finally, you may wish to stipulate whether you wish to be cremated or buried.

Guardians for your children

You can also appoint a 'testamentary guardian' to look after your children if both you and your spouse die together. (If you are not married, only the mother (or a father with a custody order in his favour) can appoint a guardian.) Although your views will not be written in stone and could be challenged by another interested party (e.g. a relative) in an application to the court, the fact that you have clearly stated your wishes and appointed someone you feel would be well qualified to care for your children will be given great weight by the court.

Before choosing, you should think about such things as age differences between the person you want to appoint as a guardian and your children, whether they have any children of their own and their religious and other beliefs. Talk it over with them to check out whether they would willingly take on this responsibility.

Appointing an executor

Your executors are those people appointed by your will to be in charge of your affairs, to administer your estate and to see that your wishes are carried out. If you are each leaving all your individual estates to each other and your affairs are not too complex, then you could become each other's sole executor. Otherwise you could appoint an additional executor. Avoid appointing a bank as their charges are very high. A business-minded friend or your solicitor would be a good choice.

The cost

It is possible to make a do-it-yourself will – many of the larger stationery shops have blank home-made will forms that you can complete. You should, however, take great care in completing the form: there are a number of technical requirements which have to be complied with for a will to be valid.

A solicitor will not charge an enormous amount for drawing up your will (at the time of going to press, charges of between £30 and £100 plus VAT (at 15%) would be common in a London firm). Many solicitors (particularly those outside London) will only charge a nominal sum if you appoint a solicitor from their firm to act as an executor. Your solicitor will be able to evaluate and advise you on your own particular circumstances, especially how you should order your affairs to avoid any unnecessary tax – not that tax savings will be of primary importance to the one who dies but they certainly will be to the ones who are left behind.

Before going to see a solicitor (try to find one who is recommended by your friends or family or ask at your local Citizens' Advice Bureau for a recommendation), it is sensible to prepare a schedule of your assets and debts in a fair amount of detail – including, for example, your pension plan, the branch of your bank and account number(s) there. Your solicitor will then have all the facts at his or her fingertips to be able to give you the best advice.

16

Buying a home

If you have been renting before, now may be the time to give careful consideration to the idea of buying a house or flat, thus ensuring that, instead of paying rent which each month disappears without trace into your landlord's pocket, you will be making mortgage repayments which will go towards paying for your own capital asset, the value of which is likely to increase handsomely over time. Buying your own home may also symbolize a real putting down of roots, a commitment to the future and to the continuance of your shared lives together.

Finding your first home

The first ingredient is, obviously, the bricks and mortar themselves. Finding a home which suits you both down to the ground can be simple or not so simple.

> 'We looked for ages to find somewhere we liked – or rather I looked. David hadn't got as much time. But we eventually decided on an area we liked and could afford and narrowed it down to about five streets. I kept phoning up the estate agents to pester them about any houses coming on the market. Finally, I tracked down one that had been put up for sale that day. We went round together – and it just felt like home as soon as we walked in the door. After staying up all night talking about it, we put in an offer which was accepted and – hey presto! – our first home.'

Of course, it isn't quite as easy as that – this couple, for example, had quite a long wait before they could move in as they both had flats to sell. But they certainly had the right idea about checking out the area first. You could try pinpointing the areas where you would like to live by driving or walking around them, finding out where the shops are, where buses and other transport runs from, checking the area out during the week as well as during the weekends and in the rain as well as on a glorious (and thus flattering!) day. But for most couples, where they live will be determined by price as much as anything else – the 20-acre château in France will have to wait for a little while.

How much can we afford?

Many people rightly feel that as their home will be their main asset and will appreciate in value with time, they are willing to stretch themselves to buy a place which feels really right and also has the potential to grow with their changing needs. Moving home is expensive both financially and emotionally – it can be a false economy to buy somewhere you'll have to leave in two years because it is no longer big enough or doesn't have a garden. And while your earnings will (you hope) increase over the years to come, your mortgage repayments should at least remain steady (subject, however, to the bugbear of changing interest rates), thereby making a large mortgage commitment more tolerable as time goes by.

These arguments are particularly tempting in times of rapid increase in house prices, such as were seen in the mid- to late 1980s. But house prices, as we also saw, can slump as well as boom, and interest rates soar dizzily. And the reasons for buying a perfect home may seem less persuasive if you are both so busy slaving in the salt mines trying to pay for it that you never see it or each other. Money worries can cripple a relationship, and you also need to bear in mind the possibility of reduced incomes if you plan to have a family together. Only you can find the right compromise – and a working compromise between your desire for a perfect home on the one hand and what your purse and nerves can stand on the other, it will have to be.

Assess the potential of the places you look at carefully and think ahead. A bigger place might work out if you could get a lodger to help with bills. (Some people can live happily with lodgers who can double as babysitters and houseminders; others can't.) Would there be room later for a kitchen extension/attic conversion? And should you risk getting a bigger place with a lot of 'potential' (as the dreaded estate agents say) in a run-down area which you bravely hope will improve in time as people like you start moving in?

Buying a home

Before you make a move, careful financial planning is essential. It is pretty safe to say that buying your own home will cost more than you ever dreamed (or feared). Although 100 per cent mortgages can sometimes be obtained (at a price), you will generally have to pay at least 5 per cent (preferably 10 per cent) of the purchase price before you exchange binding contracts to buy. As a purchaser, you will not have to pay the estate agent any commission, but you *will* have to fork out for:

- legal fees
- Stamp Duty (currently 1 per cent of the purchase price on properties over £30,000)
- Land Registry fees

To get a mortgage, you will have to pay a fee for a survey arranged by the mortgagee (and it is generally recommended that you have a separate survey done yourself), possibly a mortgage arrangement fee (generally charged by banks and sometimes by mortgage brokers but not by building societies) and often a mortgage indemnity policy (this last covers the mortgage company in the event of their having to foreclose on you and resell the house for less than the value of their charge). Then there will be your:

- first year's property insurance (which your mortgage company will probably arrange)
- contents insurance
- ground rent (on leasehold property)
- community charges (poll tax)
- connection fees or deposits payable to the various supply authorities

. . .and all this before you have even thought about removal expenses, new furniture and alterations to your new home. But do not get discouraged. Forewarned is forearmed.

Check prices, haggle and shop around *before* you commit yourself to a property. You can get a good idea of most of the costs mentioned above using as a starting point the likely cost of your new property. Any reputable mortgage company or solicitor will be willing to go through their costs with you at the beginning (make sure that you get an inclusive written estimate from them), and they will respect you all the more for your business-like attitude.

Mortgage brokers may be helpful if you have experienced difficulty in obtaining a mortgage – for example, because of your credit status or lack of deposit or because there is something unusual about the house you have set your heart on. But remember that their help *costs*. Usually they are paid in commissions from mortgagees but sometimes they also charge you a fee – and for nothing more than ringing round the different building societies and finding out what's on offer, which you could do perfectly well yourselves. Brokers may, however, be useful on advising you and helping you set up an endowment policy if that is what you want *(see below)*.

You are not bound to use the first solicitor you speak to or the building society where you have been hoarding your pennies since you were ten. However, don't cut corners unwisely by choosing a cowboy firm or company which greatly undercuts the competition – you may well pay in the end. Recommendations from friends and neighbours who have already been through it all before are often a good bet.

Depending on how comfortable their own financial circumstances are (and also how much you may have previously leaned on them), parents or relatives may not be unsympathetic to a request to stump up with a contribution to something so agreeably sensible as a down payment on a house purchase. Compromising on a simpler wedding may likewise release valuable funds to this end.

Using estate agents

A word of caution should be entered here about estate agents. Some are honourable, pleasant people who would not dream of piling on unnecessary pressure or of being economical with the truth in order to secure a sale – others are not. Unlike solicitors, estate agents only get paid if a sale goes through and the more you the buyer can be persuaded to pay, the more commission they will get. Remember that they are paid by the vendor and will basically be acting in what they see as the vendor's interest – which may not necessarily coincide with your own.

Some people will tell you horror stories about being misled by estate agents: 'We had a terrible time with them. They told us that sound insulation had been installed under the floor of the flat above – it wasn't – and then when we got into a contract race, they told us the other side was about to close, giving us mutual heart attacks! That wasn't true, either.' Make sure that *anything* important which the estate agents (or, for that matter, the vendors) tell you is subsequently confirmed *in writing* by the vendors' solicitor when preliminary inquiries are being raised. Then, and only then, can you rely upon its being true.

Once we've found a place, how soon can we move in?

This is the first question of every would-be buyer, but there is no straight answer. As your solicitor will say, it depends. The variables it depends on include:

- whether you have a place to sell.
- whether your vendors are buying somewhere else or, alternatively, whether the place is empty.
- how soon your mortgage comes through.
- how long your local authority are taking with searches.
- the respective speed and competence of *both* sets of solicitors.

Generally, however, you should expect to wait between six weeks and three months before binding contracts are exchanged, at which point you will be given a completion date when you can move in – usually 2–4 weeks after exchange. The law can rarely be accused of acting too hastily.

How should we own the property?

Your home can be owned 'jointly' – in both of your names – or, very unusually in these enlightened days, in only one spouse's name. Homes are usually purchased jointly even if one spouse is making a greater financial input. A joint purchase may be required by the mortgage company or 'mortgagee' (the building society or bank which is lending you the money to buy your own home) if you have made a joint application for a mortgage.

If for some reason you have decided that the house will only be in the name of one of you, and the mortgage has been granted on the basis that that person will be the sole contributor, the mortgagee will usually require the other spouse to sign a form to say that her (or, less often, his) rights to the property will rank below the mortgagee's. This is because a husband or wife who is living at the property would otherwise have rights to stay there which would rank above a mortgagee's right to dispose of the property in the event of the other spouse defaulting on mortgage payments. In effect, the mortgagee's consent form will be asking you to sign your rights away.

Even if only one of you 'owns' the property – i.e. only one of you has his or her name on the title deeds – as long as the house has been occupied as a shared home, the other spouse has certain rights to remain there. S/he will also be able to claim a share of the legal owner's interest in the property on the death of the legal owner or on divorce. A solicitor will advise on the steps that should be taken to protect this interest. The amount of the non-owning spouse's share will depend on your own individual circumstances. There is no law of 'community property' in the United Kingdom, unlike, for example, in some states in America, where all property acquired after a marriage is, by law, owned jointly and equally by each spouse. Here, how much each spouse would get depends on fairly complex equations, involving the needs, resources and respective contributions of each spouse.

On the basis that you will both be living at the property, sharing responsibility for it and contributing to its upkeep in some way (whether in money or in other ways such as doing the housework and looking after the family), it is better that you should own in joint names. And there are different ways in which a joint interest can be held by law.

Joint ownership: joint tenancy or tenancy in common?

Having decided to own the property jointly, you next have to decide whether you will own it under a 'joint tenancy' or a 'tenancy in common'. A joint tenancy means that the owners' shares are, in a sense, undivided and that if either dies, then the survivor will get the deceased's share automatically.

Under a tenancy in common, the shares are already divided (usually 50/50 or a trust deed entered into at the time of purchase may stipulate what each party's share of ownership is) and the owners can, theoretically at least, deal with their respective shares separately. On the death of one owner, his or her share of the property will not pass automatically to the other but will be distributed as per the terms of the will or the intestacy laws. A tenancy in common is, therefore, more usually preferred by friends or business colleagues who have bought a property together, but there is no reason why it should not be used by husbands and wives – for example, if each feels that they wish to exercise greater individual control and see their assets as essentially separate rather than shared.

A joint tenancy can easily be converted to a tenancy in common, by serving a notice to sever the joint tenancy. However, a court may sometimes have the power to override this provision if the result would be that the house would have to be sold and the family of the deceased left homeless.

In any event, it is wise to obtain advice from a solicitor about how your joint ownership of the property should be dealt with – and this should be done before you buy so that you can go into the options thoroughly.

And what about a mortgage?

Different types of mortgages have been popping up like breeding rabbits in the last few years. As banks and building societies compete ever more fiercely with each other for mortgage business, so the choice as to which mortgage will be right for you becomes ever more complex.

There are basically three different types to choose from:

A standard repayment mortgage

Under this method, your monthly mortgage payments pay not only the interest accruing on your mortgage, but also go towards reducing the amount of capital (the sum you borrowed in the first place). At the beginning of the repayment term (which tends, as with other types of mortgage, to be spread over 20–30 years), your monthly payments will mostly pay off interest, but as time goes on, you will be increasingly reducing the outstanding capital.

While a repayment mortage has much to recommend it in terms of simplicity, and can often (though not always) be the cheapest type of mortage to take on, it works best if you use it to buy a home where you expect to stay for a while. Otherwise, as you move from time to time (and the average length of family residence in a home has now fallen to approximately eight years, you will tend to take out bigger and bigger mortgages, and in the meantime, little of your capital borrowing is diminishing.

Sometimes a standard repayment mortgage is linked to a 'mortgage protection policy', which will pay off the remaining capital loan before the end of the repayment term in the event of an owner's death.

An endowment mortgage

Here, your monthly repayments will only pay off the interest on your loan, not the capital, *but* part of your payments will also include premiums on a 'with profits' insurance policy, which is usually designed to pay off the capital of your mortgage either on death or at the end of the term of the policy – which will coincide with the end of the repayment term.

The idea is that the profits should earn *more* than is needed to pay off the mortgage, thereby leaving you with a lump sum at the end of the day. However, it is theoretically possible – for example, if the payments were unwisely invested or if there were a serious and longlasting national recession – that the profits might earn *less* than is needed. Most endowment mortgages, therefore, have a clause entitling them to increase the premiums you pay during the term of the mortgage if the insurance company thinks this is likely to happen. It is generally agreed, however, that under present conditions the risk of this happening is slight.

The advantage of an endowment policy is that, as you can transfer your policy to another mortgage when you move, you are in effect 'saving up' for eventual repayment of the loan, though if you later take out a higher mortgage (which most people do to enable themselves to buy a bigger home), you will have to take out a top-up policy to cover the extra capital you have borrowed.

A further advantage of many endowment policies is that they include life cover thereby ensuring that, if one of you dies suddenly, the whole of the outstanding debt will be paid off.

A pension-linked mortgage

This essentially combines a mortgage with a tax-efficient way of saving. More expensive to service than either a repayment or an endowment, it is only worth considering if you believe that, for the foreseeable future, your income will increase steadily higher while your expenditure remains more or less the same and if you are anyway looking for a good savings scheme.

On the same principal as an endowment mortgage, again you will only be paying the interest payments and not reducing, month by month the capital you borrowed. However, you will also be paying premiums under a pension scheme, which, like an endowment policy, will give you a lump sum at a later date – when you retire or at a particular specified retirement age. The advantage of the pension-linked mortgage is that, unlike endowment payments, you are able to get tax relief on your pension payments. Because you are saving tax, your payments can be used more effectively. However, it may be that pension-linked mortgages are better suited to the self-employed who have no firm date on which they wish to retire.

Whichever type of mortgage you choose, do be careful to shop around to get the best deal, or make sure your broker does this on your behalf. Many mortgagees offer a reduced-rate interest payment for the first year or two for first-time buyers, which can help out considerably during the financially tight early months of buying a home. Do check the terms thoroughly, however: while the initial repayments are reduced, the difference between what you will be paying early on and the 'true' higher level of mortgage payment may be tacked on to your overall borrowings – so that you will have to pay this extra back some day. If your house fails to go up in value and you have taken on a 100 per cent mortgage, you could find yourself owing more on the mortgage than the house is actually worth.

Also, some superficially attractive schemes may also contain an iniquitous small-print clause entitling the mortgagee to enforce a penalty, sometimes running to several thousands of pounds, if you decide to redeem early – for example, because you have found a better deal and want to remortgage, or just because you want to move house.

Any financial adviser whom you use should be registered under the Financial Services Act – which will provide some warranty that the advice they give you will be in your best interests, and which, most importantly, will give you some form of protection if the advice s/he gives turns out to be patently unsound.

Bless this home

Despite the scarcity in our culture of rituals and ceremonies to give form to our lives, two domestic rites have survived to the present day. The first is, as we have seen, the practice of the groom carrying his bride over the threshold of their first home together. This act represents the support that he will provide for her in the home and the unity of their life together – they enter as one body, arms embracing each other. Even if you have lived in your home together for some time prior to your wedding, this custom can generate feelings of warmth, togetherness and mirth as you start to journey off together in your married life (though watch your backs!).

The second custom is the housewarming party – a celebration to usher in warmth (bodily or otherwise) and conviviality to your new home. The housewarming could be the first time you really set your imprint on your home, and the fact that you are receiving others here in your new abode can serve to strengthen your bonds within it. The party need not be expensive – get your friends to bring along a bottle and a dish of something to eat so that the cost is shared. Or adapt an American custom and turn it into a 'house shower' – all the guests bring a gift for the new house, and you two just sit back to be literally showered with useful presents!

Otherwise, how about creating your own ceremony together? In the first few days of your time together, perhaps even on the first night, you could celebrate your marriage in your new home intimately *à deux* – perhaps by cooking a delicious fireside meal together – and as you light the candles for your festive supper, ask for love, joy and happiness to be brought to your home. Ask for whatever you want to be manifested in your lives together at home – and then complete your celebration with your gourmet meal. *Bon appetit!*

17

Home sweet home (and the wretched ironing. . .)

Where your home is, there shall your heart be also.

Edgar Cayce

THE prospect of owning – or renting – your first home together is both exciting and daunting. Of course, for many, marriage may not coincide with living together for the first time. As we have seen, an increasing number of people are now choosing to live together prior to marriage, sometimes as a trial of the relationship, before deciding on a more binding commitment. Others set up their first home to move into after marriage. But for all, the practicalities of living together can come as rather a shock. Instead of the excitement and added passion of saying goodbye at the end of the evening, your time together is unending. In place of bouquets of roses and slinky black dresses come smelly socks and unironed shirts.

> *'Buying a home together was the biggest commitment for me. That was why I was so reluctant in the first place to go ahead. I knew that once I had a house with Robin, that was it. I would be in this relationship on a permanent basis. Getting married was just an inevitable stage after that. The home has always been more important – far more important than getting married itself.'*

This comment from Peter, one of our interviewees, reflects the high place in which the home is generally held by couples, especially at about the time of getting married, when the nesting instinct has a way of becoming strong. The need to create a home that will be right for you as a couple and, prospectively, as a family may come to assume an overwhelming importance, consuming all your available time and emotional and physical energy. It is a need which is recognized and

137

shamelessly exploited by the media, especially by women's and bridal magazines, which urge us to consider the form and appearance of the home rather than its meaning: the body rather than the soul. Can you *really* have a happy marriage, they subtly suggest, without a Smallbone kitchen and the finest range of Le Creuset pans that money can buy? We are asked to determine whether we will have aquamarine Austrian blinds with colour-dragged walls, ignoring to a great extent whether the designer showhouse that is thereby created, at heaven knows what expense, will actually fulfil our need and desire for a comfortable home.

Your house, flat or hovel is a physical entity with a demonstrable existence in the real world. It is made of bricks and mortar (or whatever), it requires real cash to pay for its purchase or the rent and for its upkeep, and real elbow-grease to polish its windows and clean the U-bends of its toilet.

A *home* is something else, a far more abstract and intangible concept. In an earlier chapter, we talked about how the experience of falling in love can create a sense of having come home. When our interviewee in the last chapter said, 'It just felt like home as soon as we walked in the door,' she was referring to that warm and comfortable feeling we experience when we feel safe and cherished, accepted for what we are and able to relax and unwind in peace and security.

It is certainly true that, for most of us, the home is our greatest (and perhaps only) shared asset, its significance represented by the money and emotional energy we invest in it. There is the whole question of what your home really means to both of you, and what this expresses about your relationship. For one of us, some of the closest times in her marriage have occurred while she and her husband pottered round old junkshops and slowly stripped off the kitchen wallpaper together while singing along tunelessly to old Bruce Springsteen songs.

Home, they say, is where the heart is. But whose heart is in the nitty gritty of homemaking – i.e. housework? Not so very long ago, a man's worth as a husband was assessed, uncontroversially, in terms of how well he provided for his family. Conversely, a good wife performed her side of the bargain: she was supportive to her husband, a devoted mother and, most importantly, a willing and competent housewife. In these terms was she judged. Things have changed (a bit), but nobody can deny that housework still tends to be a charged issue among couples today. . .

Men's homes

'Keep the home fires burning. . .till the boys come home,' sang homesick troops fighting a cold and bitter war on foreign soil. Without a motherland, a home, a hearth, a woman to come home to, would they bother to fight at all?

The home in all its receptive, nurturing and, occasionally, imprisoning aspects remains an intensely female and mothering symbol: in dream analysis, to dream of a house may often be to dream of a woman's (mother's) body. And in this potent image of the home as woman/mother may be located the source of the sometimes very different attitudes of men and women to their homes and to homemaking, and where the conflicts which these difficulties may sometimes cause may be unravelled.

The American sociologist Jessie Barnard in her book *The Future of Marriage* concludes that, contrary to popular myth, marriage is far better for men than bachelorhood. She presents an impressive array of supporting statistics tending to show that married men live longer, enjoy better mental health and even earn more than their unmarried counterparts. She concludes:

> *At the present time. . .there is no better guarantor of long life, health and happiness for men than a wife. . .willing to devote her life to taking care of him, providing, even enforcing, the regularity and security of a well-ordered home.*

The wife-ordered home is a benefit of which the young newlywed husbands interviewed in Mansfield and Collard's *The Beginning of the Rest of Your Life* seemed already to be enjoyably aware. While a few of their number expressed surprise or disappointment that their wives were not as proficient at anticipating and satisfying their needs as their own mothers had been, most of the men seemed to enjoy and appreciate having a home with a wife in it and all that that meant to them:

> *'Having the home is lovely – and having Caroline in it is even better – marriage is terrific.'*

> *'It's the companionship – knowing she will be here when I come home.'*

The authors conclude: '"Having someone to come home to", the presence of a wife in the home, was central to men's concept of home life, and a wife represented the very spirit of a home.'

Women's homes

A man's wife may thus represent the spirit of his home, the wife-in-the-home becoming a kind of all-purpose surrogate mother. But women rarely seem to identify their *husbands* with the home within the same comfortable composite image. For reasons which bear closer examination, women do not on the whole expect to be (and indeed are not) taken care of domestically in the way in which they make sure their men are.

Thus the other side of the Mansfield and Collard picture is a generation of young women rushing home from their paid work to attend to the all-important work of caring for their homes and their husbands. The authors calculate that over two-thirds of the wives in the survey each performed *at least* three-quarters of household chores (and this, remember, is a survey of couples in which the vast majority were childless and both partners working full time). These wives devoted their weekends to housework and did not mind their husbands' spare time being filled with hobbies ('It gets him from under my feet'). And when they felt tired and fed up about their work overload, they perceived this as being their own fault for not better mobilizing their husbands or more efficiently managing what they perceived as their own personal workloads.

The conflict is well expressed by one woman in the survey, who is quoted as saying that, although she accepted the fact that her husband did not do more, it 'got her down' sometimes. But she did not really want him to do more for 'then he wouldn't need me.' She worried about the nights when she was unable to cook for him: 'It's my fault that he has beans on toast.'

And yet these women, on the whole, did not express themselves dissatisfied with being married. On the contrary: to the extent that they felt burdened and tired (and they did), it was their paid jobs rather than their unequal share of the housework load which was perceived as being the problem. Mostly they looked forward to a time when they could legitimately leave their jobs to have a baby.

Does any of this sound even a little familiar? And if so, what is to be made of it?

A woman, to a far greater extent than a man, has to learn to care for herself – once she is an adult, other women will not do it for her (and women, after all, are the caring sex). Sometimes it seems that, if she is to continue operating healthily and happily, the home itself may have to come to stand in for that nurturing function from which she needs to benefit as much as her husband does. The home then becomes the symbol, if you like, of a woman's mothering of herself, and as such, it can be a very alluring one.

'Only a housewife. . .'

More than most roles in life, being a homemaker is what you make of it. Louisa could (though she does not) call herself a post-feminist woman. She belongs to the first generation of women to take for granted the right to university education and to untrammelled equal competition with men in the outside world, and she made the most of it. She built up her own company, but sold it after she became pregnant with her first child. Now she sees her present job as looking after the family home:

'It makes me really mad when I tell people I'm a housewife and they say patronizingly, "Oh but you used to be blah blah blah" "Oh but you're not, you're a mother." I tell them that it's true, I am a mother, just as my husband is a father – but my work at the moment is being a housewife!'

Louisa sees housework, in its various manifestations, as neither more nor less boring than most of the paid work she has done in her time. What *is* different and, for her, important about it at the moment is the extent to which she finds that looking after the home gets her in touch with the physical and with her ability to create a secure, nurturing and pleasing environment which, above all, fulfils her *own* needs.

'I used to be a person who was quite out of touch with the present nearly all the time – always looking ahead to see what I could achieve next but scarcely aware of where I actually was and how I felt. Ultimately, it wasn't very satisfying. I feel now I relate to my environment much more and that for me is very positive.'

She pauses and then continues: 'I think that, sometimes, at its best, I see housework as the outer symbol of an inner state of being which is quite precious to me.' Because her husband has now taken on the entire obligation of supporting the family, she does not mind that the housework is left to her. 'We both take parenting very seriously. . .he's out working most of the time, and when he's home, he's usually with our daughter. He can't do everything, can he?'

And yet the stereotype is not so easy to break out of. The next time we saw Louisa, she says half-ruefully that she was wondering about what she had said to us about housework: 'I mean, can I really say that I enjoy it, spending my time looking after the home? I'm really not sure. . .'

One of the unhappier side-effects of the entry of women into the domain of paid career structures has been the comparative denigration of the role of the domestic homemaker. True it may be that a great many household jobs are, without question, dull and monotonous or at least become that way from endless repetition and too little appreciation. Yet could not the same be said of the majority of paid jobs? And housework does have its fringe benefits. At least some of the time, jobs such as cooking, gardening, ordering the home and caring for babies and children have their satisfying and creative sides – which is more than can be said for many paid jobs. Plus, you are your own boss working on your own territory and can pace and prioritize yourself accordingly.

Be that as it may, millions of women who have worked in the home have ended up guiltily and defensively carrying on their traditional roles, apologizing readily to anyone who asked them: 'Oh, I'm only a housewife I'm afraid.' 'Work' is supposed to be what you get paid for: hence the expression 'working mothers' is used to indicate mothers who earn but

excludes others who work all day but whose job is caring for their homes
and children. These non-earning wives are seen as 'dependent' – which
they may be financially, but the degree to which their husbands depends
on the work *they* do goes unremarked.

An equal trade-off?

Even for women who are currently engaged in paid work, the picture is
often not so different. Earning or not, like it or not, it still tends to be
women who shoulder the donkey's share of domestic work in both its
positive and negative aspects. Thus it tends to be *women* (and women
alone) who see who does what in the home as an issue. And many a
working wife may be feeling that she is getting a raw deal and resenting
the unfairness of it all, for if women are to share in producing the income
of the family, justice surely demands an equal trade-off with the household
chores. Doesn't it?

Increasingly this may be agreed in theory between a marrying couple.
But the gap between theory and practice remains great. Another survey
about household work showed that 42 per cent of couples believed that
both partners should, for example, take turns at cooking, but in reality,
only 17 per cent of couples shared this task. This gap between belief and
actuality may be an ongoing source of secret resentment on her side and
guilt on his side, and yet both men *and* women collude in keeping men
out of the kitchens and broom cupboards. The justifications for women
working outside the home and continuing to bear the brunt of housework
within it (proffered, it must be said, by both sexes with equal eagerness
and ingenuity) include:

- *Her job is that much less demanding/more flexible than his* – and anyway
  they both agree that his work is more 'serious' as he will become
  the chief earner when a child arrives (an arrangement which is still
  unvarying in all but the tiniest minority of families). This may be
  a valid enough reason for shifting the housework burden once she
  stops work to have a baby, but in the meantime, it is a peculiarly
  circular argument. Why is her job more flexible? Because she has
  taken pains to make it that way so she can get the housework
  done.

- *She 'knows' how things should be done properly (she was 'brought up to do
  them')*. They both agree that he doesn't know how. Or he doesn't
  even notice that they need doing at all, thereby prompting the
  immortal interchange:

  He (outraged): '*But you never asked me to do it!*'
  She (more outraged): '*Asked you to do it? You have eyes, don't you?*'

And if he does then do it, naturally he'll mess it up and she will say it would have been easier for her to do it in the first place – thereby proving them both right.

- *He just prefers some jobs, and she prefers others* – a more sophisticated version of the 'some jobs are more feminine, others more masculine' line. In practice, the masculine jobs boil down to such onerous tasks as changing light bulbs, getting spiders out of the bath, washing the car, a spot of DIY and perhaps helpfully drying the dishes too – after she has cleaned, shopped, cooked, laid the table, served and done all of the washing up every day of the week.

Behind these rather self-justifying arguments lurks the truth that, despite her occasional resentment and more frequent tiredness, the wife who does most of the housework preserves the home as her special domain and retains control over domestic issues. She is also reassured that her husband really *does* need her – in other words, while she can keep him useless, she keeps herself indispensible. He, despite his occasional guilt, has the freedom of boyish irresponsibility. He has exchanged a mother for a wife – why, he hardly notices the difference! And he certainly enjoys his free evenings and weekends, well earned after his hard week's work.

Not least, husband *and* wife may both get a certain satisfaction from feeling they are fitting in with what are still generally conceived to be 'proper' masculine and feminine roles within their relationship. Three millennia or more of social programming cannot be changed overnight – her need to show she is a good homemaker (i.e. a proper woman) is entrenched as deeply as his need to show he is a bad one (i.e. a proper man). So why should they change?

With (initially) the best will in the world, resentful (and exhausted) working wives who cannot or have no desire to relinquish their careers will begin to let the housework slide. The motivation, such as it is, for pleasing and impressing him starts to fade. As the thrill of being married wears off and domestic life grinds inexorably into gear, laying the table and hoovering the hall of the love-nest have a tendency to lose whatever glamour they may once have had. She cannot compel him to care more; after a point, pride will not allow her to bully and nag him one more time into doing the things she feels he should do automatically. He seems to appreciate her contributions less and less. Her self-esteem suffers. So why should she bother, either?

The answer is so obvious: what they *both* really need is a perfect (but silent) mother to come bustling in clad in a flowery apron, whisking competently and energetically round their rather dank and dusty house until it is magically and fragrantly gleaming, a fire burns in the grate and the aroma of freshly baked bread and a tasty casserole for supper comes wafting temptingly through from the kitchen. Alas, their days of being mothered like this by someone else are long gone, if they ever happened at all. When this apparition fails to materialize, it can be all too easy to fall into the trap of both of you being disappointed and bitching at each other to vent your frustration. . .

Bringing it all back home: who does what in the housework stakes?

. . .There is no need to do any housework at all. After the first four years the dirt doesn't get any worse.

Quentin Crisp, *The Naked Civil Servant*

Sue and William have been married for three years. Sue is an arts administrator who had stopped working shortly before the birth of their baby son. William had been training as a classical musician, an oboeist, but was not yet in a position to earn a regular income from this work. When the birth of their child was imminent, he trained as a computer programmer and got a job working for a multinational company. During the interview, they sit together, their baby son sleeping in a carrycot at Sue's feet. When the subject of who earns and who does the housework comes up, they both become very animated.

'We've sorted everything out now,' says William. 'Sue does all the cooking, cleaning and shopping and I earn the money.'

'It's not true!' Sue exclaims. 'Before we were married, I earned all the money, William spent it. Before I was pregnant, I was the main earner.'

William agrees in a conciliatory tone that this is true and that they do share the housework. Sue then states that she feels that it was harder for her to adjust to the change in status than William: 'I find it hard to be able to spend money on myself now I'm not earning. I have to justify it to myself. . .I *do* do most of the housework. We both hate it. William is always willing to help, but I have to nag him. He wasn't brought up to do it.' William nods his head in agreement.

But it is not long before William, talking about the conflicting claims of fatherhood, the need to support his family and his aspiring musicianship, says that he is actually quite envious of Sue. We ask him if he would prefer to be the one who stays at home: 'I'd love it. I don't like working and that's the truth.' He adds that he thinks it has, however, been important for them as a couple and as a family that he did go out and get a job.

Sue then reveals that she has recently turned down the offer of a part-time job: 'I wanted to be with my baby. It's the one chance I've got to be a mother to him. . .yet I feel myself fighting not to lose my identity as Sue, giving my all to the baby 24 hours a day. . .'

William and Sue apparently share a scale of values in which the earner has more prestige than the non-earning homemaker. At first, they agree that it is Sue who has a hard time; she suffers from feelings of a lack of self-worth, specifically in thinking she is not entitled to spend the family money that she has not personally earned. And although they both feel it makes sense that Sue should, for the time being, take primary responsibility for the housework, they both need the reassurance of knowing that she has not been dumped with it: to this end, William 'helps'.

And yet as the interview proceeds, it becomes clear that William is (more quietly) not altogether happy with his current 'masculine' role either. For him, too, the birth of their son and the subsequent polarization of their relationship into male breadwinner/female homemaker has meant sacrifice. Trapped on the corporate ladder, he has had to place his musical ambitions on hold, and he regrets having so little time to spend with his infant son. From where he stands, the role of homemaker/childcarer doen't look like such a bad deal.

In other words, each of them is stretched tight, tired and regretting missed opportunities. And not surprisingly, each sometimes looks over to the other and cannot help but think that surely their partner has the better deal.

Sue and William both felt that Sue should be the one to care for the baby at first – and because childcare and housework have a tendency to merge seamlessly (and endlessly) with each other, she got most of the housework, too. A gender-based division of roles, with the housework mainly allocated on one side of the divide, may still have its attractions for many families, at least for a while once children arrive and one partner, almost invariably the wife, leaves paid work.

The 1971 census found that 69.6 per cent of wives were economically active upon their marriage, but after six years of wedded bliss, this figure shrank to 27.9 per cent, presumably because of the advent of children; it then picked up again to 59.7 per cent after 24 years. Only 7 per cent of mothers of pre-school children now actually work full-time outside the home, the majority working either part-time or not at all.

This traditional division of labour can be a sensible enough arrangement in itself – but only if a couple both believe that the job of homemaker/childcarer is as important and valuable as that of breadwinner. Even today, this is not always the case. A woman at home may, like Sue, voice envy of her husband who leaves the wet nappies and dribbling offspring behind every day to go to work. But it has not been as easy for men, even as they trudge sleepily off to work through Monday morning drizzle, to express envy of the traditional lives of women – epitomized by the miserable bondage of domesticity. William may be unusual in this respect – yet while we were researching this chapter, more than one man was heard to murmur softly, 'Oh, I wouldn't mind being a kept man. . .Doing the housework wouldn't be so bad after all. . .' (Any women within earshot invariably looked appalled.)

Women who become more able to voice their own needs and find men who are willing, on a mutual basis, to care for them are likely to start to feel less reliant on the home itself as a symbol of being looked after – actually, a symbol of their ability to look after themselves. And the signs are that men (however much more slowly) are changing, too. The old taboos against men expressing feelings are certainly dissolving; and as men develop more involved relationships with their children (from active participation in the birth onwards), they inevitably want to spend more time with them. Perhaps we are heading for a time when the complex relationship which so many women have with their homes – part hard-labour prison, part secure haven – may start to resolve itself into a simpler and more satisfying relationship with the home participated in by husband and wife alike and exemplified by their care for each other within it.

In the meantime, the complexities which lie behind the place of housework in married life remain great. They include the unwilling but still-potent attraction of the traditional stereotyped roles; the search for genuine equality within a relationship; the envy, acknowledged or not, that one partner often feels towards the other's different role; the unarguable reality that only women can have babies and the generally accepted belief that women are best at looking after children; the need experienced by *both* sexes to be cared for and valued. Given all this, it is not surprising that who does what in the home remains such a charged issue.

Housework is a classic area where expectations match up against reality in a very physical form – if the gap between the two is too great, your marriage may suffer. Unlike the more diffuse questions of sexual or emotional fulfilment, in the home it's easy to see whether or not your expectations are being met – you only have to look around you. The issue is simply this: whether you as a couple can together find a way of managing your home and housework that will meet your needs without creating a stranglehold over your lives.

Towards a brighter future

At the start of your marriage, it is highly likely that the two of you will both be working outside the home and will have similar demands on your time and energy. As your marriage/partnership develops, you may well find that these demands change, so the important thing is to create a flexible system which can be altered to meet your changing needs.

There is a certain Catch 22 in determining each spouse's share of household duties: (a) You'll have to divide the tasks, but (b) you need to live with each other first before deciding how each of you can best contribute to the home. You need to tread the thin dividing line between creating a rigid 'system' which works for neither of you because neither of you yet knows how the other one ticks, and falling into a haphazard, unsatisfactory way of doing things because you haven't yet decided how things should be divided.

It may be that you are both sufficiently well adapted and complement each other so much that you divide up the household chores automatically, without need of creating a structure. In this sort of perfect world, you can work things out tacitly – with the one coming in from work first starting off the cooking, the one who notices the rubbish building up emptying it (rather than just squashing in that last milk carton), the one who notices the crumbs on the carpet hauling out the vacuum cleaner. Unfortunately most of us do not consistently conduct our lives in such a mature fashion because, like as not, it will always be the same (increasingly tight-lipped) partner who 'notices' the dirt/untidiness while the other, given half a chance, falls bleary-eyed into squalid chaos (the 'you-didn't-ask-me/don't-you-have-eyes' syndrome already mentioned).

There are great risks involved if either of you becomes a supremely competent homemaker to the exclusion of the other. In the early days of the marriage, women, in particular, can urge themselves on to enormous efforts to have the perfect home; their husbands' needs may well be being met perfectly, but in the meantime they are losing out themselves. Sooner or later only a saint would be able to refrain from either backsliding or taking the resentment out on the rest of the family in other ways.

EXERCISE

Before you start getting down to the nitty gritty, this little exercise may enable you to get a better sense of your own and each other's preconceptions about housework, and may help to start dissipating some of the emotional charge that attaches to the question of who does what (and for whose benefit). It is intended to bring into the open the assumptions and expectations which you are each likely to bring into the relationship, based on your respective family backgrounds, affecting which tasks you may unconsciously see as 'masculine' or 'feminine'.

Carry out this exercise, step by step, *together*. If only one of you does it, then it will all too easily become a question of that person imposing his or her will on the other – exactly the opposite of the state of shared responsibility which is the aim of the whole thing.

First, each of you, without conferring, should write down who in your own *childhood* home was responsible for the following tasks:

- Managing finances and paying bills.
- Deciding where you would go for holiday each year.
- Taking out the rubbish.
- Making dentists' appointments.
- Noticing that the woodwork in the kitchen/living room/bedroom needed painting.
- Painting that woodwork.
- Getting the car filled with petrol.
- Remembering birthdays and sending out thank-you cards.
- Ironing shirts.
- Feeding the children.
- Disciplining the children.

Now go through the list again, this time writing down who shoulders each of these tasks within your marriage *at the moment*. To avoid the dangers of unconsciously writing down what you think *should* happen rather than what really *does*, go back to the last few actual occasions any of these tasks needed performing, and remember who really did them.

Pool your results, looking at the similarities and differences between your lists. (You may find out that you have different versions of what goes on in your own home!) Talk about what you both notice and how you feel that your own attitudes both differ from and are similar to your parents'.

Next, *talk about your expectations for your home – how you really want it to be.* You need to be honest about your expectations, drawing on the points you have both made in the exercise above, and any others that might spring to mind. If both of you genuinely like the feel of a 'lived-in' home (i.e. you share a high-level toleration of untidiness) or, at the other end of the spectrum, you are both fanatically houseproud, then you have the great advantage of like minds and just need to work out how to put those expectations into effect. More likely, you will find that there is a gap between your individual expectations – one of you wants more order, the other is prepared to live more chaotically and lazily.

Those who had left home some time ago (a group we cannot ignore as we both happen to form part of it) tend to have their own well-established routines and priorities. If a person whose idea of a well-spent Sunday afternoon is staying in bed until 3.00 pm reading a Jackie Collins novel and drinking Chianti marries someone who enjoys weekends spent ritualistically rearranging the bathroom cupboard, both will have to learn the gentle art of compromise. Selfishness is OK but within limits. No amount of hard work and exact planning will make a home if it is not infused by *some* consideration for each other – and by a sense of humour and the ability to keep things in perspective.

Back to sorting out the housework. Now you've done the hard bit, there are only three more simple steps to follow. . .

Specify what tasks you want/need to get done – and how often. This should include everything from the daily washing up through scraping the mouldy gunge off the fridge to nursing along the Gro-bag tomato plants.

By the side of each task, write down how many hours it takes per week. Stick to your guns. If freshly ironed sheets and home-baked bread really matter to you, it is no cause for shame. On the other hand, the days of the perfectly shining and spotless household are numbered: unlike our grandmothers (or mothers and mothers-in-law), few of us have the time (never mind the inclination) to spend hours scouring the outside porch step on our hands and knees. Perhaps you are happy with takeaways or boiled eggs once (three? five times?) a week. And it may be a false economy on both nerves and pocket to keep trudging miserably down to the launderette through rain and hail instead of forking out for a washing machine.

If there are some jobs which you both really loathe (ironing particularly seems to raise a universal shudder), would it be against your principles to pay for someone to come in and do them? Your budget may be tight, but even a little part-time help – maybe four hours per fortnight, which is unlikely to cost any more than a cheap meal out for two – may enable your lives together to become very much more pleasant.

Now consider whether these tasks should be split down the middle. In other words, if one of you only works part-time or, alternatively, has to commute a long way to work, you may both agree that the disparity between your time available should be reflected in the allocation of housework. Similarly, if babies or children are already a reality in your lives (or expected shortly), time spent caring for them will need to enter into the calculation as well. According to a study by K. E. Walker, published in the *Family Economics Review 1969*, the mother of a one-year-old spends an average of 50 per cent longer on household tasks than the mother of a teenager. Therefore, depending on their ages, you will need to reserve some time, perhaps a considerable amount, just for your little angel(s). Admittedly, we are talking an inexact science here, but you should be able to make a fair estimate based on experience of what the demands on you actually are.

There is no point in virtuously deciding on a straight-down-the-middle split if either of you are subsequently going to spend all your time resenting how much greater (once housework is added to all your other commitments) *your* burden is and how unfair *your* life is. We can tell you from personal experience that such a person (unless they are a card-carrying martyr) will then just spend their energies finding ways to weasel out of their agreed share instead of getting on with it. Now is the time to speak out so that the housework can really be shared fairly.

Another point: a person's notions of how much time they have available may be surprisingly distorted – either way. The only thing for it may be to sit down and actually calculate the number of hours of existing commitments you each already have – including travelling and study time, but specifically excluding hours spent in the pub on the way home!

Finally, *measure and divide up the tasks*. It's a good idea to start by allocating the tasks which one of you especially enjoys or for which you feel you have a special aptitude. (Women, this does not mean you are to agree to do everything except changing fuses and checking the oil level in the car.) Would you be happy to undertake the thing you like to do best by yourself if there is some kind of trade-off elsewhere? Or would you still like your partner to be involved?

You then need to divide the tasks that remain on a fair footing (according to whether you have agreed to split 50/50 timewise, or whatever). You could, for instance, start out from the basis that one of you will be totally responsible for washing, ironing and mending, while the other will do all hoovering and dusting. If you have tasks that neither of you wants to do, these could be alternated on a weekly basis. In the Garlick/ Howard household, Helen and her husband divide up the cooking, so that Helen cooks during the week (as she frequently works from home) while her husband cooks at weekends (when he's quite happy to spend some time in the kitchen).

A possible incentive

If neither of you feels much like tidying or cleaning up, one of us believes that a wonderful way of concentrating the mind on the subject is to invite friends around for supper once in a while. If both of you are reasonably houseproud, it's a great incentive to rush around creating order out of chaos. The other one of us shudders at the idea, feeling that the competitive spirit is what took the pleasure out of housework in the first place – if you're *that* desperate, she thinks, resign yourselves to squalor or hire a live-in maid!

To conclude, here is the solution of Jane and her husband Rick. Having variously experienced all the trials and tribulations, pitched battles, disappointments, crushed expectations and slummy living that any couple could reasonably be expected to suffer and remain together, we have now found our own solution to the vexed question of housework – a solution which is, touch wood, still working. Interestingly, we only hit on it after we had alternated going out to work while the other stayed at home and looked after the house and our very young daughter – so neither of us could deny that we knew exactly what needed doing as well as how to do it!

In the beginning of our marriage, we tried a number of systems to get the housework done. In all of them, we both viewed the tasks as a real chore, and nothing really worked well for long. We both harboured a measure of resentment, being quite sure that we were each doing more than the other (actually, I was quite sure I was doing far more than Rick!).

What we eventually started doing was putting Sundays aside as our house day. We keep the whole day clear for a leisurely clean and laundry which we do together, pottering round and having the time to chat and catch up with each other's week. As we have a whole day, we can take it quite easily, with plenty of pauses for snacks, coffee and the Sunday papers. We each do the jobs we enjoy, then get down together and share the rest.

What has made it work for us is each other's company and feeling that, because the work is being visibly shared, neither of us is getting exploited or dumped on. It has become a real ritual. . .we seem to end the day feeling quite close and happy – and we have the added joy of waking up on Monday to a clean house.

And the arrangement has an extra bonus, too, with respect to the third member of the household:

> Alexandra, our toddler, really enjoys Sunday. She loves having us both home and dusting and polishing seem to be things she

can relate to in her own anarchic way. She doesn't usually see us working, unless it's reading or writing, which to her, of course, is utterly pointless. She enjoys "helping".

To build your home together, you will need to invest your time and your energies in it. If you just view it as a place to eat and sleep with rather tiresome upkeep requirements, then that is what it will become. If you don't really live in your home, you're limiting yourselves to mere survival in it. As well as being your brick-and-mortar house, your home is the quality of the time you spend in it: loving, eating, sleeping, reading, playing music. Your home is not just your curtains, your decorations, your garden, your kitchen units. It is also your memories and your feelings about it. In the kitchen, you'll remember the time you burned the duck soup and how, as a result, you had to go out and get an Indian take-away; that hilarious evening when you sat up with friends drinking ouzo and playing poker all night; the time the cat ran up the curtains when she was just a kitten and couldn't get down again. . .These memories seem to melt into the physical framework of a house. Once people have occupied a building, their time together there is firmly imprinted within the walls. As you build your lives and your home together, so you will build up a store of memories past and present. The time you invest in caring for each other in your home and enjoying yourselves will reap rich if intangible rewards.

PART IV

TOWARDS A GOOD MARRIAGE

All of us hope to have good marriages. What that term actually encompasses can, in reality, be hard to get to grips with. A marriage which appears 'good' one day can feel downright awful another. And after the heady highs of the wedding, when both of you were working towards the same goal, the period afterwards can seem something of an anticlimax.

'I felt a bit lost,' reports one interviewee about six months after his marriage. 'I kept thinking that we should be working towards another goal – but what was it?' And his wife similarly experienced a feeling of let-down:

> 'I thought I was relatively sophisticated about marriage – after all, I'd waited till I was 27, but I still found out I had loads of expectations – and they came as a real surprise. You know, like once we'd got married, we'd be happy ever after, and that I ought to cook him a meal every night, and if he didn't have an ironed shirt, maybe it was my fault. I started acting just like my mother.'

This husband and wife, in common with many thousands of other newly marrieds, were struggling with the mixed feelings that are experienced not long after the big day. It is not until we actually do get married that we realize what our expectations about being married were and, maybe even more of a shock, that those of our spouses could be so different. The gulf between the sexes can yawn widely and questions crowd in. How do we keep our own space? Will we start behaving like 'husband and wife' or, even worse, like our parents? How do we keep sexual attraction alive now we're together day in, day out? How will we cope with children? Will s/he find someone else? And will we be happy?

Many issues have to be negotiated within a marriage. And a marriage is not made overnight. One of its strengths is that you have the *time* to deal with those issues and resolve them effectively. We have already touched on the nuts and bolts – the more practical aspects of your lives together. In this next section, we shall be exploring deeper issues: sex, children, emotional problems. Every couple will have to face problems and the success of your marriage will depend upon how well you are able to negotiate them. And as you both, in your different but complementary ways, tackle those problems with courage, goodwill and honesty, over the years your marriage should flourish.

And will it be a good one? What, for goodness' sake, *is* a good marriage? We propose a working definition: *a loving alliance where there is freedom within commitment*. Love – well, that almost goes without saying. An alliance – because as we approach the 21st century, we need to be thinking of a sharing of power between the sexes, where neither has dominance over the other. And as you work together in building your relationship and in bringing up your children, if you have them, you will need to be allies. And freedom – to express and fulfil ourselves individually and together without the need to control and possess one another. And finally commitment – that vital ingredient which represents patience, perseverance and security.

With all of these, you have the recipe for a good marriage, one that you will be working towards together. And we start off with that most fascinating of subjects. . .

18

With my body I thee worship: sex in modern marriage

When two persons love each other, nothing is more imperative and delight-ful to them than giving: to give always and everything, one's thoughts, one's life, one's body, and all that one has: and to feel the gift and to risk everything in order to give more, still more.

Guy de Maupassant

THERE'S no marriage without sex – and that's official. Once you leave the wedding reception and head off for your first night of wedded bliss, you and your partner still have a vital act to perform before your marriage really does become a marriage in the legal sense. You need sex to consummate a marriage. Thus the first time you make love together as husband and wife bonds you together in your marriage.

Unfortunately, sex has never exactly had a good press in the Judaeo-Christian tradition. It has long suffered from the taint of being a necessary evil, necessary because the sex act results in the procreation of children, but no less unspeakable for all that. But even the most puritanical have had to accept that sex is a fact of life: 'It is better to marry than to burn,' admitted St Paul, meaning that if you *had* to have sex, marriage would at least prevent your soul being damned for ever. Thus marriage became the arena for an uneasy compromise. Sex could be accepted in marriage because it was there for a reason – to ensure the survival of the human race. In marriage, it could be controlled, sanctioned and regulated by society at large.

In the age of the Swinging Sixties, when flower power blossomed and the heady aroma of marijuana and incense scented the air, free love hit the headlines in a big way. The expression of sexuality became accepted

– the symbol, the incarnation even, of freedom. Birth control became for the first time both effective and widely available. The old double standard started to erode; now even nice girls were doing it. Social commentators worried that, as men were able to 'get it for nothing', the most juicy carrot leading them to marry and to continue supporting their wives and offspring was disappearing. Accordingly, the end of marriage was prophesied everywhere. However, it never happened that way. Instead, couples went on flocking to the altar.

Sex within marriage is still seen as having a lot going for it. On the one hand, as long as both of you are faithful, the spectres of AIDS, herpes and so on will hold fewer fears for you. There is also the wider benefit of the psychological safety and peace of mind available within an intimate and secure relationship. In a long-term committed sexual relationship, the thrill of novelty and variety may wane but the insidious need to 'perform' and to impress one another also disappears. Should sexual blocks, inhibitions and problems arise from time to time, there is at least the potential within such a relationship for working through them rather than needing to conceal them from each other. And as you come to know each other better and better, your relationship becomes increasingly a place where the sexuality of each partner can be tenderly and unendingly explored.

So much for the sexual relationship within marriage at its best. But what are the issues and difficulties that you are likely to face in marriage as your sexual relationship evolves?

First romance

When two people fall in love, they are drawn to each other like magnets. Each sees the other in a special, golden light. There is magic in the air, a state of enchantment. The lovers feel beautiful and powerful. The energy field between a couple in love generates an erotic electricity. In the charmed space that surrounds them, sensory impressions are intensified: music is heard more clearly, smells are more distinct, the lover's touch is enhanced.

It is as if people who fall in love invest their beloved with a part of themselves, an idealized, perfect part which they did not previously know they possessed. Boundaries then seem to merge and disappear. Separation becomes intolerable. Self-consciousness and the fear of losing one's more-or-less painfully gained separate identity may deliciously and piquantly add spice to the sense of falling inexorably into ecstasy:

'When I first met him, I fell so deeply in love that I hardly knew what to do with myself. I found it difficult to speak to him or even be near him; yet if I wasn't near him, I couldn't bear that either! Our relationship took a long time to get off the ground, and even when we did start to go out

*with one another, we didn't have sex for some time. It somehow seemed
too important to have sex before we got to know each other a little. Yet
whenever he touched me, I felt an electric charge go through me. He only
needed to put his hand on my arm for me to feel quite faint!'*

How does the heightened sexual involvement of this couple compare to
the involvement of one contentedly married for 25 years? How can the
two experiences possibly be compared? Which criteria could you use?
Yet we often do compare them, and the quieter, less heady pleasures of
sexual love within a long-term relationship tend to be the losers in the
comparison.

It is almost as if someone has nailed a sign above the gates through
which you enter together as a married couple: 'ABANDON HOPE ALL YE
WHO ENTER HERE.' Married love seems to be perceived as a lesser
version of 'the real thing', something to be settled down to once the yoke
of matrimony has been assumed. Yet is this borne out in the personal
experiences of married couples?

In fact, none of the couples we interviewed reported any feelings of
disappointment in their sexual lives together. On the contrary:

*'Now that we're married, I feel more free to explore my sexuality; in
a way to abandon myself more in sex. I know that she won't walk
out on me – I trust her better. So I've experienced more of a feeling
of freedom in sex. I give myself permission to try out more things. I
know she won't be shocked, and if she doesn't want to do anything,
she'll tell me. But we have a good time!' [Husband after six weeks of
marriage]*

*'I find sex better than ever before. I love the fact that we live together and
we don't have to "find" a place to have sex. We can do it right here – at
home. Sunday afternoons have become great.' [Husband after 15 months
of marriage]*

*'We have gone through peaks and troughs in our sexual relationship. For
a while, after the first novelty of being in love had worn off, it was a
bit hard. But the general feeling for me is of our relationship having
become* more *intense, and the expression of our sexuality with
each other a much deeper, perhaps more confronting, and
more rewarding kind of experience.' [Wife after three years
of marriage]*

'So far, so good' was the overall message from the newly marrieds. And
indeed in the first years of marriage, the waning of passion may well be
the last thing on their minds. But if problems are coming up, what might
lie behind them?

The fear of uncontrolled sexuality

'I'm really very settled with Gary,' said Louisa. 'We have a good home and a happy family life. I'd never want to do anything to hurt him. But our sex life isn't what it used to be.'

Louisa felt that her sexuality had become semi-dormant within her marriage. Recently, however, things had changed:

> *I think I've started to change a lot as a person over the last couple of years and become more aware of feelings I had lost touch with since I got married. I've started to get more aware of my sexuality too. But it terrifies me! I look at 18-year-old boys in tight jeans on the street (18-year-olds!) and wonder what it would be like with them. . .'*

Everyone knows that adultery is an unparalleled threat to the continuance of a marriage (*see* Chapter 19). But is it also possible that the expression of sexuality within the primary marriage relationship itself might be inhibited simply by the fear, however insubstantial, of just being *tempted* towards infidelity?

We are, despite everything, still children of Freud and the Victorians: we endow uninhibited sexuality with a violent, glamorous and ruthless power to rip apart contented marriages and the very fabric of society.

If you have ever had a sneaking fear, or fantasy, that your sexuality, once given free rein, might plunge you into a series of wild extramarital affairs, thereby blowing apart the serenity of your married life, the unconscious solution may be to repress your sexuality altogether.

The truth is that we cannot control our sexuality selectively, according to conscious rational choices. If sexual feelings become repressed, even for the best of motives, this may adversely affect the very relationship which you are honourably trying so hard to protect – your sexual relationship with your husband or wife – for you may be unable to become really erotically excited about him or her either.

The problem, such as it is, stems from a monumental confusion between what one *feels* (over which one has little or no choice) and what one *decides to do* (over which there is every choice). So what if you get turned on by a man or woman in the street? Nothing will happen as a result unless you cause it to. No one will ever know unless you decide to tell them.

The question of infidelity as a threat to marriage will be discussed further in the next chapter. For now, suffice it to say that there is no reason why a *frisson* of sexual excitement – from the sway of a tightly-jeaned bottom on the street or the seductive smile of a work colleague across the office – need be any more harmful to your marriage than the sexual *frissons* provided by candlelight, satin sheets or oysters for supper. Your fidelity to your partner is precious precisely because you are a feeling, thinking person who chooses to be faithful to him or her because you *want* to – not because you have turned yourself into an insensate, unresponsive block of wood.

The pressures of time, the dangers of routine

The sex lives of many a married couple are perhaps suprisingly beset by the problem of finding enough time to spend with each other sexually. Allied with this is the ease with which you can fall into a routine in which sex is automatically slotted into the general schedule ('Darling, it's 10.00 pm on the second Sunday of the month. . .you haven't forgotten, have you?').

Gone are the days when you used to begrudge every slow hour until you could tear the clothes off each other and fall breathlessly into bed, emerging unsteadily 23 hours later. Now sex has to take its place with everything else clamouring for your attention. Reduced frequency, less time spent together sexually and a general diminution in sexual spontaneity and excitement are likely to be the result. In fact, a study of 218 married couples who visited the Masters and Johnson Institute in the United States from 1979 to 1985 found that limited time for intimacy was a primary factor in sexual dissatisfaction.

In the 1988 hit film, *Baby Boom*, J. C. Wiatt, a management consultant and successful woman *extraordinaire* (played by Diane Keaton), is at home with her investment banker lover. Both are poring over business papers late at night in bed. He turns to her: 'Do you want to make love?' She responds, still engrossed in her work, 'Do you?' She removes her glasses to look at him, and swiftly says, 'Oh, I see you do, huh.' The camera cuts to a digital clock as it flips from 11.46 pm to 11.50 pm. 'That was incredible!' he gasps. She shoots him a look of disbelief and returns to her work. The audience laughs. But how many were laughing ruefully, recognizing a portrayal of their own rushed love lives up there on the screen?

Too many other commitments crowding in on your lives may be the reason why your once vibrant sex life together has lost its thrill. But sometimes these excessive commitments can be the symptom rather than the cause of the problem. By finding other ways of spending your time, are you enabling yourself to feel more in control or safer than you might risk feeling by being intimate with each other sexually?

Security and reliability within a long-term sexual relationship are two of the greatest boons of being married, but this does not mean that you need to take each other for granted. It is surprising how many couples place their sexual relationship low on their list of priorities – well below washing the dishes, doing an extra piece of office work, paying bills (hardly exciting activities in themselves!) – and then wonder where the magic has gone. . .

Intimacy is precious and can only grow if you invest in your relationship the kind of time, care and creativity which you would have to invest in anything else to keep it thriving. Making time to be alone together should become a top priority – staying in touch and in tune with each other is an important element in keeping your sex life alive.

Sex and parenthood

Something momentous happens to many couples as their marriages mature. They become parents.

Once upon a time, and still in some cultures, sex with a pregnant woman was taboo. Today many (though by no means all) pregnant women report a distinct waning of their sex drive, especially at the beginning and towards the end of a pregnancy. Men may also find that they have ambivalent sexual feelings towards their wives at this time. Once a woman has given birth, full intercourse is generally not recommended on medical grounds for at least six weeks. And in any event, the minor and major consequences of such great physical and psychological exertion as giving birth may mean that sex is the last thing on your mind, for a while at least.

Of course, your sex drive will return, though the desire and indeed the opportunity for sex must fight for space with the many and varied demands that parenthood will make of both of you – the roar (or so it seems) of your famished infant, the dreaded patter of curious little feet approaching your closed bedroom door or the inevitable wail of 'Mommeee! Dwinkee!' from your toddler's bedroom the split second after one of you makes a tentatively romantic move towards the other. No more love in the afternoon on the kitchen table either.

And the demands of adjusting to a sexual relationship after becoming parents are more than just practical ones, great as these are in themselves. It has been said that every child's first great love is the parent of the opposite sex, a love which must of necessity remain frustrated and unconsummated if the child is to grow into a healthy adult. When you become a parent, you see your lover and partner becoming a parent too, and the transformation may kindle deeply buried babyhood memories of your own parents. This transformation may contribute to a growing closeness and comfortable interdependence between you as a couple; not unusually, it also may contribute to a kind of irrational sense that your partner is (or should be) sexually out of bounds.

Our culture has some very curious attitudes to sex and childbirth, striving to deny the intimate connection between them. Women's breasts are plastered salaciously over mass-circulation tabloids, yet women are still often prohibited from breastfeeding their tiny babies in public, no matter how demurely they carry out this procedure. Language, too, reflects these attitudes: for example, the same part of a woman's anatomy is referred to as the 'vagina' when speaking of its sexual function and as the 'birth canal' when speaking of its reproductive function, as if they were two entirely distinct organs. All this can contribute to a curious split in some people's minds.

One woman, now breastfeeding her son and otherwise having resumed a good sexual relationship with her husband, spoke with regret of how her husband never fondled her breasts any more: 'I think he feels they belong to Adam now. Anyway, I think he's anxious that, if he touched them, milk would come spurting out all over the place – and it probably would!' Other women, feeling that their sexuality conflicts with their maternity, deny themselves and their babies the pleasure of breastfeeding, wishing to preserve this part of their bodies as a sexual rather than a parental part. Perhaps they are also trying to appease the feelings of resentment and jealousy which some (but not all) husbands undoubtedly feel at their usurpation by the demanding baby.

You may feel jealous of the place your new child has suddenly taken in your partner's life or just resentful of the broken nights and the constant demands of parenthood. You may be finding it hard to adjust to the changes in your own or your partner's body. Remember that good sex is first and foremost about communication – the more open and receptive you are with each other about your wonderings and doubts, the more it will pay dividends for your long-term sex lives.

If you and your partner find it difficult to maintain your sex life in all its former glory during a pregnancy or after the birth of a child, it is hardly surprising, and certainly not something to worry about in the short term. The process of becoming a parent is very challenging on both the emotional and physical level. An intimate sexual relationship is also very demanding. It may take time, patience and mutual understanding and tolerance to discover each other again sexually, but given time, patience and understanding, it will happen.

Everything you always wanted to know about sex but never dared ask. . .!

'In no other department of life is superstition so hard to die as in the sex sphere. Half the world is still guided in its sexual conduct not by knowledge but by half-truth, traditions, superstitions and old wives' tales.' So says the American doctor Winifred V. Richmond.

However much we may think or boast that we know about sex, many of us know surprisingly little. This may be hard to admit in the supposedly enlightened 1990s, but not only do most of us have an incomplete knowledge of how we, and others, function sexually, we also often lack information on such basic things as what women's and men's genitals look like. Of course, we have an idea about how we and our partners are put together, but are we confident that we are 'normal'?

Engaging in the perennially popular doctors-and-nurses games of childhood, we may have had a chance to see and examine our own and other children's sexual organs, and we may have also glimpsed our parents in the nude. During puberty, if we were able to ignore our parents' warnings against genital touching and masturbation (how many of us actually did grow up to be blind?), we could explore how we felt and looked – maybe, for girls, with the aid of a mirror. In the locker room, adolescent boys at least had the opportunity to compare their penis sizes – and to see how far they could ejaculate compared to their peers. Later on, we could look at, touch and feel our partners' penises and vaginas. However, in all this sexual exploration, we may still have felt that what we were doing was something to keep secret, only to be done covertly. Having once been cocooned in self-consciousness, it can be hard now to throw off the inhibitions of earlier times and take a long, hard look.

The sex education most of us gained was gleaned from various sources – biology lessons (the sex lives of frogs and algae), romantic novels of the 'she swooned against his manhood' variety and rather more explicit but not necessarily any more accurate soft and hard porn such as:

> Her legs came up. . .as he began to enter her. . .It was as if a giant of white-hot steel were penetrating her vitals. She began to moan as it opened her and climbed higher into her body, past her womb, past her stomach, under her heart, up into her throat. She was pant-ing now like a bitch in heat. . .[From The Betsy by Harold Robbins]

With all this morass of false – and often frightening – information, it's a great tribute to humanity's resources that Western society has ever managed to work out how to replicate itself at all, never mind enjoying sex along the way.

Generally speaking, families do not help much either. Many women know for a fact (from irreproachable sources) that if they bathe while having a period, the 'bad blood' will rush to their heads and poison them. Others are positive that they will be severely weakened (if not blinded) by excessive masturbation (who defined 'excessive'?). And even parents who believed that they should not repress their children's sexuality still found difficulty in answering the dreaded question 'Where do babies come from?' or 'What is sex like?' In reply, they would recite to their puzzled offspring a rather hurried explanation involving a lot of incomprehensible technical information, rounded off by the assertion (spoken through gritted teeth or with a pained sigh), 'Of course, sex is a wonderful and magical thing, dar-ling.'

So. . .we decided to get back to basics and include a section on what the sex organs of men and women look like and what actually 'happens' to them physically during sex. Read on – you never know, you may have a few surprises coming.

Men's physiology

The external sex organs of a man are the penis and the testes (or testicles) contained within a bag of skin called the scrotum.

Inside the penis are three cylinders of spongy tissue, surrounded by a strong fibrous covering. The spongy tissue, in turn, surrounds a tube called the urethra. This carries both urine (from the bladder) and semen out of the man's body. While it remains in the body, urine is sterile and any traces remaining in the urethra will thus not contaminate the semen. In addition, when a man ejaculates, a muscle closes off the entrance to the bladder so that it is impossible for urine and semen to become mixed. The testicles produce sperm and also a hormone – testosterone.

The penis itself extends far into the body, nearly to the rectum. Its head is the most sensitive part for most men, especially the area around the ridge connecting the head to the shaft (the main body of the penis). Penises do not come in standard sizes. There are as many different shapes and sizes of penis as there are of men. Some are longer, shorter, thinner, fatter. Some 'lean' to one side (in old-fashioned gentlemen's dressers' parlance, almost all men 'dress' on one side or the other). Some are circumcised (the loose skin covering the head has been removed), some not. All look different when erect from how they do when they are not. But the shape and size of a man's penis, contrary to the fearmongering tales passed among adolescents, have little or nothing to do with his and his partner's enjoyment of sex. The old saying 'It's not what it looks like, it's what you do with it that counts' is as true today as it ever was.

Inside a man's body, the major sex organs are the vas deferens, seminal vesicles, prostate gland, Cowper's glands and the urethra.

The vas deferens are two tubes, one extending from each testicle to the prostate. Sperm are constantly being manufactured by the testicles and are stored there until ejaculation. Then they travel up the vas deferens until they reach the prostate, where they mix with its secretions plus those of the seminal vesicles. The prostate fluids comprise most of the semen (or ejaculate), giving it its whitish colour and smell. The semen leaves the prostate and travels down the urethra. As it enters the penis, a lubricating fluid secreted by the two Cowper's glands is added to it.

Men's sexual responses

When a man is sexually excited, the messages transmitted to the nerve ends in the walls of the arteries supplying the blood to the penis cause the arteries to become wider so that an increased amount of blood flows into the spongy tissue of the penis. Normally, blood flows steadily in and out of the penis, but once the penis is sexually stimulated, the blood flows in faster than it flows out, causing the penis to expand. Because the fibrous sheath covering the spongy tissue will expand only so far, as the tissues fill with blood, they press against the sheath, making the penis hard and erect.

In young men, the angle of an erection may be almost straight up. However, it is a little known fact that, as men age, not only do their penises grow longer naturally, but the angle of their erection drops (becomes more horizontal). Many men feel uncomfortable about this, comparing themselves to their supposedly more virile younger selves. But don't worry! The angle of erection need in no way interfere with anyone's enjoyment of sex.

Erection is the most obvious sign of sexual excitement in men, but it is not the only change. Other genital organs also become congested with blood and thus swollen. The man's testicles increase in size and pull up closer to his body. His neck, chest and upper abdomen may become flushed. His heart beats faster and the blood pressure edges upwards.

The erection is just the first stage of sexual excitement. The second stage – known as the 'plateau' – is when desire intensifies, ultimately reaching the stage where orgasm is inevitable. During the plateau phase, the man's penis increases in size, particularly the glans (the head of the penis). His heart rate continues to go up; his sexual flush (if he has one) gets darker. His testicles increase up to one-and-a-half times their non-stimulated size, and they rise even closer to his crutch. Late in this phase, a few drops of fluid may seep out of the head of the penis and occasionally sperm are to be found in this initial emission.

Orgasm – when a man 'comes' – is the release from all this sexual excitement. It is in those seconds that sexual desire and tension increase to an involuntary climax (one over which there is no conscious control). All sensations are concentrated in the pelvis and genital area to the exclusion of any other sensory inputs. And then orgasm occurs – when the desire and tension are suddenly, explosively, rhythmically and warmly released, and sperm is propelled (ejaculated) out of the urethra, either in a spurt of inches or even feet (in adolescents) or by simply oozing out.

At ejaculation, there is a spinal reflex which dramatically decreases the flow of blood to that part of the body, so that it drains away from the penis and other blood-swollen areas. At the same time, the muscular tension that has built up is released.

Ejaculation is a total body response, not just confined to the genital area. Breathing, heart and blood pressure rates increase as orgasm approaches, and they usually peak at the moment of ejaculation. Involuntary muscle movements and spasms may occur in various parts of the body, including the legs, stomach, arms and back. Ejaculation is both a physical and an emotional response; warm, tingling feelings of release and well-being often accompany orgasm.

Women's physiology

'*Vive la différence!*' countered many people when confronted by the women's liberation movement. But there are as many similarities as differences between the sexual make-up and responses of the two sexes.

Male and female sexual organs develop from the same embryonic structure. The basic genital tubercle of a baby in the womb becomes the clitoris in females and the head of the penis in males. Both organs are richly supplied with nerve endings, some of which are extremely sensitive to the touch and others are able to cause blood vessels to expand.

Women, like men, have infinite variety in the size and appearance of their sexual organs. Because women's genitals are mainly hidden from sight until they open their legs, they can seem very mysterious and fewer girls than boys tend to compare their own sexual appearance with those of their contemporaries. As a result, women may come to feel that, along with their genitalia, their very sexual selves are invisible. However, there is no time like the present to start learning about you and your own sexuality.

Internally, the major organs are the vagina, the cervix, the uterus (womb), the Fallopian tubes and the ovaries. These are all affected by a woman's sex hormones which increase and decrease at roughly the same time every month; this hormonal repetition is called a woman's 'menstrual cycle'. About once a month a woman menstruates for a period lasting about five days. The substance that appears at this time is actually the old blood-filled lining of the womb, which is shed when an egg is unfertilized.

At around the mid-point of her cycle (counting the beginning of her period as the first day) a woman ovulates: an egg passes from the ovary and travels down the Fallopian tube, ready for fertilization. She is at her most fertile from about the 10th day to about the 20th day (although many women have been known to become pregnant at other times in their cycle). Cultural taboos and personal preferences aside, there is no reason why any woman should not make love at any time during her cycle.

The external entrance to the internal sex organs is the vulva, which consists of two sets of lips, or labia, which cover the opening to the vagina. The outer lips are covered with pubic hair and contain the most nerve endings and are perhaps the only nerve endings in this region (other than the clitoris) which are particularly sensitive to touch. The hairless inner lips are, however, sensitive to pressure and stretching during intercourse.

The word 'vagina' actually comes from the Latin for sheath – revealing perhaps the tendency of men to define women's anatomy in relation to their own physiology. In their unaroused state, the vaginal walls are relaxed and touch each other; they are also relatively dry. Penetration at this time will be very painful. Until a woman is aroused, her vagina is more of a potential than an actual space. However, once a woman is sexually excited, her vaginal walls have the flexibility to fit comfortably around the penis (or another object – for example, a vibrator) that is inside them. She also secretes a vaginal lubricating fluid, thereby further facilitating penetration.

At the point where the inner lips of the vulva meet in front will be found the clitoris, covered by the clitoral hood. The clitoris has no physical function other than to provide pleasure, and although much smaller than the male penis, it has just about as many nerve endings, so is very sensitive to touch. However, the clitoris does not always get direct stimulation from penetration by a penis. The thrusting of the penis, particularly if it is positioned to rub up against the woman's pubic bone (as can happen when she is on top or if the man enters her from behind), can stimulate the clitoris through indirect rubbing. As the penis thrusts in and out, it pulls on the vaginal lips – which in turn are connected to the clitoral hood. This indirect stimulation can be sufficient to bring a woman to orgasm, or she may need or want manual or other stimulation of her clitoris.

Women's sexual responses

When a woman becomes sexually excited, parts of her body change too, very similarly to a man's, as a result of increased blood flow. The external and internal lips swell and open out to expose the vaginal entrance; the colour of the vagina itself deepens to a purplish-red. The clitoris will increase in size and diameter (sometimes length too) and a sexual flush may appear on the woman's breasts, upper abdomen and neck. Her heart will beat faster, her breath come more quickly and her blood pressure ease upwards.

Soon after the blood flow to the pelvic region increases, vaginal lubrication starts, in a process that is a bit like perspiration. A woman may get wetter, but this does *not* mean that she is about to have an orgasm, or even that she is ready for penetration. All it shows is that she is starting to became aroused. Some women lubricate fairly freely, while others do not produce so much of a flow.

If stimulation continues, the increasing blood flow makes the vagina expand and lengthen while the outer lips start to narrow. The upper vagina also expands in size and the uterus is pulled upwards. All this comprises the 'orgasmic platform', so termed by the American sex therapists Masters and Johnson, which means that the woman is becoming very aroused.

The clitoris, having continued to increase in size, may now disappear under its hood, prompting many partners to go on an unnecessary seek-and-find expedition. Even if it cannot be seen, it will none the less respond to stimulation of the surrounding area. The woman's lips and breasts also swell somewhat with the increased blood flow, and her nipples may become smaller, tighter and darker. The sexual flush may now deepen and her heart and blood pressure rates mount. Increased muscular tension may also show – for example, in a woman's face, thighs and abdomen – resulting in involuntary contractions or spasms in these parts of her body.

Women usually need continued stimulation not only before but also during their orgasms in order to reach their peaks (unlike men who reach a point of inevitability that they could not stop even if they wanted to). As her excitement level mounts and as stimulation continues, some women report feeling mounting waves of pleasure, peaking in an orgasm or in multiple orgasms. Others describe theirs as more of a directly rising wave culminating in one ecstatic orgasm. As in a man, a woman's orgasm is a reflex that powerfully releases the muscle tension that has built up and greatly decreases the flow of blood to the pelvic area. It may be accompanied by contractions of the pelvic muscles (spasms that can be felt by the penis or a finger inserted in the vagina). Women may also experience involuntary contractions or spasms in the rest of their body. There is rarely an ejaculate as such, although there can be an increased flow of vaginal juices, but some women have reported having a form of ejaculation from an orgasm sparked off from the G spot (*see* p.173). Again, an orgasm is a total body reaction and, for many women a very emotional reaction.

Coming to terms with the differences: male and female responses to sex

It has been said that the challenge of marriage is for the partners to come to terms with the essential differences between each other as a man and as a woman. Nowhere can this be more true than in bed.

To reach adult sexuality is the achievement of a mature human being, man or woman. But at the same time, adult sexual relations can echo mysteriously back to babyhood. The mother/baby relationship and the lover/lover relationship are still virtually the only ones in which our society tolerates physical contact. And our very first sensual experiences of being touched and held by our mothers may come flooding back in the experience of relaxing within a loving and sensual embrace.

Some couples are pretty brazen about it: 'Baby Rabbit loves Puddlekins for ever and ever' coo the normally sedate personal columns of *The Times* come Valentine's Day: 'Much huggies, kissies and lovies to Dumpling from her very own Possum'; 'Sugar Plum, will you marry me? From your Pooh Bear.'

The desire to go back to a trusting, intimate baby-like state in which one person merges with another may be a powerful motivation behind the adult sex drive, but it is also a frightening one, encompassing as it does the threat of losing our hard-won maturity and independence and, most of all, the fear of being exploited or rejected when we are at our most vulnerable. Today there is still a great gap between men's and women's expectations and experiences of sex. Some of the emotional differences may perhaps be traced back to this fear of regression to babyhood and the various defences which men and women separately develop to avoid this vulnerability while still allowing themselves to enjoy the relief of sexual surrender.

It is a commonplace that men have a lesser need for emotional intimacy during sex, while women want more of the cuddling, touching and holding that comes from close physical contact. Thus when a couple stop trying to please each other and start falling short of each other's expectations, he may choose to retreat sulkily to his soft porn while she seeks solace with her Mills & Boon romances – and never the twain shall meet. Why can masculine and feminine responses to pressure be so different?

Men and sexuality

In the lives of all young children, mothers tend to be a far more constant and real presence than fathers. While girls establishing their own gender identity are generally able to make use of their mothers as role models, the main task of a young boy's life is to differentiate and separate himself from his mother, to a greater or lesser extent turning his back on 'babyish' or 'girlish' intimacy.

Boys are believed to be more competitive, and a greater level of aggressiveness may be tolerated in, even expected from them than in and from their sisters. Girls, on the other hand, are believed to be more cooperative and loving. Such 'natural' tendencies are developed through praise and encouragement, boys thus being encouraged to be more boyish, girls more girlish.

As a result, boys may be taught (if not by their parents then almost certainly by their peer group and any other role models with whom they might identify themselves) to avoid showing emotions and to refrain from touching and cuddling: 'Big boys don't cry,' 'Don't be such a sissy,' 'Only girls play with dolls'. British working-class male society is, in particular, still pretty macho; and many a tearful poor little rich boy has been wrenched from his family in near-infancy, sent to an all-male, regimented boarding school and subjected to a community life which allows for only minimal expressions of emotion. The cost for adult men may be a diminution, if not in the physical enjoyment of sex, then in the finely balanced emotional dimension of sexual intimacy.

James Prescott, an American neuropsychologist, has come up with a theory that male adult aggression and violence are due (at least in part) to a lack of cuddling and of body pleasure in the early years of a boy child's life. He studied a number of non-Western societies and found that those in which male infants and children were given the most affection (by touching, holding and permitting the child to express his own emotions) were the ones which showed less violence, theft and assaults compared to those (like our own) which treated their boy children harshly or just disapproved of physical affection. These findings suggest that male aggression, as sometimes expressed in the sex drive, may be due to the way in which gender differentiation has evolved in society; it is not inborn.

Through a sexual relationship, a man may regain the intimacy of babyhood which he forfeited in order to grow up as a man. This may be both exciting and enormously threatening. And when the thought of intimate sexual congress with a woman becomes too threatening, some men retreat into a fantasy of domination and aggression, in which the partner is dehumanized (she becomes a 'bitch on heat' who is grateful for 'getting it'), sexual congress is achieved but control is reasserted rather than abandoned. Thus, the attraction of porn, soft or otherwise.

The effect of the more or less unrealistic portrayals of sex found in pornography should not be underestimated. We learn from what we are consciously or otherwise taught and from the examples and values we perceive around us. The embarrassment many parents feel about sex and their consequent inability to handle the subject openly and naturally may make children, and boys in particular, liable to be influenced by the kind of descriptions found in Harold Robbins' books (*see above*) and elsewhere. In fact, these may well be the only graphic descriptions of the sex act which they come across. If men are bombarded with images such as these as the primary indicators of how 'real' men behave, without any effective couterbalancing values, they will absorb these sources into their deepest beliefs until they become a part of their own psychological reality.

Tina Baker, a psychologist at St Mary's Hospital, London, has been researching sexual attitudes. From her interviews with men, she has identified six trouble-causing statements:

- A man always wants sex.
- It's performance that counts.
- The man must initiate sex.
- Sex means intercourse.
- An erection is needed for satisfaction.
- Good sex must include an orgasm.

Men may develop serious sex problems, says Tina Baker, depending on the extent to which they internalize these 'real' men myths, in which the emphasis is on sex as a controlling, goal-orientated act rather than as a loving experience. Sex then becomes a part of the compulsive (and automatic) drive to achieve, to dominate and to impose the will, an expression of hostility rather than an expression of love. Indeed, sex becomes a victim of the male 'taboo on tenderness'.

Because part of the ethos of male sexuality is that 'a "real" man always wants sex,' it may be very hard for a man to say 'No'. Two of the commonest sexual dysfunctions in men are premature ejaculation and impotence. Each may have physiological origins (for example, as side-effects of drugs taken for other reasons) and this possibility should not be overlooked in seeking to treat them. At the same time, however, either may be caused by a deeper psychological reason where the mind orders the body to talk for it. Thus in impotence, the body may be saying the 'No' which the mind does not dare to translate into speech. And premature ejaculation may be the result of trying to bring to a speedy conclusion something inwardly experienced as frightening.

In the meantime, there are many men who have probably been taught by their parents and society that they should not express their emotional vulnerability. Yet when they grow up, they find that emotional self-expression is precisely what their girlfriends and later their wives do want of them. It's not surprising that a good number of them feel confused at this stage.

Of the hundreds of American men who have been treated by the sex therapist Dr Bernard Zilbergeld, author of the book *Men and Sex*, many if not most reported that they had discovered intense needs for touching and physical intimacy, not necessarily leading to sex. Commented one of his American clients:

> 'I owe you a lot. Sex is fine and that's great. But there's more. This closeness and cuddling stuff is really something. I never would have believed that I of all people would like it. Never even occurred to me to try it. Our lives are better because of it. I've gotten addicted. . .'

Women and sexuality

Women are often seen as objects of male desire rather than subjects in their own right. It is not a far step then for women to become alienated from their own sexuality, seeing it as little more than a kind of adjunct to male sexuality: man is active, woman is passive; man calls the shots, woman receives, adapts and defines herself on his terms.

The cost of creating a more active sexuality can be high. Girls who are sexually adventurous still get called whores, sluts or nymphomaniacs. There is no masculine counterpart: 'He's a real stud' scarcely conveys the same message. By and large, women have accepted being defined from without, in terms of their value (or lack of it) in men's eyes. As they grow up, they see sex all around them but always in terms of what turns *men* on – Page 3 girls and striptease in the pub at Sunday lunchtime. Men feel free to comment on women's appearance and clothing (the sexiness of it or otherwise) in a complacent, even proprietorial way to which women all too often acquiesce blushingly while rarely reciprocating.

'I think that, in some way, when I've had sex with a man,' reflects one of our interviewees, 'I've had an odd feeling of having been invited into a club. But *I'm* not a member of this club – it's an all-male club. I'm a guest and really there on tolerance. I have to shape up and keep to the rules – otherwise, I know I could get kicked out, just like that.'

The larger psychological problem that many women suffer – that of trying so hard to adapt to other people's (usually men's) expectations and desires that they lose touch with their own selves – is nowhere more painfully evident than in the area of sexual desire. Here the major myth is that a man would feel so threatened if the real feelings, thoughts and desires of his woman were expressed that he would go to pieces/would be destroyed as a man/would leave her/could never forgive her. The point is not whether this is true or not: the myth has remained in force because we have all accepted it, with women judging their real feelings as greedy, selfish, weird or whatever, and accepting the need to deny them as the price of being loved.

In *Understanding the Female Orgasm*, Seymour Fisher suggests that a woman's cultural need to appease, flatter and conciliate men is ultimately due to the notion she has had instilled in her from earliest youth: that in this dangerous male-dominated world, her place is uncertain and she survives only because the male protects her. If a woman feels that she is incomplete in herself or that her survival is threatened unless her connection to a protective male is maintained, then the connection to that love-object must be maintained at all costs – not excluding the costs of concealment and manipulation.

Thus women may do their best to adapt to a masculine model of sexuality which goes something like: foreplay (brief and perfunctory) →penetration→intercourse →ejaculation→withdrawal. This model partly depends on the 'real' woman's orgasm occurring during intercourse, and this must happen sometime after penetration and either before or simultaneously with the male orgasm/ejaculation.

But not only should a 'real' woman have an orgasm at a particular *time*; she is also supposed to have a particular kind. It was Freud who proposed the notion that there were two kinds of female orgasm: the clitoral and the vaginal. The clitoral orgasm (happening as a result of clitoral stimulation rather than vaginal penetration) was held to be a manifestation of immature and adolescent sexuality, while the vaginal orgasm – the one that was complementary to the male and happened as a result of his penetration and was thus adapted to his sexual needs – was only possible in a mature (i.e. 'real') woman. Having thus wrapped up female sexuality, it was not surprising that Freud came across so many cases of frigidity in his female patients.

The controversy surrounding the female orgasm was heightened by the discovery of the 'Graffenberg spot' or the 'G spot' – a tiny area about 3 inches (7.5 cm) inside the vagina, just behind the pubic bone. This area, when stimulated, is believed by some to produce an orgasm – and not in the same way as a 'clitoral' orgasm. In addition, women frequently ejaculate a clear, watery fluid on climax after stimulation of the G spot. Although some researchers remain sceptical about the G spot, many women report that they have G spot orgasms which are more intense than other kinds.

The fact remains that there are as many different sexual responses as there are women. Some women can quite easily achieve orgasms from vaginal thrusting; others will need or want clitoral stimulation, whether by hand, mouth or whatever. Yet others are able to have orgasms at the drop of a hat – or, at least, after the briefest of strokes and touches to the ears or breasts, for example. For what it's worth, estimates (see, for example, *The Hite Report*) indicate that 10 per cent of women never have

an orgasm under any circumstances, and 20–30 per cent have orgasms in
intercourse without any other form of stimulation. The remaining 60–70
per cent report that they need additional, generally manual, stimulation
ranging from one minute to close to an hour.

The fact that many women, like men, report climaxing in dreams without any form of physical manipulation shows that it is not necessary for
there to be any direct physical contact for a woman to have an orgasm. In
a very real sense, we are constantly limiting ourselves by what we have
been told, or what we feel we ought or should be doing, or even by what
we think we can do.

While performing the necessary task of reclaiming and redefining
female sexuality for ourselves, our sisters and our daughters, we should
be careful not to throw the baby out with the old ideological bathwater.
While recognizing female sexuality and sexual needs as something distinct from male sexuality and sexual needs, we should not lose sight of
what is important, for heterosexuals, the interdependence and, to a large
extent, potentially complementary nature of the two sexes. A woman
may, for example, feel that she obtains her greatest satisfaction from full
intercourse and might be hard pressed to explain where her own sexual
pleasure ends and her enjoyment in her partner's pleasure begins. Yet
she may also have a need for longer and more tender foreplay or manual
stimulation during intercourse, perhaps continuing after his ejaculation.

One woman commented in *The Hite Report*: 'He seems fascinated by
what I tell him about myself, as if amazed that I have preferences. . .'
Note that he was not appalled, repulsed or rejecting, just fascinated and
amazed.

Until women are brave enough to start telling the truth, to stop faking
orgasms, to start stating clearly and calmly what they really want in bed –
whatever it may be – how can they know what is possible within their sexual
relations with their intimate partners? Unless women take their own needs
and the responsibility for fulfilling them seriously, how can men start to?
They are not mindreaders. In this context even a negative statement may
be profoundly positive in terms of the overall relationship, as one of our
interviewees discovered:

> *'I really felt off sex for a while. Just wasn't interested at all, but my hus-
> band wanted to. Usually I'd just have gone along with him and probably
> ended up quite enjoying it. But we had just been feeling particularly close
> and I took a deep breath and said I didn't want to. It sounds like nothing,
> but it was really very difficult for me to say it. And do you know how he
> responded? He told me that it was fine. And he said that he relied on me
> to be honest with him.'*

Although it is still not socially acceptable in our culture for women to
be as sexually adventurous as men, girl children do tend to be cuddled
and touched more than their brothers. Perhaps as a result, women on

the whole rarely dissociate the expression of sexuality from emotional closeness. For women, the need for sexual fulfilment may manifest less strongly as a thing in itself and more as part of a greater desire to be wooed and for intimacy, cuddling and closeness. Loving, gentle touching – 'foreplay' so-called but why should it not be an end in itself? – may matter more than hastening full steam ahead towards the goal of orgasm, which anyway will be over in a few moments.

To a greater or lesser degree, this need for intimacy is likely to be met during the early courting period of the relationship. It is later that a gulf may develop between his desire for sexual gratification and hers for emotional and physical intimacy. As one of the sociologists Mansfield and Collard's interviewees put it:

> *'Sex doesn't make me feel warm and secure. I'd rather he give me a cuddle, that makes me feel warm and secure more than anything else. . .I tell him I love him but* he *don't tell* me.

Back to the values of hard-boiled porn versus soft-boiled romantic fiction?

Towards a shared sexuality

> *Intercourse is synonymous with communication or communion, consummation may speak of an urge towards completion or perfection, union is to join together as one and to know is to really understand one another.*
>
> Jean Shinoda Bolen, *Goddesses in Everywoman*

Many of us in present-day culture have become almost disembodied, losing the sense of ourselves as existing within our own bodies. In this age of television and passive consumerism, we live increasingly in our minds, losing touch with the simple but profound pleasures of physicality. How to unlock the door again?

Your sex life can only be superficially described by the number of times you have had sex, how many orgasms you each had, how long they lasted and so on – this is 'accountancy sex', sex by numbers. It cannot help you discover what is right within your own sexual relationship. For enjoyment of sex comes from within; it's what *feels* good to you and what feels good to your partner and never mind anyone else.

As women are finding their sexual voices, they are becoming able to express their sexuality as one aspect of a relationship which also includes emotional and sensual aspects. And more and more men, too, are beginning to realize that the separation of sexuality from emotion may work in a relationship where the partners are perceived as unequal or as having so little in common that they meet primarily to have children and for masculine sexual relief – but it will not, cannot, serve in a relationship of sexual partners who are both friends and intimate companions.

As a couple living together and committed to each other sexually, you have the opportunity to discover your sexuality, not cast in the mould created by past generations but as a process of being together which serves, nurtures and revitalizes the needs of each of you individually and together. Orgasm is an extraordinary experience but it is only a part of the entire experience of sexual relating. There are many other ways of being together sexually, many opportunities for pleasure of all kinds once the 'tyranny of the orgasm' has been banished.

We are concluding this chapter with exercises adapted from the 'sensate focusing method' evolved by Masters and Johnson's work with couples in the 1960s (with thanks to Bernard Zilbergeld). The purpose of these is to free yourself from the goal-oriented sexual experiences we have all learned too well. The myth is that, to be successful in sex, you have to have an orgasm every time. In these exercises, concern about having an orgasm will disappear. Instead of concentrating on this end-goal, you will be learning about how wonderful the journey is in itself. The time you spend with each other is designed for glorious *sensual* pleasure.

'Touch is an end in itself,' said Masters and Johnson. 'It is a primary form of communication, a silent voice that avoids the pitfall of words while expressing the feelings of the moment. It bridges the physical separateness from which no human being is spared, literally establishing a sense of solidarity between two individuals.'

EXERCISE

In all of the exercises described below, each of you will have the chance to touch your partner all over his or her body. The idea is to give you the freedom to really enjoy exploring your partner's body sensually, by touch. This could be by stroking, rubbing or kneading with your hands, licking with your mouth or using your feet or wrists – be as inventive as you like. You will each find out what you like 'doing' and what you like to have 'done' to you.

Don't worry about achieving any specific goal. The exercises are not competitive. Your 'goal' is *not*, at this stage, sexual intercourse or orgasm. This is primarily an opportunity for you to explore and learn – and a golden opportunity at that. You have no other end in mind other than to experience touching and being touched. The giver simply focuses on touching, the receiver on being touched.

As a preliminary, you will have to decide who will first be the toucher and who will be touched. You will both have your chance. Once you have decided, giver and receiver must not change roles during the exercise. The person being touched must simply be passive, receiving the other's touching and physical exploration, unless otherwise stated. (To avoid too many repetitions of 'his' and 'her' in the instructions we have started with the woman being the giver first and the man second.)

You should carry out the exercises in a warm room, with a comfortable place for one of you to lie down – a bed or couch or even the floor if this suits you. You will also need a lubricant. (The Bodyshop do a nice massage lotion. If you use scented oil, it might be wise to start off with a relaxing rather than a stimulating one!) Finally, a soft blanket or other covering to keep you warm will be required.

Make sure that you will not be disturbed. Lock the door if need be and don't answer if someone knocks. Turn on the answering machine if you have one (if not, take the telephone off the hook). Make sure you have enough time – set aside at least half an hour for each session. The receiver may well feel so relaxed after the first session that you may want to arrange another time for the first giver to receive his or her own session.

It does not matter whether you do or don't get aroused during the exercises. Some people find the experience of being completely passive uncomfortable at first, particularly if they are always used to being 'in charge'. Stay with it, even if you feel ill at ease in the beginning. Just remember that the exercise is not a prelude to anything else. It is what it is. Read the exercises through together a couple of times so that, before you start, you are comfortable about knowing what you should do.

First session

The giver strokes, rubs and touches her partner with whatever part of the body she chooses, doing whatever she likes and whatever she feels intuitively is right. The receiver is to accept the caressing passively, only speaking if he is in discomfort or even pain, in which case he should request his partner to stop doing whatever is hurting him.

The giver's purpose is to discover what she likes to do to her partner's body, exploring with different types of body movements. During this first session, avoid your partner's genital area – the aim is to take the focus off the genitals and discover other parts of the body from which you can gain pleasure. Later, if you wish, you can repeat the exercise, this time allowing yourselves to touch the genital area.

The giver can use the lubricant if she wants to, learning how that also feels for her. She should also be aware that, as the receiver relaxes, his body may become cold. If so, he should ask the giver to cover with the blanket the rest of his body, which she is not exploring at that time. She may also want to place the blanket over a part of his body if she feels it is getting cool.

Spend at least half an hour per session; you can go on for longer if you like. When you have finished (and at the end of every session), talk to each other for at least several minutes about how the experience felt and share your feelings. You should say what you enjoyed and what you didn't (if anything!) and also if you came across any problems – for example, if you found it hard taking the initiative or being passive. This way you will be learning more and more about each other's likes and dislikes.

Second session

Now repeat this exercise when you feel ready (this may not be the same day, particularly if the receiver wishes to relax), this time swapping roles. Do this exercise at least once each before moving on.

Third session

Set up the same conditions as for the first session, but this time, the receiver is in charge. He will direct the giver as to where and how he wants to be touched, stroked, licked, etc. While the giver just follows his instructions. (Again the first time that you do this, avoid stimulation of the genital areas. These are off limits for the time being.) Again, spend about 30 minutes on this session.

The receiver is to utilize this time to discover more about his own body. If there is anything he has ever wanted to have done to him in terms of touching and stroking but has never dared to ask – for example, to experience how it feels to have his toes licked – now is his chance! Try new places and techniques even if you are not sure how they will feel.

Make sure, receiver, that your directions are followed out exactly as you want. If the giver is not doing what you want, tell her how you want it done – even if you may have to tell her several times. Remember the receiver is in control, so he should be as clear as he can be in his demands. The receiver is, of course, also able to ask for the lubricant to be used and to be covered with the blanket if he wants.

The giver is to do whatever is asked, as long as it is not repulsive or physically uncomfortable for her. If she does not understand, she should ask the receiver for clearer instructions. This is a wonderful opportunity for the giver and receiver to learn about communicating with each other.

Once the exercise is over, again spend time talking to each other to share your experiences. Find out in particular what it was that you both liked and didn't like (if anything) this time around.

Fourth session

Again, follow the instructions for the third session, but swap roles.

Where do we go from here?

You have both been very patient in giving yourselves the time to learn about the whole of each other's bodies – not just the bits between the legs.

Once you have completed the sessions, you can throw away the rule book and feel free to touch each other's (and your own) genital areas and to have intercourse. The aim of the exercises is to involve the whole of your body in *sensual* as well as *sexual* intercourse in the days and nights that lie ahead.

19

Forsaking all others: the challenge of monogamy

Then, instead of the two of them. . .there are three of them. First it is stimulating and fun and it goes on that way for a while. All things truly wicked start from an innocence. . .You lie and hate it and it destroys you and every day is more dangerous, but you live day to day as in a war.
                                    Ernest Hemingway, *A Moveable Feast*

I N the early heady days of marriage, the possibility that you or your spouse will be unfaithful is pretty unthinkable. The whole subject of sexual infidelity is fraught with fear and loathing – far better to put the whole squalid business out of your mind. In our interviews with newly married couples, infidelity, not surprisingly, proved to be the most confrontational subject of all. Questions about whether they viewed fidelity as important in their marriage and – even worse – what effect they thought actual infidelity would have were met universally with some demonstration of shock and upset. The most minimal reaction was a sharp intake of breath; other interviewees laughed nervously, left the room or indicated they would rather not talk about it at all.

On the face of it, the possibility of infidelity is *not* unimaginable for most people: the reluctance to talk publicly masks a private unwilling acceptance that either or both partners may be unfaithful. What proportion of married people this might involve is anyone's guess. Figures range from a mere 16 per cent of Italian husbands (who were asking the questions – their mothers?) to (in Aurette Lawson's study *Adultery: An Analysis of Love and Betrayal*) a startling 78 per cent of British husbands. Perhaps more reliable are the figures supplied by Relate (formerly the Marriage Guidance Council), who say that no less than 60 per cent of husbands and 40 per cent of wives in Britain will be unfaithful at some point in their marriage.

The advent of relatively safe contraception, increased time spent outside the home and the reduction of social condemnation and sanctions have all served to increase infidelity's occurrence, with the sharpest recent increases being recorded by wives. Yet married people rarely seem to anticipate becoming its victim, instead remaining ostrich-like and swearing that 'It'll never happen to us.' Our interviewees' replies to questions in this area were typically:

'I'm hoping I'll never be tempted.'

'I think I've played the field long enough.'

'I'm sure it'll never happen to us. If it does, though, I think that would be it – an end to the marriage.'

'Sex is too important. Anyway, with AIDS around, it's like playing Russian roulette.'

The stakes are indeed higher with the spectres of herpes and the infinitely more terrifying AIDS. Yet the emotional cost, too, is always high. As and when the catastrophe strikes, the shock is breathtaking, appalling, unbearable. And infidelity is a grave threat to the marriage itself: one-third of all divorce petitions are brought because the marriage has irretrievably broken down due to one partner's adultery.

This reaction to unfaithfulness is hardly surprising given the fact that a vast majority of people – 83 per cent according to a survey in *Options* magazine in August 1988 – feel that extramarital affairs are wrong.

Yet when we also consider the estimates of actual infidelity, there appears to be a great chasm between how we as a society feel that we should behave and how, when it comes to the crunch, we actually do behave.

Different people have different reasons for getting involved in affairs. In the recent past, the high statistical 'evidence' of marital infidelity, could place pressures on those who chose to remain faithful – they could find themselves thinking that there must be something 'wrong' with them for not joining in the attitude of the times. In the 1960s and 1970s, much was made of the notion of 'free love', the idea being that if we could all get rid of our petty jealousies, we could open ourselves up to more and more sexual relationships and thereby enrich our lives. The greatest advocates and exponents of this theory were George and Neena O'Neill who, in their book *Open Marriage*, rejected the concept of marital infidelity and encouraged, to the point of evangelism, everyone to engage in extramarital affairs. However, the breakup of the O'Neills' own marriage not long after their book's publication was a pointer to the huge stresses and strains that a marriage has to bear when one or both partners choose infidelity.

The good news, such as it is, is that more marriages survive adultery than are destroyed by it. Infidelity need not end a marriage. The law implicitly recognizes this by insisting that a divorce petition cannot be brought on the basis of adultery alone; there must be an additional element. The person asking for the divorce must also declare that he or she finds it intolerable to live with the adulterer – to adultery must be added intolerability.

While an extramarital affair usually, perhaps invariably, signifies that things have gone wrong between a couple, it does not necessarily signify 'The End'. An incident of infidelity, if it *can* be tolerated and dealt with responsibly within the relationship, can be a unique opportunity for change – to put things right at last. A permanent separation is often the last thing that an adulterer has in mind. Indeed, once the cat is out of the bag, unfaithful partners are frequently surprised and appalled to discover how much pain to their partners and how much perhaps irreparable damage to their marriages they have caused.

Why does infidelity happen, and happen so often? For some people, in some relationships, is it inevitable? And in the grey dawn of the aftermath, is it possible to pick up the pieces and restore, even restructure, the wounded relationship?

The slippery slope

Being in love has many symptoms, one of which is tunnel vision. When you first fall in love, the idea of taking another lover may be far from your mind. But sooner or later, being married begins to feel different from being in love. The first sweet, fierce pangs of romantic love start to fade and are replaced by the quieter pleasures of married love. Then, perhaps in the first year of marriage, perhaps much later, a moment of temptation arrives for most of us.

There may still exist a few fortunate people for whom that moment has never come, either for themselves or their spouses. Not for them the thrilling but alarming bodyshock, a few months into married life, when their glance lingers overlong on the physical contours of a complete stranger, and their eyes meet for long seconds. Not for them the temptation to linger a little too long over a business lunch with an attractive acquaintance, drinking just a little too much, laughing a little too meaningfully and suggestively, with the frightening, thrilling, wickedly tempting 'What if. . .' reverberating through their minds, hearts and bodies. Blessed are the pure of heart, for they shall not be tempted to commit adultery. For the rest of us, life is not so simple.

Associations with people of the opposite sex, up to and including the point of a little mild flirtation, are one of the pleasures of living. But will you be able to allow yourself that pleasure without feeling that you will run amok and astray? For many overscrupulous or fearful people, such innocent titillation is a pleasure which they feel that they have to forgo on marriage, and they tailor their behaviour accordingly. For women, the Plain Jane syndrome may take over. 'I have a married woman's wardrobe now,' says one woman, three years married. 'Full of a married woman's clothes. Perhaps I'll look at something a woman's wearing in the street and think, how fabulous. . .but not for me.'

For 'married women's clothes' read dowdy and dull clothes. What is this wife (once a glamorous and stylish woman) afraid of? Is she tailoring her behaviour in an attempt to assuage the feelings of jealousy in her spouse – who doesn't want anyone else to look, never mind stare at, his wife? Or does she herself fantasize that, if she walks down the street clad in the little black number which she has denied herself and gets a wolf whistle from a construction worker, she will be overcome with lust and fall headlong into the nearest skip with him for a quick one? Perhaps she is saying that she doubts her ability to say (and mean) 'No' if that moment should arise. So she structures her life and subdues her own sexuality to make sure that it never does.

Similar repression can be seen in the husband who loses all interest in his appearance after marriage. He puts on weight, 'forgets' to shave at weekends (although bristle-kisses bring his wife out in a rash) and lets out great trumpeting farts with reckless abandon. He, too, is suppressing his sexuality. 'Now we've got married, why bother? I don't need to impress her – or any other woman – any more.'

Infidelity may strike such fear in people that, in seeking to avoid it at all costs, they push away with the utmost severity the merest suggestion, the remotest *possibility* that sexual attraction might exist between themselves and someone outside their marriage. This inevitably affects their own self-image as a sexual person and may indirectly affect their sexual relationship with their husband or wife. However, there is all the difference in the world between thinking and doing. *Pace* Jimmy Carter: people do not commit adultery in their hearts; they commit it in bed.

To feel sexual towards another is not morally wicked, nor is it destined to wreck a marriage. In fact, it can bolster people's self-esteem, make them feel good about themselves and, in this respect, have quite a positive effect on the married relationship. We all are sexual beings, attracted towards attractive people. Who can say with exactitude when social, even emotional relationships with third parties become relationships with adulterous overtones? The person who is very afraid of temptation may block off all meaningful relationships with others; and then the marriage will have to take the burden of that person's hidden resentments and may start to feel like a trap. Ironically, it is *this* situation which can be the most conducive to actual, harmful infidelity.

Spouses are entitled to expect a lot from each other, and generally speaking, they *do* expect a lot, including fidelity. Yet what they cannot expect is that each will be everything to the other. We all search for different needs to be fulfilled: to natter with old friends, to discuss the meaning of life and love, to go fishing and share a drink or two with buddies, to compare gardens and children. No one person is able to fulfil the whole of another's needs. If you expect this of your partner, you may end up blaming him or her (and yourself) for failing to achieve a uniquely impossible task.

The problem of marital infidelity is *not* the problem of being attracted to another person. If you do feel that tingling in the groin, there is no need to jump between the sheets straight away with the person who turned you on. You can take home that attraction and make it an extra plus in your lovemaking with your spouse. In fantasy, you can have the best of both worlds: the pleasure of being attracted to and by someone else and the security of enacting that pleasure with your own partner. All of the fun and none of the guilt.

Breaking the boundaries

Fullblown actual marital infidelity is sometimes, but not always, about the failure of love and respect for the marriage partner. It is *always* about the failure to respect boundaries.

It has been said that there is no creation without limitation. The maintenance of strict boundaries is what enables people to play and to be creative. An artist's limitations, or boundaries, are the edges of his canvas, the properties of his paint and, to a greater or lesser extent, the artistic conventions of his age. A child plays, safe within the boundaries which his parents have established. They know when to say 'No!', and their 'No!' protects their child from external dangers and from the results of his own over-enthusiasm. They also know when to tell him that play is over for the day and that it is time to go home.

Later on in adult life, we may go to a formal dance which involves a set of prescribed steps in which couples meet, embrace and draw apart. No one minds watching their husband or wife dancing temporarily with another partner, as long as the rules (not too close, not too often) are obeyed, the boundaries observed. They know that, at the end of the dance, each dancer will leave with the partner s/he came with. At the dance, society oversees sexual attraction, regulating it, containing it and making it safe. Dancing is playing.

The task of growing up is, in part, the task of internalizing the first boundaries set for us by our parents. In growing up, we learn to say 'No' for ourselves when we need to, learn to delay instant gratification instead of snatching it like eager, impulsive children who have no thought for tomorrow.

Marriage provides a set of very clear boundaries – one of the clearest of which is fidelity. In order for marriages to work, every married person must internalize these boundaries within him or herself. Otherwise adult spouses will be like children watching their parents (spouses) to see what they can get away with the moment the parents' (spouses') backs are turned, heedless and oblivious of their own potential ability to damage what may matter most.

The struggle for power

Adultery is an attack on the adulterer's marriage and upon the married couple. This is probably true even when the partner who has been unfaithful goes to great lengths to hide it from the other or, once discovered, insists that it was a momentary lapse, a passionate fling which had nothing to do with reality and the married couple's life together.

In relationships in which a power struggle has commenced, it is often those who feel themselves to be the weaker partner who begin an affair. For those who feel undervalued, unappreciated, unable to reach their partners, infidelity is a powerful act of retaliation. It changes the status quo of the relationship, giving the strategic initiative and (despite the acknowledged wrongdoing) an enhanced status to the unfaithful one. Sometimes, painful, angry and destructive contact can seem better than none at all. At least it proves you exist.

Whichever partner is unfaithful, the infidelity is a way of keeping the other partner at bay and of attaining a dominant position. Both before and, especially, after the adultery is out in the open, the adulterous partner (though guilty) feels triumphant and attractive. The spouse (though angry) feels useless, inadequate and helpless. S/he may even feel at fault, and end up personally shouldering most of the blame for what has happened. Such self-blame can, however, be marginally more comforting than the feeling of utter helplessness.

'My wife doesn't understand me': a husband's adultery

Higamous hogamous women are monogamous,
Hogamous higamous men are polygamous.

William James

The notion that men are automatons, governed by deep sexual desires which erupt uncontrollably inside them, may, today, have lost some of its credibility. However, men *do* seem more inclined than women to commit adultery – and in greater numbers than ever before, if the statistics are to be believed. For instance, the Relate figures show that half again as many men as women cheat on their marital partners. Yet the marriages of male adulterers are often important to them, providing a much-needed sense of security.

Men seem to follow one of two patterns of adultery. The *polygamous adulterer* typically keeps a wife and a long-term mistress, and may be content to let this state of affairs drift on for months or years, occasionally for decades. In sophisticated circles, all three may all be on the best of terms;

more usually, the wife may suspect but have no certain knowledge of the mistress's existence, while the mistress is a willing or at least acquiescent partner in the deception.

The man in such a triangle may feel himself in an enviable position. After all, polygyny (that is, a polygamous relationship involving one husband and two or more wives) is still the preferred marital pattern in a great many of the world's cultures. The possession of several wives is, in many countries, an indication of a man's wealth, success and potency. He has variety, he has power; he can play one woman off against another. He possesses them; but they cannot possess him.

The *casual adulterer*, on the other hand, goes in for occasional or sometimes frequent one-night stands or brief affairs. More than likely, he does not want to rock the boat, but he feels like playing some 'away matches'. The door is always open, the getaway car revving at the kerb. Some casual adulterers weigh the risks carefully as to whether they will be found out, and the possible consequences if they are. Others let it all hang out outside the home, being compulsive flirts and compulsively unfaithful. In the incessant search for new conquests, they look for constant reassurance about their own attractiveness. However, the judgement of one woman or a few or many is never enough; these men continue, hopelessly, to look for affirmation of their own self-worth from without rather than within. If pushed, the casual adulterer may offer some biological explanation of his behaviour based on hormones and uncontrollable urges. Such men, along with Oscar Wilde, can resist anything but temptation.

The Casanova Complex by Peter Trachtenberg is a study of the author's, and other men's, compulsive promiscuity. Trachtenberg compares such behaviour to an eating disorder in which women become the 'food' yet seem to have no ability to nourish. Instead they are ingested, regurgitated – and so on to the next. Some men (and fewer women) also become addicted to the thrill of the chase, almost as if it were a narcotic fix, and they are never happier than when in the first throes of a love – or lust – affair.

Some of these men may end up by cutting off all sexual feelings towards their wives. She is preserved as a wife and mother: respected, honoured, loved even but not desired. His sexual desires are safely confined to casual affairs in which women are desired, pursued, conquered and then abandoned at will.

This split between wife (madonna) and mistress (whore) was vividly explored in the short film, *The Red Dress*. The philandering husband, played by Michael Palin, plans to buy his mistress an alluring designer dress – in erotic scarlet. However, his plan is foiled when his wife (portrayed as exclusively involved with their children) spots him in the boutique and rushes in to exclaim over his generosity in buying *her* such a beautiful gift. Even worse (for him) she decides to wear the dress to an office party at which his mistress will also be present. Palin tries to change her mind, arguing that the dress simply isn't suitable for *her* – but in vain. She looks stunning, and during the course of the evening, Palin, blind to the charms of his mistress, finds himself wracked with jealousy and then desire for his wife, and he falls in love all over again. The result is a happy ending. Yet but for the fortuitous sighting of the dress in the shop window, this husband would have joined the thousands of others who prefer to expend more time, energy and money creating an exciting life outside marriage rather than put the same resources into creating a successful relationship within it.

What the polygamous adulterer and the casual adulterer have both contrived for themselves is an escape hatch from the demands of married life, from intimacy. Intimacy is a state of openness and undefendedness, a state in which you offer all that you are – all your fears and insecurities as well as all your dreams, talents and beauty – to your partner, in trust. It is a vulnerable state to be in, and for men especially, whose upbringing and role models do not accustom them to intimacy, it can be frightening. The man who commits adultery knows that it keeps him away from intimacy, for he has been able successfully to keep one entire area of his life secret from his wife (even if she knows about his affairs). And he is also safe from his illicit partner(s): whether engaging in one-night stands or an ongoing adulterous relationship, the demands of secrecy and the awareness that he has, of necessity, a separate existence from his lover(s), keep him, in his eyes, distant and protected.

As we have seen, men sometimes find it easier in a relationship to express love via sexuality (rather than through cuddles and affectionate physical touching). It is not, therefore, surprising that they also sometimes express hostility through sexuality – in other words, through adultery. Infidelity is a hostile act. The hostility, however, is often concealed and it smoulders on, acted out in recurring hostile acts. The discovery, expression and working through of whatever underlying hostility may exist can be difficult and painful for both husband and wife. The marriage which is strong enough, and involves a wife who is brave enough to enable this to happen and to withstand it, is the marriage which stands the greatest chance of survival.

The demon jealousy

A monster begot upon itself, born on itself.
William Shakespeare

No discussion of marital infidelity would be complete without touching on its co-conspirator in crime: jealousy.

Problems in the early days of marriage are far less likely to be spawned by unfaithfulness than by one partner being irrationally jealous. For some people, security comes in the shape of the wedding ring – their fears of their beloved straying dramatically recede once they *know* their partners have given lifelong promises. For others, less secure, the wedding is when the pain begins: the throat-strangling, often groundless, worry that they will be betrayed. Nights out together lose their attraction as one spouse immediately bristles and interposes if the other is friendly towards, say, the waiter or waitress. Nights out apart become impossible as the partner left behind imagines all sorts of intrigues in store for his/her supposed faithless partner.

A smidgin of jealousy can support and indeed enliven a married relationship. If one partner flouts the rules of the marriage game and, for example makes outrageous suggestions to an outsider, a healthy demonstration of territoriality on the other's part can be saying loud and clear: 'Hey! Hold on a minute! You're going too far!' In so testing the boundaries of a relationship, we can find out what is OK and what isn't. The thrill of a demonstration that you are loved and wanted can add spice to your relationship. No harm done here.

However, the damage starts when the jealous spouse loses track of what s/he can control and what s/he can't, and unhealthy jealousy rears its ugly head. If the jealous spouse is getting upset over his/her partner's completely innocent behaviour, resentment will soon set in.

Coping with jealousy

- *If you are jealous*, discuss with your spouse how you are feeling – as frankly as you can. Explain that you are feeling insecure and need to build up trust. Work out strategies to enable you to do this. You can, for example, ask your partner to reaffirm how much love s/he feels for you. But ultimately you will need to deal with your own feelings of insecurity. Enhance your confidence and self-worth by developing your own interests and finding out what you really would like to do – rather than having excessive time on your hands to worry about what your partner is doing.
- *If you are the one with a jealous partner*, try not to let this inhibit your behaviour. If you capitulate to unreasonable demands now, you are only setting the scene for a tightening of the noose later, but don't cause trouble by deliberately going out of bounds. Tell your spouse how much you love and care for him or her. Try to find out what s/he is feeling. And take heart: it is likely that once you have been able to build up your trust together, your partner's jealous fears will diminish.

'I felt all empty inside': a wife's infidelity

Women are less likely to commit adultery than their husbands. They are also less likely to be forgiven. In the past, this has been reflected in the law. Although as far as grounds for divorce are concerned, men and women are now treated identically, this has not always been the case. The divorce laws introduced in England and Wales in 1857 made a wife's adultery sufficient grounds for a divorce, but a husband's adultery was only sufficient if coupled with either cruelty or desertion. Until very recently, an adulterous wife risked losing custody of her children – a punitive judgement upon which her behaviour as a mother had no bearing. Even today in unrepealed statutes of several American states, adultery is still against the law – but only if committed by a wife. In times past, an adulterous woman faced the hideous penalty of death by stoning – an archaic remedy but one still championed by the quasi-heroine of Carol Clewlow's 1989 novel *A Woman's Guide to Adultery*. Rose makes the other female characters in the book (all of whom are involved in extramarital affairs) confront the fact that they're helping their men inflict pain on other women. 'A woman taken in adultery should be stoned,' she says, 'by other women.'

The statistics bear out the common belief that men commit adultery rather more lightly or at any rate more frequently than women. (Or are they just more willing to brag about it?) In any event, the gap is closing. Annette Lawson, in her survey of adultery, quotes the highest incidence of female unfaithfulness: 67 per cent of wives (as opposed to 78 per cent of husbands). However, the women in this sample were quicker off the mark than their male partners: on average, a wife strayed after 4.5 years of marriage, whereas her husband, on average, would wait a further seven months (5.2 years) before so doing. While there are other, more reassuring statistics (see, for example, the Relate predictions above), the fact cannot be denied that women of today are far more likely to have an affair or fling than their mothers were.

However, the reason for the increased incidence of female adultery cannot simply be put down to the fact that women now have greater opportunities to meet men because, increasingly, they work outside the home; although it must be said that those who do are inevitably exposed to a greater number of temptations.

The rules of the sexual game traditionally demand that men actually proposition women. If a man feels the urge to commit adultery, he usually has to make the first move; women don't have to take the initiative. A woman may be faced with insistent demands from an attractive (or less than attractive) colleague and, tutored from an early age to say 'Yes,' may find it hard to resist. Even if she does say 'No!', her refusal, again according to our home-grown national mating rituals, may only be seen as temporary. Comments one interviewee, 'I was amazed, after I got married, that the office Romeo still saw me as fair game. I suppose I thought I would be immune once I was married. That there would be a sign saying "Keep off!" Naïve, I was. He seemed to see me as *more* of a challenge.'

As women move into male-dominated worlds, it is likely that their inner reasons for adultery may come to resemble more closely those of men. However, for the most part men and women still have different motivations for getting sexually involved outside marriage. As we have seen, men may start an affair in a bid to avoid the intimacy of marriage, which they may feel that their wives, or simply their marital state, are forcing upon them. Women, on the other hand, are more likely to be unfaithful in an attempt to *rediscover* the intimacy which may have disappeared from their marriage, leaving them feeling empty and lonely. A man may want to conduct an affair simultaneously with his marriage and anticipate no problems except the risk of discovery. A woman who begins an affair may, consciously or unconsciously, be testing out an alternative to her marriage, perhaps as a first step in fortifying her along the road to marital separation.

It is rare for infidelity to come out of the blue. Usually the process of disengaging, of losing interest in the relationship, has begun much earlier. As such, marital infidelity is a symptom, not an underlying cause of marital breakdown. Once a marriage has become cold and unhappy for one partner, it will inevitably be so for both. Then, both husband and wife will start to fantasize about happier relationships and more responsive partners: the grass on the other side of the fence appears ever greener.

While in defensive retreat from an unhappy marriage, the reasons men and women give for their inconstancy differ. In her research for her study of marital infidelity, Annette Lawson gave a checklist to both men and women and asked them to check off the statements which most closely corresponded to the thoughts they had in their mind when they decided to commit adultery. The men's most common thoughts were, 'With care, this needn't harm the marriage' and 'I was curious about sex with someone else.' The women most commonly thought, 'I felt compelled by my emotions' or 'My spouse and I were growing apart.'

A woman may be unfaithful as a desperate last resort. Perhaps undertaken to try and reassure herself of her own desirability as a woman, or in retaliation for her husband's real or imagined affairs, her affair may be an attempt to wake up her marriage, to kindle some response – jealousy, anything – from a seemingly indifferent partner. A couple who have taken each other too much for granted or who have been afraid to voice their anger and hostility may have thereby succeeded in becoming invisible to each other, neither noticing the other partner as an individual. In this scenario, infidelity may precipitate a necessary crisis in an aimlessly drifting relationship, a crisis from which both partners and the marriage itself may emerge stronger and wiser, if a little sadder. But for this to happen, courage, hard work and radical restructuring will all be called for.

Sally and Roger had been married for 11 years before Sally had an affair. Throughout their marriage, the struggle to make ends meet had been hard. Not being able to work out how her contraceptive cap should fit, Sally had become pregnant on their honeymoon at the age of 18 with their daughter Sandy. She had not been happy as a mother initially, keenly feeling the loss of her youth and the freedom to do what she wanted. Then, three years later, at Roger's insistence, she had become pregnant again and gave him his longed-for son.

The marriage did not flourish. Roger, wanting to provide his wife and children with a secure financial future, worked harder and harder in the family firm. He and Sally fell into an uncomfortable routine, though neither of them particularly realized it. He worked late but would want his dinner ready on his arrival home. He rarely spoke to Sally more than was necessary, and she became increasingly introverted and frustrated. Always willing to do anything for his son, he largely ignored their daughter.

> 'Our home was divided into two camps – a battle between the sexes. My daughter and I on the one side and my son and husband on the other. Life was getting to be intolerable. One day, I went round to my Mum and Dad's and just cried and cried. Then, of all things, my Dad asked me if I'd ever thought about having an affair. He said that, of course, I'd got to stay with Roger because of the children, but that didn't mean I couldn't enjoy myself on the side, just as long as it didn't break up the family!'

The opportunity was not too long in presenting itself. Roger had to go away on business. One of Sally's friends suggested they go out dancing. Her parents babysat the children and Sally went out – and found herself a man.

> 'It was fantastic at first. Because I'd got married so young, I'd never really had any confidence in me as a woman. And then here was this man who thought I was great. Bill and I used to meet up when Roger went away, whenever we could. But then I started thinking that maybe I should leave Roger. So I decided to tell him. I asked Roger to meet me in the park – I was afraid if I told him at home that he'd hit me or something. And I did tell him there – that I'd been seeing someone else.'

Roger did not react the way she thought he would. He broke down in tears, crying there and then and then for days afterwards.

> 'He fell to pieces – couldn't go to work. He just kept saying "Why?" I felt terrible, but then one day I just lost my head and told him why. I told him I was fed up with the way he treated me and Sandy, fed up with the way he treated the house like a hotel. Fed up with the whole damned thing and then I just walked out – walked off to stay with my parents. I thought he could look after the kids for once.'

In that outburst, Sally started to get more in touch with the anger she had been suppressing for so many years. She had wanted to hurt Roger – to hurt him back for all the times he had hurt her through the years. And hurt him she had.

She stayed with her parents for a week, giving herself time to decide what she wanted to do.

> *'My parents were OK. They left me alone – I think my Dad felt guilty. And one of the things I realized when I was on my own was that I didn't want to be with Bill, not at all. Despite everything, I still wanted to be with Roger and the children. I wondered what I'd done – and I wanted to give it another go.'*

She went back home, and over the next few days, she and Roger started talking to one another – and listening. Sally found out how Roger had been scared when Sally got pregnant – that he wouldn't be able to cope – so he'd thrown himself into his work. Sally told him how she'd felt – and how she'd wanted to hurt him. They had years to catch up on. Trust in each other had never been given a chance to develop. They had had good times together but only before, not really after, they were married.

One night, after they'd exhausted themselves talking, Roger hesitantly extended his hand and said he was sorry. Sally took his hand and said she was sorry, too. They both cried. For the first time in years, they were able to see each other as people, no longer as just 'husband and wife' or 'mother and father'. That was the turning point.

Sally's case may be the exception that proves the rule. When women are unfaithful, their infidelity is far more likely to break up a marriage. Roger and Sally did not, from that moment on, live happily ever after; they are still struggling to come to terms with each other with the aid of marital therapy. Roger is trying to find out whether he can ever trust Sally again. Sally is wondering about her own destructiveness and about whether Roger will ever be willing or able to mend his ways and give her what she wants and needs. Sandy is having problems at school. But Sally and Roger are still together. So far, they have survived. And they think that their marriage may survive, too.

Coping with marital infidelity

If you are thinking about beginning an affair. . .

. . .then don't. It is a fundamental betrayal of the fidelity which you promised to your marriage partner and which s/he is entitled to expect of you. However much you enjoy the affair, however much it means to you, you will almost certainly feel very guilty and you will carry your guilt around with you for a long time. You will also, again almost certainly, be making your partner suffer real pain. Is it worth it?

'I feel as if I can't help myself' is one of the great self-serving myths we tell ourselves. Take a firm grip on yourself. You *can* help yourself. What are you unwilling to confront in your marriage, what has gone wrong? People who are genuinely involved and fulfilled with one person do not feel compelled to hop into bed with another.

You may have to do some uncomfortable soul-searching, and to sit down and talk seriously to your partner. Perhaps you will have to make some difficult decisions about the future of your relationship, but these cannot be avoided. An affair will only complicate an already complicated situation in a messy, undignified way.

If you have already begun an affair. . .

. . .then most of the above still applies. What are you avoiding? A difficult situation involving three people has been created. It may be making you happy in the short term; you may be in love. But sooner or later, you will have to face the consequences of what you have done.

You would not be reading this unless you knew in some part of you that decisions have to be reached. A situation like this which just drifts on and on will become increasingly intolerable to all concerned To confess or not? To end the affair or not? To arrange a separation, on a trial or on a permanent basis? To give the marriage another go? Only you can make these decisions. The more you are able to understand what has happened and why, the less likely you are to repeat the infidelity, in this marriage or in a subsequent relationship. Try, if you can, to get in touch with your feelings, which probably include anger against your husband or wife and the desire to attack him or her. If your marriage is strong enough for these feelings to be openly expressed and explored together, it stands a good chance of survival.

Infidelity and confession

If your partner does not know, you will have to decide whether to tell him or her. This is a decision which only you can reach and your decision to do so must be taken responsibly. Have you previously discussed together whether or not to be open and honest about infidelity? Do you already have any agreements in this area? To tell him or her will be placing a burden on your partner of your own creating. Some people may genuinely feel that they just do not want to know. Some adulterers may feel that, if they do not tell their spouses, all honesty in the relationship will disappear. In many cases, marriages tangled up in lies start to die for both partners, and unless you are able to reach some kind of truthful relationship with each other, yours may be one of them.

You also have to risk your partner's perhaps quite unpredictable reactions – and not knowing whether he or she will ever forgive you. Where love and caring are well and truly dead and the marriage is reduced to a shell for one or both partners, no amount of reparation or forgiveness will save it, and once the betrayal is out in the open, one or both may decide that the marriage is over. But others, particularly where children are involved and where caring is not dead on either side, may feel that they still have something worth saving.

If you suspect your partner of having an affair. . .

. . .you may feel compelled to find out one way or the other. When confronted, if your spouse denies that s/he has been having an affair, of course you will want to believe him/her. But will s/he tell you the truth? For an adulterer, reality and fantasy may start to merge together and the whole truth might not be told. On the other hand, your spouse may be quite innocent and you the victim of your own jealousy rather than of any infidelity.

Suspicion can be the hardest thing to live with, poisoning not only the actuality but all possibilities, the present as well as the past and future. Even if it is the death of perfect trust, some people find that verification of a partner's unfaithfulness can be a relief. At least everything is then out in the open, and a firm base is provided from which options for the future can be honestly considered.

You probably would not feel suspicious if something were not already going wrong. But many things can go wrong in a marriage; partners can withdraw for many reasons. For instance, it is not unknown for one partner's guilty fantasies about starting an illicit relationship to be projected on to the other, making the fantasizer quite certain of the *other's* guilt. Either way, something is wrong which will not simply go away, which requires thinking about and talking about. Perhaps a counsellor or a marital therapist will be able to help you to sort out reality from fantasy and to rebuild the trust in the relationship (*see* Appendix 2). To paraphrase the song, you can't go on together with suspicious minds. . .

If you know your partner has been unfaithful. . .

. . .then you may go through several emotional stages. None can be rushed and you will have to allow time for each of them.

The first stage may be shock. Infidelity is truly a catastrophe, and the discovery of it can bring about a state akin to physical shock, including feelings of exhaustion, coldness and detachment from reality. You may find it impossible to concentrate on anything. All you can do is be gentle with yourself, and allow yourself to be cared for, searching out whatever love and support may be available. Support from others in your life – friends, family, work colleagues – can be terribly important.

Remember that you do not need to tell them what has happened unless you want to. However, talking to a sympathetic listener (some people choose a complete stranger with whom to entrust their life story, feeling this way somehow safer) can be a wonderful relief.

The second stage, which may follow on from the first or alternate with it moment by moment, is a state of extreme emotionality, especially grief, anger and hatred (including self-hatred). These feelings need to be explored and expressed – preferably with your partner – if they are not to harden into bitterness and enduring resentment. The predominant feeling may be one of overpowering sadness. After all, something has died for you. And a death requires a period of mourning.

Finally, when you are ready and able, you will need to consider your position and your future. Of course, a great deal will depend on your partner's attitude. Is the affair over? Did you find out or did s/he confess? Is s/he genuinely sorry? Will it ever be repeated? Do you trust any such promise? Like the others, this final, resolution stage cannot be rushed, and you may not be ready to confront the issues involved until at least some of your more powerful feelings have subsided. Do not allow yourself to make a decision in the heat of the moment which you may come to regret.

Taking back power into your own hands

One of the most difficult features about being the victim of infidelity is just that very word – victim. You may feel powerless in your partner's hands; in fact, your partner may, deep down, have intended you to feel just this way when s/he started off the affair – in an attempt to gain the upper hand.

While your partner *has* made a serious attack on some of the agreed boundaries of your relationship, leaving you feeling stripped of the identity which you derived from it, you need not surrender into helpless passivity. It is all the more important that you take this opportunity to create your own clear, individual boundaries, based on your present needs and what you think would work for you in the future. This is often very hard for women who are accustomed to putting first the needs of others, especially those of their husbands and their families. Men may also have difficulty in getting in touch with their inner feelings – particularly if these have been repressed for a long time. However, work out what you need and stick to it, regardless of what your partner or others tell you. Do you want him/her out? Do you need time to think? Do you want a clear statement from him/her about future intentions?

Time apart can be invaluable – particularly if the relationship has become very messy. You can then concentrate on your own thoughts and feelings without the distractions provided by your 'guilty' partner. Once you feel strong enough, the two of you will almost certainly need to spend time together talking and working out what has happened and why. Be honest about your own feelings and open to what your husband or wife has to say about theirs. This is a chance to really find out about each other – which you will need to do before you can decide what to do about the future.

The emotions aroused and the pain suffered can take years to pass. However, eventually, another relationship may be built – less innocent than the first but, perhaps, stronger. In many ways, you and your partner may have much to learn from the experience – greater tolerance, understanding and honesty on which to build anew.

20

For the procreation of children

Ah, the patter of tiny feet. . .I always wanted a midget for a butler.

W. C. Fields

BABIES are suddenly back in fashion. There has been a proliferation of films (*Baby Boom* and *Three Men and a Baby* to name but a couple) about high-powered female executives and feckless high-living males faced alike with the alien demands of the super-ego baby. However, Hollywood is simply jumping on to the bandwagon of a late-20th-century phenomenon: another baby boom. By the end of the 1990s, the number of four- to nine-year-olds in Britain is estimated to grow from 2 million to 2.4 million. More little offspring than for many a moon, will, it is predicted, be celebrating (with orange juice, of course) New Year 2000.

Away from the public arena, couples face alone the decision about whether they do, or don't, want children. The choices we face today are very different from those of our parents' generation. Then the choice lay between whether or not to have sexual intercourse – if you did, you knew you ran the risk of getting pregnant. The pre-pill generation could not rely on being able to make love without making a baby. Nowadays, with reliable contraception available for all, the dilemma is very different. Couples have to make a conscious choice to throw away the packets of pills, cap or whatever, and actively try to conceive.

Couples, once married, now delay having a baby for longer than previously. In 1971, the average period elapsing between the wedding and the birth of the first child was 20 months. By 1979, it had increased to 30 months, and since then, the interval has undoubtedly widened further. The statistical change indicates the growing dependence of most households on two incomes, or at least couples' unwillingness to let go of the advantages that two incomes provide. Gone for ever are the days when a wife automatically stopped work upon marriage and longed for a baby to release her from at least some of the loneliness of domestic drudgery. Now, it seems, priorities are reversing – domestic and family plans have to fit in with career aspirations rather than the other way round.

The practical factors need careful consideration. Put bluntly, children are no longer economic assets; they are ruinously expensive, and the expense has in the main to be borne by the couple themselves. At a time when every penny is needed, the loss of one income when the woman stops work (as most women do, for a time at least) can hit a new family hard: 'We wanted to buy a nice home when we got married, and took on the highest mortgage we thought we could afford. Now our mortgage has gone up five times, and it's all we can do to cope with it. I'd love to have a baby – but we'll have to wait for some time yet.'

In times of rocketing house prices and mortgage rates, it can be hard to work out a simple solution to the problem of coping financially. On the brighter side, however, a considered delay before the conception of a first child will almost invariably be beneficial to your emotional life as a couple, particularly if, before marriage, you did not live together for very long or at all. A couple need to get to know each other. It takes time, care and consideration to create a strong and durable relationship, and too much stress coming too early can set back the development of mutual trust. No matter how well prepared you are, the arrival of a baby will be enormously demanding. The more you have been able to build up your emotional resources within your relationship, the more likely you are to find that those first months and years of being a threesome are turbulent and happy rather than turbulent and miserable.

The decision to conceive

Once you have made up your minds to go ahead, you are by no means at the end of emotional turmoil. That momentous and exciting decision is usually followed by months, and occasionally years, of waiting and anticlimax. No one can choose the precise moment of conception. It comes when it comes – a decision arrived at by your body, not your conscious mind. For a couple accustomed to planning and organizing their lives, perhaps on a tight schedule, the uncertainty of that wait, knowing the profound changes that pregnancy will effect, can itself be extremely unnerving. Right from the beginning the process is governed by planning and foresight on the one hand and uncertainty and the surrender of control on the other. It is a funny balancing act. And as it starts, so it continues, throughout the pregnancy and on to the birth, and parenthood itself.

A considerable number of first pregnancies are, however, more or less unplanned. Many couples may start relaxing their strict use of contraception, perhaps switching from the pill to a slightly less reliable barrier method such as the condom – a change which is anyway now recommended on medical grounds prior to conception. Contraception may then be 'forgotten' on an increasing number of occasions. . . 'After all, it doesn't *really* matter if we have a baby now.'

The decision to conceive can be made calmly and rationally, but when conception actually occurs, the ensuing emotions can be quite startling, as Kate and David found:

> *'After being married for seven years (we got married just after leaving college), we decided that we'd waited long enough. We'd talked about the decision over a very long period – years, I suppose – but I wanted to wait until David, too, was really sure. It took me a couple of months to get pregnant and I started panicking, thinking I never would – though I've since found out it takes four to six months on average anyway. Then I remember doing a test early in the morning in the bathroom, and coming into the bedroom to tell David, who just said, 'Wow! This is it then.' He – and I – were thrilled, frightened and proud all at once.'*

Wanting a baby: men's and women's responses

From a materialistic or cynical perspective (and ours is, after all, a materialistic and cynical age), it could be seen as strange that, given all the expense and bother involved, the vast majority of couples positively do want to have children.

In fact, the indications are that women want them a lot more than men do. This may be because a man's biological clock does not tick away at the same speed that a woman's does – other things may now, perhaps, be equal, but our bodies are not. Men do not have monthly cycles which serve as constant reminders of the state of their fertility. As a result, when a rational and practical couple consider the pros and cons of having a baby now, and decide it is not a good time, she may still say, 'Let's try anyway.' And he will find it hard to understand.

Less prompted as they are by their own biology, men on the whole can seem to be more lukewarm than their wives about the idea of becoming parents, especially now that the dynastic importance of carrying on the family name and/or the great need to provide more bodies to labour in the fields (both previously strong masculine inducements to parenthood) have waned. For the prospective father (as for his own father), no matter how financial responsibilities have previously been shared between the couple, becoming a parent is still almost invariably about the husband becoming the family provider. For the time being (in the absence of a flesh-and-blood baby to love), the benefits of fatherhood remain unclear to say the least.

It is, therefore, not surprising that the financial and practical ramifications may now loom far larger for him, even when the couple have previously shared similar material values and been able to reach consensus without difficulty. So he remains rational, rather distant and detached when she starts wondering, yet again, about having a baby. Yes, of course, he wants children. . .some time. . .maybe next year. . .or, even better, in a few years when things are easier. . . She, on the other hand, remains completely unconvinced by this notion of things getting easier. She can think of plenty of reasons why now would be a good time, but rational reasons are no longer her governing priorities. Her desire, her *need* for a baby, is immediate and palpable. The need comes from deep within her and, as far as it is concerned with anything beyond itself, is concerned with questions of her identity as a woman and her prospective identity as a mother. At the same time, precisely because of the profundity and importance of the subject, it may be tangled up with very many other issues in her life. . .

A good reason for having a baby?

- Margaret's elder sister had just had a baby. Margaret envied her the attention and the special treatment she thereby gained within the family. Margaret needed to prove her maturity, her ability to bear and care for a child to her family and to herself. She hoped that her baby would bring to her the fulfilment and real feeling of success that she saw in her sister.
- Sharon had just handed in her notice, feeling disillusioned and bored with her chosen career. She toyed with the idea of starting her own business but lacked confidence. At this point, she became pregnant and shelved her plans.
- Karen, whose mother had died the previous year, had recently married a wealthy but often-absent businessman with a teenage family from his first marriage, to whom she was now the stepmother. Karen felt invisible. She became pregnant, feeling that she needed someone of her very own who would make her feel loved and treasured and special again.
- Maria and her husband had been drifting apart, and he had recently started an affair. The other woman was shocked when she heard about Maria's pregnancy – she had understood that Maria and her husband were virtually separated. That ended the affair, and Maria's husband made a renewed commitment to their marriage.
- Sarah had had two abortions in her 20s and recently underwent an operation to remove a tumour in her breast, fortunately benign.

She was feeling insecure about her sexuality and her ability to function healthily as a woman. The news that she was pregnant was immensely reassuring to her.

Whether they can identify with any of the women above or whether their own motives are entirely different, most women move towards their first pregnancy propelled by a complex mixture of reasons. Of course, it is easy for people who do not want a baby or are not in a position to have one to stand in judgement over which reasons are acceptable and which are not. However, life – and procreation – are rarely so simple.

It is certainly true that the advent of a baby will not shore up a failing marriage as, each year, many couples discover to their cost. Even more assuredly, nor will a baby automatically provide the feelings of love, security and fulfilment that a would-be parent feels she missed out in her own childhood. As every mother and father knows, the emotional nurturing and consideration demanded of parents seem to be exhaustingly one way at first. Nevertheless, any situation examined deeply enough may present several different interpretations and aspects.

Take Sharon, the woman whose career was at an impasse. Some people, especially her work colleagues, felt that she was copping out by becoming pregnant, giving herself an escape route from the decisions which clamoured to be made about her future career. But Sharon herself had found that both her salaried work and the new prospects on the horizon were becoming increasingly meaningless. She compared them to her recurring wonderings about what having a baby might be like, and found them lacking.

True, she was intimidated by the thought of starting her own business. Yet she felt that, despite this, if she were really excited about it, she would have taken a deep breath and gone ahead anyway. As it was, it just felt like a gigantic, unattractive, exhausting effort. She had tried hard to talk herself out of her longings for baby; she herself felt the accusation of copping out painfully. Yet she came to feel that this was a judgement by people who, for their own reasons, needed to see their careers as being more demanding, exciting and creative than the work of conceiving and bearing a child. Sharon had once felt like that too; but she had changed. During her pregnancy, she was slowly able to come to terms with the new realities of her life and her changed values, priorities and ambitions. She discovered a new kind of self-respect which did not depend on her career-derived status and achievements.

There are no good or bad motives for having a baby. In themselves, motives do not determine how successful you will be as a parent and how fulfilling you will find parenthood. Being strongly motivated may matter when the decision to conceive is made; but when the baby arrives, the reasons for that decision melt away and you are left to discover whether you have within yourself the capacity to be what the psychoanalyst Bruno Bettelheim has called the *'good enough parents'*.

A capacity for parenthood

The capacity to be a parent may be one which is more in evidence in some people than in others, and is partly determined by the quality of your own parenting as a child. Nevertheless, parenting is not something that you either have or haven't got – it can be learned and developed.

Our education system fosters the *intellectual* growth of the person and the development of practical and mental skills and understanding. Parenthood demands a different kind of functioning: an *emotional* maturity, an ability to understand and to empathize with the needs of your child while, at the same time, looking at each situation objectively and acting in your child's best interests. This may sound as if every parent has to be perfect; indeed, having a child is a privilege and not a right and deserves to be more widely regarded as such. Yet most new parents do – often to their own great surprise – take to it naturally and even easily.

Becoming a mother. . .

When you were a childless woman juggling career, adult relationships and other interests, you may have seen pregnant women and mothers with young children as a race apart. The transition from the world which virtually ignores the existence of children and their caregivers to a world which is centred around them is not easy.

The changes triggered off by bearing a first baby are widespread and can feel overwhelming. They affect your body, emotional state, close relationships, career prospects, earning and spending potential, self-image, other people's preconceptions of you and just about everything else you can think of. It can all come as rather a shock.

For a start, there are the physical changes, brought on not only by the growing baby and womb but by the flood of hormones that are necessary to sustain them. In the early months, pregnancy may be concealed from outsiders, yet the pregnant woman, apparently carrying on as usual, may find it hard to concentrate on anything else. Constant tiredness is common as is nausea. When one of us, Jane, was still working as a solicitor and pregnant for the first time – I found that I'd be in the middle of interviewing a client and suddenly my stomach would heave. I'd stand up and say 'Please excuse me for just one moment.' Then I'd rush out to the loo, throw up, splash water on my face and come back into the room looking, I hoped, as calm and composed as ever. I wouldn't say that it was particularly easy, but I did manage.

Some people believe that the nausea experienced by about 50 per cent of pregnant women may indicate an ambivalence between wanting and not wanting to have a baby. However, nauseous or not, a majority will feel ambivalent to some degree. For a woman involved in demanding work (and this means most women, at least into the first few months of a first pregnancy), the prospective transition may be difficult to negotiate and may feel like a deprivation. What will be gained may be imagined but not yet clearly; what will be lost soon becomes all too painfully evident.

The woman who works will be obliged, at least temporarily, to step sideways out of her job. She cannot know for sure how long she will be away: for every woman who actually returns to work within three months of having a first baby, there are several who tentatively plan to do so but change their minds after the birth. Statutory maternity leave holds a woman's job open for a fixed period after she has given birth, thereby giving her a much needed breathing space in which she can come to a decision about whether to return to it. Furthermore, discrimination against women on the grounds of pregnancy and childbirth is now illegal. Yet, despite these safeguards, the very uncertainty of what will happen to their careers (not to mention their incomes) may create great anxiety for women during pregnancy. The more competitive their work, the more they will inevitably feel under pressure.

There may well be times during your pregnancy when you feel super-energized, confident and effective. You may have a fit of domesticity during this period, plunging into an orgy of redecoration and refurbishment centred around but not confined to the new nursery, or you may discover that your work becomes sweeter and more absorbing the closer you get to leaving it. But you would be unusual if there were not times when you feel tired, emotionally, even tearfully, vulnerable and dependent on others, especially upon your partner.

For pregnancy to be a positive experience, some women find they need to create a space in which they can peacefully nurture themselves and their unborn child, reflecting and meditating upon the mystery of the new life which is being created within them. Perhaps they may take up yoga, country walking, sewing or just rocking quietly on the back porch. If you are always rushing around shouldering the burdens of the universe and proving to everyone, including yourself, that you are just as competent and alert as you ever were, you may find it hard to create this space. Relax. Breathe. *You are having a baby*, for heaven's sake!

The miracle of creation

Conceiving, bearing, and nurturing a child is a supremely creative act. A newly pregnant woman may start to discover a new sense of female identity and strength which bears little or no relation to popular notions of strength (masculine, goal-orientated, rational, achieving, etc.). Your changing relationship and concern with your own body and feelings and with the baby growing inside you may also tend to make you less anxiously aware of external circumstances, including other people's opinions. Because many women spend far too much time worrying about what people think of them and trying to please others, this can be a very positive change for them, resulting as it does from a sense of inner confidence in the validity of their own moods, desires and experiences, whatever they may be. These powerful, positive feelings may be intertwined in a complex way with intense bouts of tearful insecurity and the need for reassurance. They are none the less powerful for all that.

Pregnancy is a time of transition. It may feel as if you are always looking back – to the times when your clothes fitted, when you could run about, could plan the future with reasonable certainty – and, at the same time, always looking forward, with a mixture of excitement and apprehension, to the onset of labour and to the great unknown beyond.

Change, even when longed for, upsets the routines of life. On the stress chart on page 28, you will see that pregnancy ranks at 40 points; the gain of a new family member adds another 39. Sometimes the urge is to deny the traumatic nature of the change or to focus on the things you *can* control and organize – going to antenatal classes, decorating the nursery and so on. These things are important and necessary, but it is also important not to dwell on them instead of dealing with the emotional consequences of unforeseeable and uncontrollable change.

Sometimes people such as relatives, doctors and health professionals – in effect, people who should know better – take a rather patronizing, dismissive attitude towards your changes of mood and emotional intensity. 'It's just the hormones, dear,' they say. 'Don't worry about it. You'll snap out of it.' But the emotional changes are as important as the physical ones, and in any case, they are interconnected. They are there to be experienced and understood, not denied or just 'put up with'. Becoming a mother to a tiny demanding baby is a very specialized and special job. It is a great change from the state of non-parenthood and it requires a special kind of emotional sensitivity and empathy to the speechless and helpless. Drawn into an inner reverie with your unborn baby, this state of mind may now be taking form within you.

Finding the mother within

For women, there is a yawning gulf between being a parent and not being a parent that simply does not exist for men. Women line up on each side of the chasm, studying each other across the great divide – with envy, with hostility, with non-comprehension, with admiration. They are looking at themselves, at what they could be or could have been, and aren't. What you lose when you become a mother is the childless woman you once were. Perhaps some of what you valued in her – her slenderness, vigour, competitiveness, singlemindedness, ambition, spending power – you may rediscover later. Nevertheless, she herself is gone for ever, and she may need to be mourned.

A 32-year-old woman, a mother for the first time, holds her new baby up to the mirror and compares their faces:

> '*I'd never felt remotely old before. But looking at her blooming skin, I can see the lines on my own, where time and experience, giving birth even, have taken their toll. I feel proud of what my face shows, but a little sad too. I know that today is still mine. But tomorrow will be hers.*'

When you become a mother, your relationship to your own mother suddenly comes into the foreground. You have always known her, first and foremost as a mother, perhaps only as a mother to the exclusion of being able to imagine her in any other role. In the past, this may have enabled you to feel very different from her, to contrast yourself (no doubt favourably). Now all that is changed.

Most women, even if their relationship to their own mother and their experience of being mothered were good, will have ambivalent feelings about the mother/daughter relationship. For the woman who did not get on with her mother and finds little to admire in her, the task is that much more difficult. The more support she has from elsewhere – husband, friends, perhaps other relatives, a mother-in-law, perhaps a sympathetic family doctor or a counsellor – the more able she will be to discover a role model which is right for her. Sometimes a woman may need to explore her own babyhood and childhood and her relationship with her mother before she can feel free to be the mother she wants to be herself, and in this case, psychotherapy may be particularly helpful.

Friends can be particularly supportive at this time. Women with babies, who may have been invisible to you before, suddenly materialize before your very eyes. The sharing of your dramas with them will inevitably ease them:

> '*Down our street, four women all had babies within six months of each other. We've all become incredibly close – they're the best friends I ever had. If I've ever felt I couldn't stand it any more, they've just been there. I know I could leave my baby Jack with any of them just to have an hour or two on my own. They see me at my best – and my very worst. Crisis forms strong friendships, I guess. This has been the best time of my life.*'

You may need to look carefully at all the 'shoulds' in your head about being a parent. If you tell yourself that you 'should' be a perfect mother, you will certainly fail – just like every other woman in the history of the world. If you can allow yourself plenty of room, permission to learn through trial and error, a willingness to be open to your baby's helpless needs and the kind of support that builds your own confidence instead of telling you what to do, you may surprise yourself:

> '*I thought I'd really prepared myself for being a mother. But I was knocked over by the sleepless nights, the exhaustion, walking the wailing baby up and down when my body was screaming for peace and rest. And all the mess, the living in chaos. She seemed to need so much,*'

and sometimes I just didn't know. . .her tininess frightened me. I'd wake in the night and reach over in a panic to check she was still breathing. . .Then I remember one evening when she was two months old. The three of us were lying peacefully in bed. She was between us and she looked at me very directly, clutching my little finger, and she smiled. And I remember thinking, everything's going to be all right after all. . .'

Becoming a father

For women, pregnancy may be a release or an escape from work. For men, the converse applies. Whether their wife works or not (and only 7 per cent of mothers of the under-fives do work full-time), most fathers take the obligation of supporting their families very seriously.

George, a father-to-be, is a furniture restorer. His wife Susie, who has finally given in to his longing for a child, is an author of romantic novels. When she found out she was pregnant, she became nervous about whether they would be able to support the child. George, however, sees it this way:

> *'I've always been a bit easygoing about money, letting punters take as long as they like about paying – much to Susie's annoyance. But it's suddenly come home to me. I'm going to be a father. I've got responsibilities. It's a reason to work even harder so's I can look after my family. I tell her – she doesn't need to worry.'*

Sometimes prospective fatherhood involves making a binding commitment to secure, well-paid work with a good future and letting go of more exciting but precarious hopes and dreams. Steven, in his late 20s, was a musician, working in a highly competitive, pressurized and financially precarious profession. He left his band when his wife became pregnant and took up a full-time office job. Perhaps he will return to music once his wife has gone back to full-time work, but it will not be to resume where he left off. For the next few years, fatherhood means focusing all his energies on the support of his family.

In our society, the world of pregnancy, babies and young children is still an almost exclusively female one. Especially in relationships where there is not a great deal of verbal communication about the subject (and this is an area in which men may feel notoriously shy, uncomfortable or inarticulate), men may easily feel detached from the whole process. There may, in addition, be personal circumstances that can prevent a man from becoming wholeheartedly involved in conception, pregnancy and childbirth.

Belinda was Robert's second wife. She had always expected and wanted children and took it for granted that, once married, they would start a family. However, it was at this point that their sexual relationship started to deteriorate. It was a long time before Robert dropped the bombshell: he told Belinda that he might not want another child. Although he loves his son from his first marriage very much, the child had been conceived when the relationship was breaking up. Robert had not wanted a baby; he had felt that his son's conception was a ploy by his then wife to make him stay. He had felt tricked, exploited and deeply angry. All these feelings had gone underground and were now surfacing in his relationship with Belinda. Fatherhood for Robert had been something that had been done to him; a decision had been made which had immense implications for him, but over which he had not been consulted. It was hard for him to choose freely to become a father the second time around; he had a lot of anger, pain and guilt relating to the failed marriage which he had to work through before he could come to any decision at all.

A woman's urge towards motherhood may seem so powerful that a man feels swept along by it, unable to consider the question personally. He may be unlikely to articulate this feeling – after all, 'real' men do not feel overwhelmed by their women – and he may simply withdraw and become passive about the whole business. He may even inform his wife that it is her decision entirely.

Unlike her, he undergoes no physical or hormonal changes during the process. In fact, he may carry on just as before and may even feel that the new responsibility of being sole breadwinner justifies his ever deeper immersion into work to the exclusion of anything other than mild interest in the forthcoming event. His withdrawal may also stem from envy (of the life-giving process which he sees taking over his mate's body) and fear (of being rejected and excluded from the intense mother/baby relationship once the child is born). These may not be feelings he is able to talk about; he will need to come to terms with them in his own time.

And anyway, once the baby arrives, things may suddenly look very different. This may be especially true if he has been present at the birth and is able to become involved with caring for the new baby. He may be surprised to discover how proud and passionate is his attachment to his new son or daughter.

Sometimes, unusually, a man may feel a personal and intense desire to become a father even before his partner has felt the same strong desire to become a mother. Anthony went on holiday to Italy with his best man immediately before his wedding. He and his prospective wife had talked about the timing of children, and he had been considerably unenthusiastic about the prospect of conceiving in the next year. An incident on holiday changed his mind.

> *'One morning, I lay on the beach watching a group of fathers playing in the water with their kids. For the first time, I had a feeling that I was really missing out by not being a father. I had an idea about how fulfilling I might find it for myself.'*

Not every man undergoes such a radical change of mind. It is important that the two of you talk through the decision to conceive, to make sure if you can that any doubts are voiced and that the event is mutually planned. A father-to-be is not, after all, just a sperm-producing machine.

In our culture, men are not trained or socialized into becoming fathers. And, like the little boy who draws a picture of his mother, two sisters and himself to represent his family and never thinks of including his father who is away at the office every day, they have few role models. More often than not, men's recollections of their own fathers are of men who are away all day, every day. A day is a long time to a child. Perhaps the father became of increasing importance to the pre-adolescent and adolescent boy; nevertheless he remains largely absent from the mother-dominated world of early childhood.

Thus, men find themselves without any example in their personal lives on which to base an intimate relationship with their own child other than what they themselves experienced in the mother/child relationship. This can create anxiety about losing their hard-won sexual identity and about being unmanly, and they may end up distancing themselves from the whole process and even from deeply felt love for their child. Men, understandably, do not want to be mothers. They want to be fathers. But it may not be clear what being a father really means.

Social change and the women's movement have opened the door far more for women to enter the previously masculine world of careers than for men to enter the female world of involvement with young children. Nevertheless, that door is now ajar. For every man today contemplating his potential relationship with his own children, the possibility of what being a father means for him has to be worked out personally and creatively.

When two becomes three: your changing relationship as a couple

A baby is an unknown factor – until it appears. How you, as a couple, cope with the advent of your baby and the process of two becoming three will depend primarily on the kind of relationship you had beforehand and, in particular, on how well you were able to respond to the prospective changes during the transitional period of pregnancy.

Within your relationship as a couple, increased feelings of interdependence, reliance and appreciation can be very satisfying, drawing you closer together as you plan for the unfolding of your lives together as a new family. Various studies of couples expecting their first child have borne out the finding that, although in a troubled relationship a first pregnancy will only increase tension and acrimony, for the majority of couples it tends to be a satisfying and happy time. Many couples actually report an improvement of relations between them during this time.

> 'When we found she was pregnant, my first thought was, I'm really married now. No way can I leave the relationship now if things get difficult. Yet it didn't really feel like a trap – it seemed more to make us stronger.'

> 'My husband really enjoyed my pregnancy. I think, perhaps, I was so dependent on him, and he could be really sure of me. Maybe it's the first time he hasn't ever needed to feel jealous. He's so proud and happy at the moment; really very secure. Very considerate about me. I wonder if it'll last. . .[she laughs].'

> 'Our roles have really changed. Once we both left for work in the morning, now he goes and I'm at home. Soon I'll be at home with the baby. Emotionally and intellectually we relate to each other in the same way, but there is this great change which really affects the way we see ourselves and each other. For him, I suppose the change is not so great, just more responsibility. But I know it is going to take quite a lot for me to come to terms with it.'

The process of becoming parents is one which tends to polarize couples. What happens when you become a mother is very different from what happens when you become a father. . .

The baby outside and the baby within

Eric Berne, the founder of transactional analysis, described three primary modes of relating to others. The *parent* mode is authoritative, sometimes authoritarian ('Daddy/Mummy knows best'), and can also be nurturing and supportive of others. The *adult* mode is cool-headed, sensible, and emotionally detached. The *child* mode is impulsive, creative and anarchic; it is emotionally open and vulnerable and can be simultaneously wilful and profoundly dependent.

> When I was a child, I spake as a child, I understood as a child, I thought as a child: but when I became a man, I put away childish things.
>
> I Corinthians 13:1

In return for the privileges it bestows upon adults, culture demands that childish things be put away. But as Freud remarked, the child we once were lives on in all of us. One of the reasons that intimate and loving relationships are of such crucial importance to most people is that the emotional, creative and sometimes needy child who lives within each of us may be expressed, responded to and contained within them.

A childless couple in a contented relationship have the satisfaction of knowing that, when they need it, they have first call on their partner's consideration and emotional resources. By and large, they are prepared to take care of each other, in the happy expectation that their partner, in his or her own way, will do the same for them.

The love that the partners have available for each other is not necessarily altered by the birth of their first child; indeed, it may be deepened and intensified. But suddenly between them is a creature, whose own childish needs and uninhibited expression of them bear no relation to his or her tiny size. This can turn the existing dynamic between the couple upside-down and back-to-front.

> '*I remember looking at my son and seeing how helpless he was and thinking how he depended on me for life itself. I mean, I could have just locked him in a room and not fed him and he would have died. It's an incredible responsibility.*'

Recovering from giving birth, a physical and emotional trauma which in any other circumstances would entitle her to pampering, concern and a lot of rest and relaxation, the new mother is suddenly required to devote 110 per cent of her time, energy and attention to her little charge. She had no idea that looking after a baby could be such hard work. The simplest tasks take six times longer than they used to. Bedmaking, washing up and tidying that once were disposed of in half an hour's brisk activity remain neglected. Sometimes she notices and cares; mostly she does not. Her empathy and sensitivity are tuned in to the needs of her baby for whom she is starting to care with a passionate intensity which surprises her. Yet, particularly if she has not yet met up with other mothers in the same boat, she misses adult company and her old life. She feels isolated and longs for the turn of her husband's key in the door. She is having to adjust to a major life change.

He is likewise trying to adjust to his new role as a father. He may be feeling enormously and intuitively involved with his new infant; he may be feeling tentative and unsure. He has not gone through the trauma of birth himself, although if he were present at the event, it may have affected him very deeply. He has not felt the baby growing within him as a physical presence, and for him, its sudden debut may be hard to come to terms with.

On top of all this, he probably has to return to work and to pick up his old life almost immediately. If he has an exceptionally enlightened employer, he may have been given a week or so off, but then it's business as usual. He is expected to carry on as before. Perhaps, shouldering his increased financial responsibilities, he may even be expected to take on overtime. He and his wife used to meet in town for a night out or return home from their respective offices for a drink in front of the television and a leisurely supper. Now when he walks through the door, tired after a hard day's work following an almost sleepless night, his wife is lying on the settee looking even more exhausted and the baby is crying. The dirty breakfast plates are still in the sink and the house is a mess. Wordlessly, she hands the baby over to him, and then bursts into tears. . .

The baby's tiny helpless kicking body, the intimate smells, sounds and closeness evokes in the mother strong unconscious memories of herself as a baby and of the mothering she herself received then. The new father may have similar feelings, and he may, furthermore unconsciously identify his wife with his own mother. The children within both the man and the woman may be feeling insecure and needy, but faced with the non-negotiable and startling actuality of the new flesh-and-blood child, their requirements must be relegated.

The mother is giving all the parenting she has in her to her new child. She may feel that she has little or no personal resources left and turns to her husband, her intimate partner, for love, reassurance and nurturing. If he can respond, non-judgementally and supportively, by giving her whatever it is that she needs, she will feel more empowered to mother her child. But sometimes her partner may feel too threatened or too needy himself to be able to respond appropriately.

Sometimes a couple may have themselves functioned until the birth within a parent/child dynamic. Particularly at risk on the birth of a real baby is a relationship where a responsible, perhaps over-protective woman has previously played parent to her man's entertaining, creative but emotionally freeloading child. Such a man may feel that his own place has been usurped. Unable to discover a new role, he may feel excluded and alienated by the intense, almost sexual relationship between mother and baby. His wife increasingly turns from him to their child, resentful and disappointed at his persistent demands on her when all her mothering is now directed elsewhere. What *she* needs is a husband, not another baby! Such a man is going to have to grow up in rather a hurry, if his relationship with his wife is going to survive. He will need to discover and bring forth from within himself an adult to see the situation clearly and a parent to take care of his wife and child as well as his own needy childlike self.

No doubt the majority of men suffer some feelings of jealousy and exclusion in the early stages of parenthood. This is natural enough and does not prevent a husband from functioning with love and tenderness towards his wife and child. How well he will be able to do this depends on his own personal resources of maturity and on the relationship already established between the couple.

Being parents

Perhaps nowhere is there so much potential for guilt as in the effort to be a good parent. Just about everyone – the child's grandparents, your work colleagues, other new mothers, child psychologists, militant feminists, the Pope, the old lady next door – has a personal opinion about what being a 'good parent' means and often an undeclared vested interest, too. Few will be reticent about expressing their views.

New parents may end up feeling like the old man, the boy and the donkey in Aesop's fable. They tried every combination: the old man rode and the boy walked; the boy rode and the old man walked; they both rode the donkey; neither rode the donkey. Every strategy was met with public criticism and alternative suggestions by the crowd along the way. Eventually, they ended up carrying the donkey. The moral: If you try to please other people, you will fail and you may end up committing yourself to a course of action which pleases nobody.

One eminent child psychoanalyst, Bruno Bettelheim, has come up with a notion that, for once, gives reassurance to parents. He believes that they should not attempt the impossible but rather should simply try to be 'good enough parents'. Bringing up a child, says Bettelheim, is a creative endeavour – an art, not a science. There is no single 'right' way of doing it, no set of instructions to follow. Instead each parent must think for him or herself at every turn, responding to the individual needs of the child rather than according to any predetermined prescription.

One dilemma that new parents commonly encounter is the vexed question of the mother returning to paid employment. Should she go back? If so, when? And who will look after the baby? Other people's attitudes may inevitably affect your own values, as will, strongly, the parenting you had as a child. Once upon a time, women with young children were made to feel very guilty if they had jobs. Now, in certain milieux, things have come full circle and it is the woman who declares that she wishes to stay at home and be a full-time mother who may be subtly disparaged and seen by others, and perhaps by herself, as letting the side down. Of course, financial pressures may be important and heavily tip the scales in favour of the mother's eventual return to work, whether part-time or full-time.

Your own common sense will probably tell you that, if you make a decision which you or your husband (or both of you) know in your hearts is wrong, whether that decision is for you to stay at home or to go back to work, it will affect all three of you adversely. The thought that you are doing the 'right' thing will be of small consolation. Babies and very young children do need regular, consistent, familiar care, and a good amount of this on a one-to-one basis. They also need, and deserve, to be cared for with ungrudging love and with personal involvement. In the past, the mother was seen as the obvious person to satisfy the majority of these needs. This is often how it still turns out, but sometimes, for whatever reason, this isn't practical and/or desirable. In these cases, it is much more important simply to ensure that your offspring's needs are, one way or another, lovingly provided – by whomever.

There is a Doonesbury cartoon that shows a married couple settling down for the night, talking about their childcare arrangements. 'Why do you feel so good about it when I feel so bad?' she asks with furrowed brow. 'Simple,' he replies. 'I'm doing much more than my father so I feel great. You're doing less than your mother, so you feel like a failure.' And, with that, he smugly rolls over and turns out the light.

Decisions about childcare, and the guilt that went with this power to make decisions, were once the province of women, and while they keep this uneasy power to themselves, few men will interfere. But times are changing. Superwoman starts to come apart at the seams and realizes that she just can't do everything herself. Fewer men now feel it is unmanly to display an interest in their children even in their daily care, and employment prospects too are becoming more flexible with part-time work, jobshares, self-employment and working from home increasingly viable options. Within these parameters, a number of creative solutions are possible.

- Alan and Alice split the care of their daughter. Alice, who was breastfeeding on demand, stayed at home with her until she was six months old and then she found a part-time job. Careful planning enabled Alan to set up a job-share, the hours of which were arranged to dovetail with those of Alice's job.
- Bernard and Cathy had more or less decided before their son's birth that Cathy would return after six months to her well-paid and demanding job as an advertising executive. Cathy found being a mother enormously rewarding. Taken aback by the pull of love towards her son, she could not face returning to work. She and Bernard tightened their belts, sold the second car and took in a lodger (who also doubles as a babysitter) and now Cathy is expecting a second child.
- Nicholas felt bored and frustrated by his work in the Civil Service, especially since the birth of his daughter whom he adores. He came to envy Matilda who, until that point, had been at home with the baby. Now Matilda is back at work and Nicholas is at home looking after their toddler as well as fulfilling a long-cherished ambition to write a novel, which he is able to do in the afternoons when his little girl goes to the day nursery.
- Mary and Steven were both actors, although Mary's career was

going less well. By the time their baby was born, she had more or less lost interest in it. Staying at home with her child, she had time to knit his clothes and discovered a previously unimagined skill for designing and marketing them, too. Steven got a long-running job in a West End thriller which enabled him to be at home most days to look after their child when needed. Within three years, Mary had built up a thriving business employing ten outworkers and selling to Harrods and Macy's.

Be creative. Be flexible. You do not know what may be possible until you try. We turn finally to Kate, whom we first encountered at the beginning of her first pregnancy and who is now expecting baby number two: 'Despite all the hard work, the tears, the things I thought I'd lost – like freedom – it's been well worth it. Whatever you give, your child gives back to you double. Nothing else in the world is so good. Anyway, it must be OK, otherwise why would I be doing it again?'

21

For better or
for worse:
troubleshooting

*You were born together, and together you shall be for evermore. You shall
be together when the white wings of death scatter your days. Aye, you shall
be together even in the silent memory of God.*

Kahlil Gibran, *The Prophet*

IT had been the most traditional of June weddings. The sun poured in
through the windows of the reception hall, its light bouncing off the
emptying champagne glasses and throwing lacy patterns through the
bride's filigree head dress on to the damask expanses of the bridal table.
A small tired bridesmaid sat on the floor playing with a piece of frayed
ribbon. Rows of faces were upturned towards the bride's father, still on
his feet and about to conclude his speech: '. . .and so I know that everyone
will join with me in wishing this couple in their marriage, *should it last*, the
very greatest happiness. . .'

It is today widely appreciated among the marrying population that one
in three marriages come to an end in divorce, that the average life of a first
marriage is only ten years (and of a second marriage only seven) and that
one in five children will live through their parents' divorce. These statistics
have entered our collective consciousness fundamentally and radically:
they are the uninvited guests present at every starry-eyed wedding.

Is the point simply that marriages today, once they are dead, can be
easily ended and thus these failures are more visible? Or are we, as a
nation, actually getting worse at making long-term relationships work?
Or is it just that couples marrying today have come to expect much more
from their relationships and are less willing than their parents to put up
with something that may, sooner or later, fall short of their ideals? For
whatever reason, the transience of many modern relationships and the
soaring divorce rate certainly do seem to affect the way in which we
experience the daily realities of our own marriages, both the times

215

of closeness and happiness ('Will it last? Can it last?') and the times of bitter fights and misunderstandings ('So that's it, then? I bet you're just going to walk out on me!').

Most people still agree that marriage as an institution is worth preserving – and, more to the point, keep voting with their feet all the way to the altar. Yet it seems that little specific insight, advice or support is available to help people create what will be, for them, a good (and lasting) marriage, leaving aside such vague injunctions as 'Try to keep romance alive in your marriage' (wear perfume at breakfast, say it with flowers and so forth).

An enormous mystique has been created around the ideal of a good marriage, which has comes to mean not just a *good enough* marriage, but a *perfect* marriage – like soul, you've either got it or you ain't. When difficult times come along, as they surely will, there may be a sense of doom; failure seeming, in retrospect, inevitable. Then through lack of understanding, lack of support and lack of room to negotiate, adjust and grow, the couple may find themselves being propelled – to their shock, alarm and ultimate resignation – into relationship breakdown.

From argument to catastrophe

Sometimes couples discover that a fundamental incompatability – in terms of what they each individually want from the relationship and what they are each prepared to put into it – is too great for their marriage to endure. Perhaps one or both of them lack the personal and emotional resources to meet the continuing challenge of intimacy with the other; if one partner has irrevocably turned his or her face from the marriage, nothing the other partner says or does will bring that person back. In such circumstances, divorce, however painful, must come as a release – the sooner the couple are able to address the situation honestly and to call it a day (preferably *before* the arrival of children), the better. But now with what is effectively 'divorce on demand' being relatively freely available, has the pendulum now swung too far in the opposite direction with divorce becoming too easy, too available – the commonplace solution when the going gets rough?

All long-term relationships go through bad patches:

> *'I used to think every argument was a major catastrophe until we were married. Now, if it doesn't get resolved over the years, then it might end the relationship, of course. But there isn't the same sense of panic. It feels as if there's a lot more room to work things out between us than before we were married.'*

This man does not feel that getting married has provided a cast-iron certainty that the relationship will endure no matter what; nor indeed is this something he wants. He does, however, believe that the commitment he and his wife have made to each other will enable their relationship to weather conflicts which might otherwise have had the potential to destroy it. Another husband, however, is not so sanguine:

'Well, sometimes we get into sticky patches. We're in one now, actually. It gets very discouraging. I find myself wondering, what's the point? I suppose I could imagine myself walking out one day, trying again with someone different. . .'

Marriage is supposedly a permanent relationship. It has been said that it takes 10 to 15 years to make a marriage: a concept that may be hard to grasp if what psychologists and advertising executives claim is true – that the attention span of the average person is now just under two minutes. In all areas, consumer choice rules: Your cooker needs mending? Why bother – throw it away! Get a new one! Buy now, pay September! When a quick 'out' becomes the universally advocated panacea to all ills, small wonder that instead of staying in there we succumb to defeatism, closing ourselves off from the difficulties which have been created and from the frustration and pain which they cause us.

Yet have these advertising slogans reached our hearts? Is there not in all of us the longing for a lifelong commitment? A 1982 survey in *Woman* magazine revealed that one-third of all the divorcees questioned wished, in retrospect, that they had tried harder to save their marriages. These findings were confirmed by a recent study by Gwynn Davis and Mervyn Murch which discovered that over one-half of divorced men and nearly one-third of divorced women openly (if unilaterally) admitted regret about having got divorced. This is a startlingly high figure given that such a feeling cannot be easy to confront even privately. It indicates that divorce may not be the panacea it may tantalizingly look like from within the pain of a marriage in difficulties.

After a person has left a conflict-filled marriage, s/he may find that it is not as easy as s/he had anticipated to create a fulfilling new relationship with someone else. Tensions may be carried over into the new relationship, to erupt with disastrous consequences once the passion of romance has once again started to cool and the work of developing genuine intimacy again looms. The prognosis for second and subsequent marriages is not good, and this is as strong an argument as any for staying with your existing relationship, allowing it time and working at it – at least until you feel that all possible avenues have been explored and you have given it your absolute best.

Divorce is no picnic. People whose marriages end, no matter which one initiates the separation, feel helpless, angry and betrayed, emotionally wounded and psychologically undermined. The sense of failure may be very great. Thei careers and their health may suffer; their finances almost certainly will. Homes may have to be sold, possessions divided;

very few divorcees can maintain the same standard of living which they enjoyed when they were married, and subsequent marriages may suffer financially as well as psychologically from the unresolved burdens of the first failed one. And for couples with children, the outlook may be considerably worse, the possibility of putting it all behind and making a new start greatly reduced. Even if both ex-partners have been superhumanly successful in keeping their children out of their battles and negotiations, even if the desire to retaliate is gone or can be contained elsewhere, the problem of the children still remains, as do the grief and guilt consequent upon having blown their small worlds apart. It is not always the case that what is best for parents is best for their children, however much we would like to persuade ourselves that this must be so.

These problems are very real. Frequently they are glossed over, perhaps out of misplaced kindness to people in marriage difficulties. However, it is better to go into them very carefully at a time when you still feel that you have a choice about whether or not to stay in the relationship than to find out too late. Then, even if the marriage does fail, at least you will be free of the nagging thought that perhaps, somehow, it could have been different. If, on the other hand, you seriously decide to renew your commitment to your marriage, you may discover that there is a lot more life left in it than you had thought.

So what should you do if your marriage seems to be foundering in deep water, even heading for the rocks? The first priority must be to step back, take a deep breath and try to make some sense out of what is going on.

Coping with the relationship in crisis

Once upon a time, your fights were lovers' quarrels, quick to flare up, quickly and sweetly mended. When was it that the bickering started to become more frequent, more prolonged and more painful?

Danger signal 1: increasing conflict

Sometimes a couple may realize in retrospect that there was some event – perhaps a discovery, a betrayal of trust – great or small – which precipitated, quite unconsciously at first, an uncoupling process. Sometimes the process starts to happen imperceptibly, with disproportionate heat being generated between husband and wife over apparently trivial incidents. The rows between them start to occur more frequently and seem more threatening to the basic fabric of the relationship.

If you think that your relationship may be in or is approaching this stage, you should listen quite carefully to what is being said between you. Are the arguments genuinely about what they seem to be about on the surface? Or is something else being said underneath, such as 'I don't trust you now'? For unless the two of you can get to the root of what is going on and why, you will be edging into the second stage. . .

Danger signal 2: non-resolution of conflicts

The bickering is now tailing off into a more or less frozen silence with arguments resuming with increased bitterness sooner or later. Or the kiss-and-make-up is of the most perfunctory kind, fooling no one. At some point, the will to sort things out – the belief that things *can* be sorted out between you two – seems to ebb away.

The source of conflict may be great or apparently trivial. Why couldn't he answer the telephone instead of leaving her to heave herself, dripping wet, out of the bath? He thinks her mother is an old bat and refuses to go and visit; she feels he could make more of an effort. She wants to stop work to have a baby; he is determined they should go on as they are for the time being. She cannot help feeling jealous since she found out about his regular lunches with an unknown woman; he maintains she is making a fuss about nothing.

Given goodwill between the couple, creative solutions to these problems would be within reach. But goodwill is fast disappearing, along with the inclination to search for solutions and the ability to find them. A sort of fatalism starts to attach itself to the relationship, as each partner increasingly begins to view the other's interests as being fundamentally opposed to his or her own. They push each other further and further into their separate corners, emerging only to attack each other once more, each sure of their own rightness. So they progress to the next stage.

Danger signal 3: blaming each other more and more

The more threatening the deterioration of the relationship, the more frustrating and venomous the blaming becomes. Backwards and forwards it goes as each becomes increasingly unwilling to listen to what they perceive as malicious and unwarranted attacks by the other.

Sometimes the couple blame each other with equal vigour; sometimes one of them by common, unspoken consent takes all the blame on his or her own head and seems to fall into a passive, self-flagellating hopelessness. Such a state may nevertheless conceal an enormous amount of *hidden* anger and blaming directed towards the other person.

A couple hooked into blaming are increasingly robbing each other of their humanity, turning their erstwhile lovers into stereotypes and caricatures of their true selves. 'If she thinks I'm a selfish inconsiderate pig,' he says to himself, '*I'll* show her how a selfish inconsiderate pig really behaves. . .' And how! Each obligingly starts to act out the caricature created for them by the other, thereby lending more credence to the name -calling as the circle grows more and more vicious. The script that the couple are now acting out is the classic good guy/bad guy scenario. In this script, there's no mistaking the baddy. He's the one in the black hat and three-day-old stubble. He's the one who isn't me. . .

In making all the couple's problems their partner's fault, the blamer frees him or herself from the uncomfortable inner doubts which a closer self-examination might have entailed. By the time things have reached this point, some serious individual soul-searching is called for, together with a shared willingness to call a halt and make an effort to see the other side of the story, if the relationship is to be made viable once again.

Danger signal 4: withdrawal

One or both of you is disengaging from the relationship. Perhaps you're not sure you want it to end – but you're exhausted and sure that you've had as much as you can take for the time being. You have hurt each other to the point that you feel unable to trust each other any more. You are unwilling to risk any more intimacy with your partner.

Intimacy can be frightening because it opens a person up to such a risk of betrayal. The greater the intimacy, the greater the possibilities for being hurt. It is not easy at any time to trust another person enough to create genuine intimacy with them. When someone has hurt you or let you down badly, it may seem impossible to think of ever opening yourself to that person again.

Back in Chapter 1, we met Mary and Mark. Beneath her veneer, Mary was just as afraid of intimacy as Mark. Nothing in her family background had persuaded her that it could be a fulfilling and rewarding experience. However much she had consciously come to value and desire one, to her unconscious mind the idea of a deeply involved relationship with another person was implicitly connected to the threat of being controlled, intruded upon and taken over.

By choosing such a reserved and withdrawn man as Mark, Mary contrived never to have to deal with these fears herself. Instead, as the relationship deteriorated, she could attack them in Mark, criticizing his coldness and trying to make him change, secure in the knowledge that he never would and that she would therefore be both safe from intimacy – not to mention being able to retain a self-image as a warm and open woman. Mark thus ended up carrying all of Mary's fears of intimacy as well as his own very genuine fears of the same thing.

If real intimacy between you seems desirable yet no longer possible, then like Mark and Mary you may have got stuck into a situation in which one of you always seems to be pushing the other to be more open (the withdrawn husband/hysterical wife syndrome), for this is how it often pans out. The person doing the pushing feels angry and frustrated, the one being pushed feels bullied and resentful. What would it now take to get *both* of you to open up to the other again?

Danger signal 5: communication breakdown

By this time, a once living relationship feels dull and lifeless: even fighting can't get you going any more. It may seem that there is nothing more to be done except to call it a day and arrange for a decent burial.

The bridges connecting the couple seem to have been burned, and they feel that they can no longer communicate with each other in any way. They may seek solace elsewhere – in an affair or in work commitments – or just close up. Sometimes the failure to communicate leads to violence, with one person lashing out at the other in fury and despair. The violence then sets in motion a spiral which can only lead to yet further hurt (both emotional and physical) and disillusionment.

Time is running against any couple caught up in this whirlpool. The time to stop the rot is now, not in two weeks' or six months' time when the gap between you may have widened further and what goodwill still remaining between you may have dissipated even more. It may not be easy to revive and restore your relationship – but given energy, courage and commitment, it may still be possible. . .

Steps towards restoring your relationship

Refocusing

You are probably feeling confused about your relationship. Your tension, anger (whether expressed or not) and distress may be having an adverse effect on your health, and you are likely to be feeling tired and depressed generally. You may have reached the point of feeling that everything is just too much bother. This may not feel like the moment to start working creatively on your relationship, yet important questions are chasing each other round your head:

- Is there, at bottom, enough shared ground underneath the pain and hurt to make the relationship worth preserving?
- Are you honestly prepared to make a commitment to get your relationship back on its feet again, with all that may entail?
- And do you believe your partner would be prepared to do the same?

Answers to these questions will have to be found before you can move forward. You may be able to do this most effectively if you can set aside time for yourself as far away as possible from the present stresses of the relationship. Then you will be more able to look at it from a realistic perspective.

First, you may have to teach yourself how to relax. The ability to relax on demand especially at times of emotional or any other crisis is a precious and undervalued skill. Here's how:

- Get in the mood by taking a solitary walk, having a warm bath or doing a few yoga exercises.
- Then make yourself comfortable on cushions or a bed in a quiet and private place where you will not be disturbed.
- Close your eyes and let your body become heavy. Go through each part of your body – from head to toe or in the opposite direction – noticing where the stiffness is, tensing this part and then letting it go completely.
- Imagine that your mind is a lake. Allow it to become still and quiet. When troublesome thoughts appear on its surface, just notice them and allow them to float quietly away.

Once you feel really relaxed, allow yourself to start considering the negative aspects of your relationship: the quarrels, the mistrust, the fears, the lack of understanding. Then let them go. Breathe deeply again and feel them drain away from your mind and body. Then consider the positive aspects of the relationship, past and present: your shared life together, the happiness you have brought each other, the depth of the intimate understanding and knowledge you have of each other and the trust and love which you have sometimes experienced. Again, take as long as you need to let each thought and memory come up, and then let them drain away.

Then relax again, and for several minutes just concentrate on your breathing, while allowing your mind to dwell on the relationship and to consider what the possibilities for change and growth might be.

When you are ready, open your eyes. You may want to write down some of the thoughts and feelings that occurred to you so that you can think about them further.

Reopening communication and creative listening

These two go together because communication is a two-way process: listening just as much as talking.

Every single individual whom either of us has ever encountered or assisted in the process of divorce has named 'failure of communication' as one of the principal or most likely causes of relationship breakdown. Without successful communication, any efforts you make to ensure your relationship's survival are almost certainly bound to fail.

Unless your partner is a professional clairvoyant, it is no use assuming that s/he automatically knows your gripes and what you want and need from the relationship. You will have to take your courage in both hands and declare yourself – as simply, accurately and unblamingly as possible. Women may have a reputation for being more in touch with their feelings than men, yet it can be very hard indeed for a woman to state simply what she wants from another to that person's face – after all, women are taught to put the needs of others first. A man may find it very hard to express his feelings at all; he may have avoided doing so for years, and emotions, especially his own, may look like extremely alien and unfriendly territory.

You will need to be patient and forbearing with yourself and with each other as you reopen long-closed lines of communication. The following may help you do this:

- *Choose your timing.* The inclination to sit down and spend time talking must be mutual. This will not be the case if your toddler is rampaging round the house unattended, if one of you has to leave for work in 15 minutes, or if you are exhausted at the end of a hard day and longing to go to sleep. Pick a time when you are both comparatively relaxed and willing to be open with each other.
- *Be specific.* Specific questions and problems can be dealt with. Generalized moaning and whinging can't.
- *Take responsibility for your own feelings.* The less you appear to be blaming your partner, the more s/he will be able to hear what you say. For example, it may be just as true to say 'I don't feel heard' as it is to say 'You never listen to me!'
- *Be truthful and don't hold your punches.* Without real honesty at this point, any communication between you will just be a waste of time. You may regret your insincerity later and perversely resent your partner even more (which isn't really fair on him or her). The truth may be very uncomfortable, but it is better spoken straight rather than hinted at and then left hanging over your heads like the sword of Damocles. You are commencing what has been called the labour of love: the willingness to allow a great many, perhaps forbidden thoughts and feelings to come to the surface of a relationship in the interests of strengthening and deepening it. And that takes time and courage.
- *Listen constructively.* This is one of the greatest gifts of love that a person can give another. So often what we call listening is a half-hearted 'Mmm. . .uhuh' while our heads are full of our own concerns. Or perhaps we hear selectively, or imagine our partner has said something which fits in with our own thoughts when in fact s/he may have said something entirely different. Often we interrupt to reassure, argue or put another point of view without ever really taking in whatever our partners are attempting to articulate.

  Genuine listening requires a willingness to be open to what the other person is really saying while ensuring that your own internal voice, with its constant stream of opinions and judgements, remains silent. This is an astonishingly effective technique and not remotely passive. Do you and your partner listen to each other? Honestly? Here is a simple but very powerful exercise to try out:

EXERCISE

Ask your partner to talk about an issue in your relationship that really concerns him or her – for, say, five minutes. Listen. Really concentrate on what your partner is saying, and for the whole of that time, *do not interrupt*. You may find it surprisingly hard not to chip in with your own comments but keep quiet: it's only for five minutes after all.

At the end of the agreed period, repeat back what your partner has said as accurately as you can remember, paraphrasing where necessary. If you get something wrong or miss something out completely they may now interrupt, but *only* to put you right about what they actually did say. You should then repeat what they have just told you.

After you have finished, repeat the exercise, swapping roles.

A period of separation

This may sometimes be the answer if you feel your relationship has become stuck and messy, your altercations repetitive and unhelpful, and you yourself drained and at the end of your tether. Remember, though, that separation can be risky. Sometimes time and distance apart may make the rift between you seem even more absolute, and the trial separation then paves the way for a final one. Whether this happens to you or not will depend on whether the separation has a clear purpose, as well as on the level of commitment you each still feel to the relationship. And these are things that may either increase or decrease in the breathing space which you have created.

Direct your time and energies to contemplating the relationship and what might possibly enable it to become viable and worthwhile again. Also use the time apart to relax and recharge your own batteries. Before you expend energy on others, you need to take care of yourself.

Professional help

Once upon a time, communities were far more close-knit and a couple in trouble might have an entire network of people on whom to call for help. No doubt at times the same couple would also have their work cut out resisting unasked-for interference.

Nowadays the problem is usually reversed. A couple whose marriage is in difficulties may find themselves adrift upon a sea of loneliness with the wreckage of other people's collapsing marriages and the news of ever-increasing divorce statistics all around them. Occasionally a friend, relative, doctor or vicar may be able to offer you the sympathy and advice that you need, but this may not go far enough. You may realize that what you require is objective professional assistance from someone who specializes in working with couples in crisis.

Sometimes people struggle along in the face of difficult odds, caught up in the web of a problematic relationship which they have no real hope of seeing clearly, let alone untangling singlehandedly. It may take courage to pick up the telephone and make the first appointment, but it is not an admission of failure to go to a counsellor or a psychotherapist. On the contrary, it takes maturity to confront your fears and problems and to obtain the support which is most likely to help you resolve them.

Thankfully, modern attitudes are making professional relationship counselling far more acceptable – even, in some circles, fashionable. You can consider going to see a professional not because you 'need' to (whatever that may mean) but because of your commitment to greater clarity and an enhanced quality within your life and relationships. For further information about counselling and for a list of helpful organizations, see Appendix 2.

Relate (formerly the Marriage Guidance Council), specializes in treating relationships which have run into problems. Here is a man, quoted in the *Observer Magazine*, describing what seeing a counsellor from Relate did for his marriage:

> '*It was a shock when discord struck. We started to row about everything – her cat, my children, money, sex. . .We still loved each other but we couldn't get on. When Vicky suggested Marriage Guidance, I agreed. I wanted to stop behaving like a bastard, but I didn't know how to go about it.*
>
> '*The counsellor was fantastic. She always directed us to the root of the problems. I realized that if I got angry with Vicky, I had to look at myself. I admitted that a lot of my behaviour was based on fear. . . I still have insecurities but I'm no longer dictated to by them.*
>
> '*Sexually, I've stopped being so greedy and selfish, and it's opened up facets of enjoyment I'd never have believed possible. By shifting my attitude, I now get as much from giving as taking. We still quarrel, but nowadays we bleed, we don't haemorrhage.*'

22

For mutual society, comfort and help: love and friendship in marriage

> Piglet sidled up to Pooh from behind.
> 'Pooh!' he whispered.
> 'Yes, Piglet?'
> 'Nothing,' said Piglet, taking Pooh's paw. 'I just wanted to be sure of you.'
>
> A. A. Milne, *The House at Pooh Corner*

SINCE the day that man first put quill to scroll, whole forests have been felled so that epics, novels, poems, plays and texts extolling the agonies and ecstasies of romantic love might be written. In recent years, books exploring, analysing and offering advice about what happens when relationships go wrong have come to consume almost as many trees. But is there nothing to say about the quiet, deep pleasures of love and friendship within a secure marriage?

The lives of most people consist of two acts broken by an intermission. Act I is the story of a child, born helpless and slowly learning how to be autonomous and independent. In the intermission, the child leaves the parental home and whiles away some time experimenting with independence from the freedom and sometimes squalor of a bedsit. At the beginning of Act II, the young adult finds a partner, creates a home and brings a new generation into the world. The new parents watch their children grow and eventually leave home themselves. The parents grow older. Perhaps, if they live long enough, they will one day return to the state of helplessness in which their lives began.

Thus, Act I mirrors and complements Act II. In Act I, the individual

226

grows to maturity in the space provided by the relationship of his parents; in Act II, he creates a new relationship in which a new family will be reared. In order that children may grow and mature healthily, they need a secure environment created out of the love and commitment of the adults who care for them. An adult, too, needs to know that s/he has a special person to love, be loved by and to rely on, and may realize this need within a mutually fulfilling marriage. The adult creativity and growth of each of the partners may then flourish in that space created by each other's love, faith and support.

Of course, very few childhoods are fortunate enough to unfold in the best possible environment, one that is at all times secure, loving and supportive of the best interests of the child. Few of us grow to adulthood unaffected by the difficulties we experienced growing up in our own particular parental homes. A child can do very little to change his environment. He has to accept the one he is born into and make the best of it. He can respond, adapt, reject or rebel against it; what he cannot do is create it from scratch. An adult, potentially, can. With marriage comes the opportunity to create the environment that you want, both for yourself and for your children. This may be so in theory. But how real is the opportunity, how genuine the choice?

In this book we have seen how people sometimes seek out marital relationships which echo their parents'. They thereby demonstrate that they are attracted like magnets to what is familiar, however stifling or uncomfortable that may be. This in itself may not seem very positive, and yet what Freud called 'the urge to repeat' also indicates the movement towards growth and maturity which struggles towards the light within every human psyche. Our unconscious seeking out of relationships and environments similar to the ones we faced helplessly in our earliest years allows us to keep working through the same issues which confronted us then. Now, with the benefits of fresh insight and increasing maturity and stability, we can hope to establish more creative choices and more successful responses. Marriage, because it is an intimate relationship, at once so similar to and so different from those relationships of our childhood, provides a unique forum for growth.

What is a good marriage? It must be a reliable one, in which each partner knows that the other will be there for them when they are needed – to listen, to support, to strengthen and to gladden. Equally, there must be a willingness on the part of each partner to open their hearts to each other, to share and communicate their joys, fears and difficulties. There will certainly be times when the relationship is painful, confrontational and difficult, but it is alive, and the pains will be growing pains.

At any point in a marriage, moment by moment, there are opportunities for the couple to give up. You can walk out, close off, go on the attack and deny responsibility for your own actions while loudly blaming your partner for theirs – until, finally, the relationship becomes an arid, static caricature of its former promise. There will be episodes in the best of relationships when these things, and worse, happen: when the partners, however briefly, become deadly enemies. As we have seen, only when such episodes are prolonged and frequent and the partners are unable or unwilling to work at resolving them will the marriage falter and eventually, perhaps, die.

More than just a shell: routine and reliability in marriage

A woman on the eve of her wedding expresses one of the most commonly held fears about getting married:

> '*I think what I'm most afraid of is that the love we feel now, which is so real for both of us, will become no more than just a shell. Not suddenly, after a fight – I can live with fights – but gradually, worn down by years of boring routine, taking each other for granted until we just don't see each other any more. Then our marriage will be dead. Just like my parents' marriage – dying, without anyone really noticing. They stayed together for us children, because they thought they should, but it was dead all right.*'

The fear is that time itself has the power to destroy a relationship, stifling it of challenge, excitement and creativity, wearing it down to a shadow with mindless routine and banality, killing it slowly, surely and ever so quietly as one or both partners, growing in their separate lives, leave it behind.

If you think of your marriage as just something to slip into now and then like a familiar, worn-out pair of slippers and to put aside at will, you may one day find that it has indeed (in the way of all slippers) fallen apart in your hands. Routine is what happens when a couple cut off, when they carry on living as if they were involved in a relationship while emotionally they have become disengaged and detached. The body may be there but the spirit has fled.

Routine is very different from reliability. The latter presupposes a willingness to remain emotionally open and available within a relationship. In his book *Marriage, Faith and Love*, Jack Dominian, the psychiatrist and writer on marital relationships, talks about emotional availability within marriage this way:

> *Self-realization within marriage is a mutual process between the spouses and requires patience, effort and sacrifice. The pace and rate of growth will differ for the partners and it will be an expression of love to have the ability to wait for one's partner to advance to the same level as oneself. So much marital breakdown is due to unilateral growth which leaves the other spouse behind and consequently produces alienation between*

the two. A loving commitment attempts to appreciate in depth the level of development of one's partner and requires a sincere attempt to respond to it. Then the feeling expressed so often in marital breakdown – that 'he/she doesn't understand or care about me' – will be heard less often.

One of the most profound and powerful of human needs is the yearning for a consistent, reliable and loving connection with another person. Babies have this connection with their mothers, first within their bodies and then outside them but still closely bonded. As young children grow, they learn to tolerate temporary frustration, learn about relationships which involve give as well as take and learn eventually to care for others. Ultimately, providing that their own developmental needs have been sufficiently met along the way, adults will be able to provide the same kind of constant reliable, loving care to their own helpless children.

As Dr Dominian points out, different parts of people grow at different rates. Some parts grow slowly, if at all, and within most people (however maturely they may function as adults and parents), there remains a part which continues to crave loving reliability from another just as the babies they once were needed the same so many years ago.

Marriage is potentially the forum within which the dependent needs in everyone may be met, just as it calls forth at different times the loving parental parts of people and the adult, creative, sparky and sexually mature parts too. At some times, the dependent needs are likely to preponderate, at others the needs for independence, separation and initiative. Neither set of needs should be underestimated.

Reliability is the glue which holds a relationship together. In a marriage's solemn promise of permanence and stability – 'to have and to hold from this day forward. . .till death us do part', as the Anglican wedding service so gravely and movingly expresses it – lies its function as a healing, living relationship. A couple who marry promise implicitly or explicitly to make available to each other their minds, hearts and bodies, and they promise to renew this commitment every day of their lives together. The extent to which they succeed or fail in this endeavour will be the extent to which the marriage thrives or founders.

Marriage partners: friends at last?

In modern marriages, in all their infinite varieties, couples relate to each other sometimes as mutual dependants, fulfilling complementary roles and relying on each other accordingly, and sometimes more competitively. For example, a couple may start off in a competitive relationship, both working outside the home and striking a rather wobbly balance between their identities as individuals and their identities as partners in marriage. But then with the birth of their first child, they may be plunged straight into a dependent relationship with each primarily defined by the now complementary roles they rely upon each other to play. They may experience this transition as either a weakening or a growth point in their changing relationship.

There is, however, a third type of relationship that may evolve within a marriage. Friendship within marriage does not preclude either of the other two ways of relating: dependent and competitive. But it has to have space to grow – it can't just be plunged into.

M. Scott Peck, the psychotherapist author of '*The Road Less Travelled*', talks about love as a willingness to extend oneself to nurture one's own or another's spiritual growth. This type of love, he says, is volitional rather than emotional, resulting from a commitment to love rather than the experience of a wave of loving emotion:

> *Couples sooner or later always fall out of love, and it is at that moment, when the mating instinct has run its course, that the opportunity for genuine love begins. It is when the couple no longer feel like being in each other's company always. . .that their love begins to be tested and will be found to be present or absent.*

And so we return to the point from which this book started: love as a decision. The person who can say that their partner is their friend as well as their husband or wife is blessed if by this they mean that liking and respect as well as love are living presences in their marriage, and that theirs is a lifelong and secure commitment. But how does friendship within marriage develop?

The need for equality and respect

Lovers do not need to be equal: a master may fall in love with his slave, or vice versa. In the past, friendship within marriage was rare largely because men and women just did not see themselves as equals. What they demanded from each other was circumscribed by their complementary roles: a wife who was expected to revere her husband and to run the home and her life around his convenience could expect no similar regard extended to herself.

Sometimes, when two people are in love, a sense of inequality may pleasurably intensify the feelings for one or both parties. But friendship requires equality, and the kind of respect that one feels for an equal. It is exactly the opposite of the state of affairs when each partner takes the other for granted, thinking only of their own personal needs. Where there is mutuality, a person will be aware of their partner's needs and desires as much as they are aware of their own, and will value them as equally important.

There is still no better precept for successful relationships than the biblical precept to do unto others as you would have them do unto you. Not because it is morally admirable, but because it works:

'I would have to say that my family were all extremely self-centred people. But Nick [her husband] is different. He's considerate, he'll bring me a cup of tea in the morning and rub my back without me asking him to. And he's not a moaner, he just gets on and does things or else leaves them be. When I find myself about to start having a moan at him nowadays, I think twice.'

Friends will decline to engage in the great power struggle for ascendency, a game which can never truly be won as it only succeeds in undermining both players and making them feel more insecure, not less. This is because they want the best for each other. The relationship is inspired by the belief that the well-being of the one may only be achieved with the well-being of the other.

The need for playing

Play and its close relation, humour, are about living in the moment. In play, the present not the future is what matters. Instead of end-gaming – mentally always zooming ahead to the end result: what will *they* think of it? how will I look? am I a success? – a couple who can be playful with each other have the freedom to explore new and different ways of being and to recreate their world as a colourful, exciting place. If, as a result, they do not take themselves too seriously, this is probably no more than saying that they do not take difficulties too seriously either and can keep a sense of proportion (even when all about them are losing theirs).

It is precisely because play is *not* serious that it can be used to explore possibilities and to share ideas and fantasies that you might otherwise feel inhibited or uncertain about exploring together. For instance, a couple who can be playful with each other sexually, thereby escaping from the tyranny of performance and orgasm, will open up for themselves an intimate way of relating which can be funny, moving and tender all at the same time.

The absence of a sense of playfulness in an adult relationship, a surfeit of seriousness and an orientation towards achieving rather than simply being, can make the world seem drab and dull. Then every expenditure of energy within the relationship becomes an effort. Problems may be focused on to the exclusion of everything else; in the absence of colour and variety, they are all that is left to make life interesting.

Playing is a luxury which can only happen within a secure and trusted relationship. Adolescents who dress exclusively in black and walk about with a copy of Sartre's *La Nausée* stuffed ostentatiously in their trouser pockets thereby indicate their seriousness and also their insecurity. Being in love at the beginning of a relationship is also a surprisingly serious business. One is on show, self-conscious, constantly assessing the other and being assessed. So much is at stake! On the other hand, a couple secure in their relationship, who are able to be playful and humorous with each other, make room for the healthy, creative children within them both -- thereby elbowing out the negatively over-dependent, whining or capricious childishness which may otherwise assume tyrannical control.

The point of playing is that it is exquisitely point*less*. Because of this, unlike going to the supermarket, washing the car or dusting the picture rail, it will not scream to be attended to. You need to make time for it; by doing so, you make time for each other.

The need for separate growth within the relationship

'If I continue to endure you a little longer, I may by degrees dwindle into a wife. . . .' muses Millamant in Congreve's *The Way of the World*. For some couples, any twitches of independent feeling or thinking, any sign of conflicting wishes may need to be strangled at birth, so deeply threatening are they to the couple's concept of what makes a 'good' marriage. But this 'good' marriage is likely to be dull and stultifying: a symbiotic Siamese-twinship. Whole areas of experience may die between the couple, areas in which there is the possibility that a spark of individuality might flare into life, and which are consequently too threatening to allow.

Where there is trust and mutual appreciation, a couple will not feel threatened by each other's different attitudes and interests. The relationship stays alive because it is one between two growing, involved and complex people who are constantly feeding and developing it, not one which is being used by one or both as an institution behind which to hide from the rest of the world.

Margaret Grimer, a counsellor of over 20 years' experience with the Catholic Marriage Advisory Council, says of her work with couples contemplating marriage:

> '*The aim is to have fewer no-go areas. People are so afraid of disagreeing . . . if they could only see disagreement as a growth point, something normal and usual. It doesn't mean a breaking point. What will happen is that the limits get pushed out – and that can only be healthy for the relationship.*'

The need for commitment

A marriage is not made at the moment when the wedding officiator pronounces you husband and wife. It is made at the moment of commitment – which may be saying that it must be made daily to be made at all.

Commitment may develop gradually over a period of time, it may be a moment of decision or the effect of some important shared venture such as buying a house or conceiving a child together. Such an event, important in its own right, also symbolizes your commitment to each other. Commitment may just sneak up on you silently and you suddenly realize: This is it then. We are committed. Could we ever not have been? For one day you have looked across at that person, that stranger placed by fate to snore serenely in the bed beside you; and you have found that your life is inextricably intertwined with his or hers for ever more. And that, as they say, is a long time. For good or ill, come what may, you are a couple. You are married.

Without commitment, one lives at the whims of the moment, a slave to the search for pleasure. Commitment is the willingness to persevere with the relationship, to accept the rough with the smooth, giving yourself no easy way out when the rough times preponderate and, through confronting difficulties in your relationship, to reach beyond them. Then, of course, a whole new set of challenges will be waiting just the other side of the hill. Commitment is hard work.

This 30-year-old man was interviewed shortly after his wedding about his decision to get married:

> 'I was at the point in my life when it made sense to make a lifelong commitment. . . .it was connected with wanting a child, but that wasn't foremost at the time. . . In the past, relationships would go so far and no further. I didn't want to go through that meeting – learning to trust – falling out – stopping again. It hurt too much. I wanted to find the right form to take it deeper.'

Without stability, there is no security. Without the willingness to change, there is no growth. And without limitation, there is no creativity.

Afterword

Recipes for success?

WE asked a number of the couples we interviewed for their last word on what it takes to make a good marriage.

Few couples seemed to feel daunted by this task. Almost everyone was ready with their own piece of distilled wisdom; many commented on why 'other people's' marriages didn't work. Advice ranged from Jane's uncle's recommendation to her and her husband, in his speech at their wedding – to 'follow what her grandfather used to call the two bears: bear and forbear' – to the suggestions printed below:

BOB AND ANNIE. A couple just about to celebrate their tenth wedding anniversary 'despite' having married while at university (when Bob was 19, Annie 21). Bob and Annie defy the usual warnings against marrying young: they consider themselves happily married at a time when many of their friends are either getting divorced or just starting out on the marriage trail themselves.

> Bob: 'Adaptability and flexibility. We've each got to accommodate the other's point of view.'
> Annie: 'I'd agree with that wholeheartedly. Also though, you shouldn't expect too much. People today have got too great expectations.'

BARRY AND MANDY. A couple in their early 40s; a second marriage for him. Two children, both boys, aged 10 and 8.

> Barry: 'I remember Mandy saying to me, after we'd had a huge fight, "You know, you've got to work at relationships." That hit me really hard – I'd never thought of it that way. I thought you got married and then. . . well, sort of that was it. It hadn't occurred to me that we, I, had to work at the marriage. But that's what it is – a lot of hard work. There's a lot of fun too, of course.'

LESLIE AND SHIRLEY. Now in their early 60s, Leslie and Shirley moved to Scotland many years ago and have run their own garage business since then in one of the most beautiful parts of that country. They have three children and several grandchildren.

> Leslie: 'Never go to bed on an argument. We always try to make up our

rows before we go to sleep and say 'I love you' to each other. Sometimes it comes out through gritted teeth, but I think it's still important to say it; it means something to us. It means I'm reminded each night that I do love this woman, my wife. I think people very often forget about saying they love each other, so we have a routine so we do always remember.'

IVOR AND MAUREEN, married for over 30 years and, at the time of going to press, about to welcome their second grandchild into the world. The subject inspired Maureen to burst into verse:

> *'Take commitment, sharing, compassion and love.*
> *Mix family and friends with the above.*
> *Sprinkle honesty, trust and good communication.*
> *All these ingredients make a good marriage relation. . .'*

JOANNA AND NICK. Married for almost three years:

> *Joanna: 'To keep on seeing him as the person he really is – not taking him for granted. And never to let the sun go down on our anger.'*

ANNA AND STEWART. The couple in Chapter 9 who created their own ceremony.

> *Anna: 'Always keep talking, a willingness to share yourself with your partner and a willingness to grow. . .yes, and that you remember to be kind to each other.'*
> *Simon: 'To take care of each other in the widest sense of the word. And finding new ways to remind each other that life doesn't have to be that serious. The only other thing I'd say is to make sure that you keep time to be with each other, and also time to be alone, to give the relationship space.'*

PETER AND ROBIN. The couple we met in Chapter 2.

> *Peter: 'I think we've got a good marriage. Maybe compatibility; but that's easy to say. Friendship, really. You've got to be friends first; to like someone as well as love them.'*

We have a dream of marriage as it may evolve in future years. A dream of two whole people coming together, both with their own unique, individual talents and qualities that are fully recognized and allowed expression within marriage. Of a marriage that is enriching rather than belittling; where each partner is allowed and encouraged to grow by the other. Of a marriage that is a safe haven from the world outside and nurtures and cares for the individuals within it, allowing them both to go off and face anew the challenges outside. Of a marriage where each person is trusted and wholly and unconditionally accepted. Of a marriage where each is fully committed to the other and, as a result of this total commitment, each is able to expand freely and explore their shared love and sexuality. Of a marriage that forms the healthy basis for children to develop within it and which is strong enough to bear the inevitable pressures of family life. Of a marriage where humour, love and laughter reside as well as sadnesses and anger – where the whole gamut of human emotions are allowed their place.

We do not see this dream as an impossible ideal which can never be reached. Instead, we believe that every couple has the potential for such a marriage – the raw material is there right in front of you in the form of you and your partner. None of us can expect an instant transformation. Think of your marriage as a garden, with the soil, the seeds and all the other things necessary to create a beautiful haven. You will not create that garden overnight, but you can plant the seeds which will enable it to develop into a place of beauty.

Appendix 1

A guide to dealing with your income tax affairs

THE tax law in the UK is complex and not easy to understand, even for the experts. Indeed, the very word 'tax' can be guaranteed to send a shiver down the spine; in terms of popularity, tax must rank on a par with dry rot and malaria. This is not to say that the subject of tax can be safely avoided: again, like dry rot and malaria, tax problems can worsen out of all proportion if left too long. You cannot be absolved from your responsibilities for tax: dealing with it is one of the unpleasant aspects of being an adult. None the less, tax can be managed in such a way as to control its unpleasantness: the key to doing this is to face it head on and deal with any problems at an early stage, before they get too much for you. Here, we shall be looking at the best ways of managing your tax affairs and giving an easy guide to what tax is all about.

Then and now

The situation pre-1990

Up to very recent times, whether or not married women wanted to deal exclusively with their own tax affairs, they had no option: under their own names, they simply could not. However enlightened their relationships and however successful their careers and businesses, when it came to tax, married women found themselves thrust straight back into the Dark Ages.

Married men were given the power – and the responsibility – to deal with all of their wives' fiscal affairs. To be sure, a couple might arrange to be separately assessed, yet even so, if a married woman wrote individually to the Inland Revenue, as sure as eggs are eggs, the Revenue's replies would be directed to her husband. Some wives perhaps saw the system

239

as relieving them of an unwelcome chore: many others found it deeply affronting. A journalist for a women's magazine comments:

> 'It made me feel invisible as a person. I would write to the tax-man; he would write back to my husband. He would even send my husband a cheque for my tax rebates. I felt furious but impotent. I used to end up blaming my husband, although obviously it wasn't his fault. If my husband and I hadn't eventually come to an arrangement that I would always open any letters that looked as if they came from the Revenue, I don't know what would have happened.'

And separate assessment only related to earned income. Thus a wife with a low personal income from investments married to a husband with a high one could find herself paying tax at *his* highest rate on her income, however paltry it might be. Her husband would also have been able to find out about her savings, even if she wanted to keep them a secret.

The problem cut both ways, too. Occasionally, married men found themselves faced with tax demands relating to their wives' (unknown) extra income, which they found themselves obliged to pay. In the eyes of the tax authorities, husbands had no legal let-out from being forced to bear what should have been their wives' tax burden, at least while the marriage was still in its existence. (Although one wonders how many marriages would ultimately be able to withstand such widespread concealment anyway.)

The 1990 changes

Happily, as from 6 April 1990, all has changed. From that date, all married women will be as responsible for dealing with their tax affairs as their unmarried sisters have always been.

Now, instead of a husband automatically being entitled to a 'married man's allowance' (which was considerably higher than the single person's tax allowance), all people, whether married or otherwise, will each have a personal allowance. In addition, married couples will be entitled to a married couple's allowance, which can be tacked on to one of their own individual allowances. (usually the husband's).

The 'do nothing' approach?

Particularly if you are employed and pay tax under the PAYE (pay as you earn) system, it is tempting to take the line of least resistance: to let sleeping Inland Revenue dogs lie. If you are employed, your employer will deduct tax and National Insurance contributions at source (i.e. before you get your salary). With regard to the new tax changes, if you are an employed married woman with no extra income and entitled to claim no extra tax allowances, all you will have to do is to plan, with your husband, whether you can reduce your joint tax bill any more. As long as you never receive an income tax return, you can remain blissfully unaware of the complexities of the UK tax system. And if not?

The rub lies in the phrase 'If you are an employed married woman with no extra income and entitled to claim no extra allowances'. This means that if you are:

- self-employed
- receiving extra income aside from your salary
- able to claim any extra allowances (*see* pp. 243–4)
- have just received an income tax return

you will need to acquaint yourself with the tax system. In the following pages, you will find an easy guide to dealing with your tax affairs, cracking the tax jargon codes and ensuring that you play the system to your own maximum benefit.

Managing your tax affairs

Question 1: what is 'income' for tax purposes?

This may seem like a strange question, but the fact is that not all of the money you may receive is taxable as 'income'.

The following **are** classed as income for tax purposes:

- earnings from your work
- spare-time earnings
- fees for work you do
- any profits you make from your business
- any other earnings from being self-employed
- pensions
- most Social Security benefits as well as payments under the Enterprise Allowance scheme
- rents from letting out property
- regular payments from someone else (e.g. maintenance payments or covenant payments)
- investment income (e.g. interest from your bank or building society account, share dividends, unit trust distributions)

The following **are not** classified as income (though, depending on the amount, sometimes capital gains tax or inheritance tax may be payable – if you are in doubt, speak to an accountant):

- presents or gifts
- money you borrow
- money you inherit
- gains you make on something you sold for a higher figure than you bought, unless this was part of a business venture or part of your business (any profit you make on the sale of the home you use solely as your residence is not currently taxable)
- betting or lottery winnings (unless this is your 'business')
- premium bond prizes

Certain other sources of income are specially seen as tax free. These are, broadly speaking, some income from particular investments (e.g. the first £70 from a National Savings Bank ordinary account, or from National Savings Certificates), certain types of income from the State (e.g. Social Security benefits and pensions and rate rebates, grants and scholarships), certain overseas income and some 'perks' at work (e.g. luncheon vouchers up to the value of 15p per day).

So, once you have an idea of what is your 'income' for the taxman's eyes. . .

Question 2: How will I be taxed?

The tax year

Income tax is an annual tax. The *tax year* runs from 6 April to 5 April, so you must assess all your income which arises between those dates to calculate your income for any one tax year. However, if you are self-employed, your accountant may advise you to choose different dates for your business's own tax year; you must agree this with the Inland Revenue.

Confusingly, the Inland Revenue date their tax forms a year ahead. Thus a tax return headed, say, 6 April 1990 to 5 April 1991 will require you to declare income from the previous year (i.e. 1989– 1990).

Calculating tax

It is best to think of your income in terms of 'bands'.

Once you have deducted from your *gross income* (i.e. all the money that has come to you in any one year):

(*a*) any monies you have received which are not viewed as income (e.g. gifts); and

(*b*) any income which is tax free

you are left with your *net income*.

From this figure you should deduct any expenses that are completely due to the running of your business, any payments to a pension scheme and any investments under the Business Expansion Scheme. (*See* Question 5.) Then you will end up with your *taxable income*.

Question 3: How much will I be taxed?

From your taxable income, you should deduct your *allowances* (see next question) – e.g. your personal allowance plus the married couple's allowance (if appropriate). You can then calculate the actual tax to be paid by referring to the tax bands for the relevant year.

For example, for the tax year 1989/90, tax was assessed at two rates (or proportions of your income):

Any taxable income earned up to £20,700: 25%
Any taxable income earned over this sum: 40%

With the new changes in the tax system, you and your husband may be able to cut down your joint tax bills by:

- transferring income producing assets (like accounts that pay interest on a property you rent out) from the higher earner to the non-earner.

- switching interest paying accounts to those that pay interest *gross* rather than *net* (e.g. National Savings Bank investments)

if one of you is paying higher rate tax whilst the other doesn't pay tax, or only pays at the basic rate. Changes should be made as soon after 6 April 1990 as possible to get maximum benefit. See an accountant for further details.

Question 4: What allowances can I claim?

A surprising number of people fail to claim the tax allowances to which they are entitled. If you find that you have not been claiming a relevant allowance, you can reclaim the tax wrongly paid for up to six years previously (i.e. six years after the end of the tax year in which the original assessment was made).

The main allowance which everyone can set off against tax is the personal allowance. In addition, a married couple are entitled to an extra allowance. This Married Couples' Allowance will automatically be set off against the husband's income unless the husband's income is insufficient to use it up, when it (or the remaining part of it) will be set against the wife's.

There are further allowances for single parents (though none for bringing up children when both parents live together) and various allowances for men and women over retirement age, widows and widowers, blind people and people looking after dependent relatives. Check your eligibility, etc. with your accountant or the Inland Revenue if it sounds as if any of these may apply to you.

Question 5: What expenses can I claim against tax?

Basically, any expenses you incur solely in the pursuit of conducting your business as a self-employed person (*not*, usually, as an employee – though your employer can claim expenses on your behalf) and which the Inland Revenue agrees are legitimately tax deductible.

There are exemptions for company cars, and if you are self-employed and run a car as part of your business (i.e. it is used for purposes other than just getting to and from work), you may be able to claim as expenses a substantial part of the cost of running and maintaining it, and even part of its initial cost. If you are an employee earning more than £8500 and have a company car, you will be taxed strictly on the value of the benefit obtained. Your employer has to declare this benefit to the Inland Revenue. If you earn less than £8500, you will not be taxed any extra.

If you work from home, you may be able to put in a claim for a proportion of your rent, telephone bills, stationery, heating bills, etc. However, if you own your home, do not formally designate a part of it exclusively as an office and deduct a proportion of your mortgage payments accordingly; if you do, you may have to pay capital gains tax on a proportion of your profit when you later come to sell.

Training fees, study materials and so on, if they are related to earning work in which you are already engaged, *are* deductible. If, for example, you are just starting out in business and the deduction of training fees means that you are running at a loss, you can carry the loss forward to other income earned in subsequent years.

If you are an employee, from July 1988 for your own personal pension, you will have paid the premium net of basic rate tax, although if you pay higher-rate tax, you have to make a claim at the end of the tax year for extra relief. (Prior to July 1988, you paid the gross premium and received tax relief by way of an adjustment of your tax code.) If self-employed, you will pay the gross premium, but effectively your tax bill will be reduced at the end of the day. Premiums for life assurance policies taken out before 14 March 1984 also receive tax relief, the deduction being made at source.

The following are *not* deductible:

- money you pay to someone for looking after your child(ren) while you are working (and the benefit of workplace crèches will also be taxed).
- restaurant bills even if incurred while entertaining clients.
- training fees relating to a prospective line of work that you have not yet got off the ground.

Claiming expenses is one area where a good accountant may be worth his/her weight in gold. S/he may advise you to claim for expenses you may never have dreamed of, and will also know how to present them to the Inland Revenue in the most favourable light – many expenses are allowable depending on the Revenue's discretion and so professional presentation may make a difference.

Remember to keep receipts for *all* expenses you claim, preferably filed by the month in which they were incurred.

Question 6: Which tax office will deal with my affairs?

The tax office which will deal with your tax matters will not necessarily be the one nearest to where you live. It depends upon your individual circumstances.

- *If you are an employee*, your tax file will be assigned to the particular tax office dealing with the area where you work (or the office where you are paid from, if this is different – e.g. the company's headquarters). If, however, you work for a big organization, your Inland Revenue tax office may be one of the large London Provincial districts (which are based outside London – for example, in Salford, Manchester, Bradford). These offices deal solely with employees' tax affairs.

  If you are a government employee, your affairs will be dealt with by one of the Public Departments in Cardiff.

  You will be able to find out from your employer (usually either from the accounts or personnel department) which tax office deals with your affairs and, very importantly, they will also be able to tell you what your *reference number* is. Without this, it is very hard for the Inland Revenue to trace your file. If you can't find out your Inland Revenue reference number, quote your National Insurance number.

- *If you are self-employed* (e.g. a sole trader or in partnership), your place of business will determine which tax office deals with your affairs.

- *If you are unemployed*, your file will still be dealt with by the office that dealt with your former employer.

- *If you derive income mainly from pensions or investments*, and if you are receiving a pension from a former employer, your tax affairs may well be dealt with by the local tax office nearest the pension fund base which pays your pension. Otherwise, generally speaking, the tax offices of those with pensions or investments will be the one most local to their homes.

Local PAYE enquiry offices

As it is likely that your tax office will be hundreds of miles away, the Inland Revenue have set up local PAYE enquiry offices, so that you can call in and discuss any problems. You should be able to locate the one nearest you by looking in the telephone directory under 'Inland Revenue' (or ring Directory Enquiries), or you can get the full list of addresses and telephone numbers from any tax office.

Question 7: What about tax forms?

Tax returns

There are several different types of tax return, the special form sent to you by the Inland Revenue for you to complete and return to them to advise them about your income. Remember that many of the questions may be irrelevant to your particular circumstances – you only need to fill in the parts that are applicable to you. It may take a little time to read through, but it will be worth it.

- *Form P1*: This is the most straightforward and is issued to the majority of employees. If you are employed and your tax affairs are relatively simple, this is the form you will get. It is unlikely that you will be asked to complete and return a Form P1 every year.
- *Form 11*: Again designed for employees, this is issued to those with more complex tax affairs – e.g. company directors or taxpayers in the higher bands of tax.
- *Form 1*: This is for partnerships, to include all the income of the whole partnership and to show how that income has been divided between the partners. This is extra to Form 11 (which will need to be completed individually by each partner). Form 1 also covers other special circumstances – for instance, the tax affairs of the trustees of a settlement or the executors of a deceased person's estate.
- *Form R40:* This is sent to people who claim a repayment of tax each year.
- *Form R232*: This will be sent if you have to advise the tax authorities about someone else's income – e.g. a child's.
- *Form P11D*: This shows the benefits you have received in kind (e.g. a company car) and expense payments if you are an employee earning more than £8500 per annum.

If you are sent a tax return form, you are required to complete, sign, date and return it within 30 days – a rule which is more often honoured in the breach than in the observance. In practice, the Inland Revenue will not penalize you if your tax return is a little late, but if you fail to send it back until after the end of the tax year, they can impose penalties.

If you have not been sent a tax return form but have received income that the Inland Revenue know nothing about, you must tell your tax office about the extra cash. Failure to do so within one year after the end of the tax year in which the income arose makes you liable to pay a penalty.

Notice of Coding

- *Form P2:* If you are an employee, you will usually be sent a Notice of Coding. This shows the code number you have been assigned, which your employer will use to calculate the tax to be deducted from your pay. The basis of calculating the coding will be explained, usually on an accompanying leaflet.

Notices of assessment

These are forms on which the tax man works out how much you owe and demands an 'assessed' amount of tax. This may be either an estimate or a figure based on a tax return which you have already submitted. Check the notice carefully – if you think it is wrong – (for example, if your personal or other allowances or your expenses have not been deducted correctly) – you can appeal.

If you have been asked to pay an estimated amount which you think is well in excess of the actual amount due, you (or, preferably, your accountant) should contact the tax office *immediately* and make sure that you file a correct return straight away.

Question 8: How do I deal with the Inland Revenue

It is quite common for people to pay too much tax. For instance, you may have been allocated the wrong tax code or otherwise have paid too much tax under the PAYE system. If there have been some difficulties over your tax in the past, or even just changes in your status, when you change jobs your new employer will have to pay you under an 'emergency' code, which usually means that tax is deducted at the basic rate from the whole amount of your income, ignoring any tax allowances you can claim. You may also find that you have been paying too much tax either for this and/or for past tax years because you have not been claiming all the tax allowances to which you are entitled.

In all of these circumstances, you can claim back the extra tax paid (up to six years in the past if appropriate).

To reclaim, you should write to your tax office (marking the letter or tax return 'REPAYMENT CLAIM' at the top, preferably in red) to explain why you are making a claim and how you calculate the amount of your repayment. If your tax rebate is £25 or more, you may be entitled to interest, if your claim goes back a long way. The tax authorities usually deal with repayment claims on a priority basis – however, they may need prompting.

Whenever you write to the tax authorities, always ensure that your letters are marked with your tax reference number, and always keep a copy for your own file. Inland Revenue officers can be very slow in dealing with correspondence, so do not expect an immediate reply.

Question 9: Where do I go to get help and advice?

If you need advice or information about PAYE, contact your local PAYE office. Your local Citizens' Advice Bureau (CAB) may well be able to give you some basic help.

There are also a number of excellent tax guides on the market, if you want to go into the area of tax in greater detail. However, watch out for the information in them being out of date, particularly since all the revolutionary changes of the last year. The *WHICH? Book of Tax* is quite readable as well as thorough (contact the Consumers' Association on 01–486–5544). Many insurance companies and financial advice companies also produce their own yearly guides, which are updated soon after the Budget in any year: the *Allied Dunbar* book is a good one.

If, however, your tax affairs are in a mess and you feel quite inadequate to cope with the problems of sorting them out *or* your tax affairs are quite complex, you should consider using an accountant. To find a good one, try asking around your friends and acquaintances (preferably, if you can, those who are in the same line of business). Otherwise, your bank manager, your solicitor or your financial adviser (if you have one) may well prove to be a useful source.

Appendix 2

Where to go for help and advice

General information

S OME of the organizations listed below offer their services free, others make a voluntary or compulsory charge. A first contact will generally be without obligation and you should check the situation then.

Counselling and psychotherapy

Counselling is primarily provided by the organizations below marked*. They will aim to help you individually or with your partner through non-judgemental listening, support and, hopefully, clarification.

Psychotherapy generally aims to go deeper than counselling, getting to the root of why the problem has arisen in the first place – sometimes by tracing it back to your childhood. It tends to take longer and be more intense than counselling, which is usually orientated towards present-day, sometimes short-term issues. Although, unfortunately, anyone can call themselves a psychotherapist, properly trained psychotherapists or psychoanalysts have a longer and more rigorous training than counsellors.

There is no centralized clearing-house for psychotherapy at present, but all the organizations below marked** provide it and should be able to help you or to refer you to another (especially if you live outside London). Otherwise you could try personal recommendations or talk to your family doctor. You could also try your local Social Security office or the psychiatric ward of your local hospital; staff there will be aware of the local network in your area and should also be able to refer you on. Psychotherapy on the NHS has the advantage of being free, but in today's economic climate, it is not always easy to qualify, and there may be long waiting lists even if you do.

If you have any doubts at all about the qualifications of a person you have contacted, a good safeguard is to check whether they trained at or belong to an organization which is part of the Standing Conference for Psychotherapy (formerly the Rugby Conference).

There are many different orientations in psychotherapy – Freudians, Kleinians, Jungians, Gestalt, psychodrama to name but a few. Various paperbacks have been published which contain descriptions and useful addresses to help you find the psychotherapist who will be right for you – as an individual, a couple or a family. Particularly recommended are *A Complete Guide to Therapy* by Joel Kovel and *A Consumer's Guide to Therapy* by Lindsay Knight. You should be able to order either without difficulty from your local book shop if they do not have them in stock.

Legal advice

If you want to find a solicitor, you are best advised to rely on personal recommendation or visit a few local ones, checking out in person the costs, whether you like them and so on. If you wish to consult a solicitor who specializes in family law, telephone the administrative secretary of the Solicitors Family Law Association on (0689) 50227 for a list of local members.

The organizations

Only the head offices of the organizations are listed here. Many will have local branches, however, and you could check in the telephone book first or ask the organization itself.

Alcoholics Anonymous, P.O. Box 514, 11 Redcliffe Gardens, London SW10 9BQ, tel. 01–352 3001.
or
P.O. Box 1, Stonebow House, York, tel. 0904 – 644026.
Branches throughout the country.
Association for Group and Individual Psychotherapy**, 1 Fairbridge Road, London N19 3EW, tel. 01–272 7013. Provide mainly individual psychotherapy and may operate a sliding scale of fees for those in need.
British Association of Counselling*, 37a Sheep Street, Rugby CV21 3BX, tel. (0788) 78328. Will advise about registered counsellors in your area and will provide general information.
Catholic Marriage Advisory Council*, 1 Blyth Mews, Brook Green, London W14, tel. 01–371 1341. Run premarital groups, also counselling for people whose marriages need support. Often a shorter waiting list than for Relate (*see below*) and not confined to helping only Catholics. Branches throughout the country.
Department of Social Security. In the first instance, contact your local office; you will find this in the telephone book. For general enquiries,

there is also a freeline 0800 – 666555; they may be more informed and more helpful on such matters as what constitutes eligibility for benefit, etc. You could also try your local CAB or neighbourhood law centre.

Inland Revenue (Public Enquiries Room), West Wing, Somerset House, Strand, London WC2, tel. 01– 438 6622. (*See also* Appendix 1 on managing your tax affairs.)

Institute of Family Therapy**, 43 New Cavendish Street, London W1M 7RG, tel. 01–935 1651. Provides counselling for the family, both in groups and on an individual basis.

Jewish Marriage Council (JMC)*, 23 Ravenshurst Avenue, London NW4 4EL, tel. 01–203 6311. Runs courses for engaged couples and provides family-oriented support and counselling for Jewish couples. There is also a branch in Manchester.

London Centre for Psychotherapy**, 19 Fitzjohns Avenue, London NW3 5JY, tel. 01–435 0873.

National Childbirth Trust, Alexandra House, Oldhams Terrace, London W3 6NH, tel. 01–992 8637. Provide help of all kinds for prospective and new parents, from antenatal classes through maternity mail-order to locally organized support groups for you and your new baby. Branches throughout the country.

National Council of Citizens' Advice Bureaux, 115 Pentonville Road, London N1, tel. 01–833 2181. Extremely useful organization. Your local CAB will be able to advise on many things, from legal rights to debt management. Branches throughout the country.

Relate* (formerly the National Marriage Guidance Council), Herbert Gray College, Little Church Street, Rugby CV21 3AP, tel. (0788) 73241. Provide premarital counselling and counselling for those whose marriages need support. No religious or ideological basis. (*See also* the discussion of a counsellor's work in Chapter 20.) Branches throughout the country.

Samaritans*, 46 Marshall Street, London W1, tel. 01–439 2224 or look in your local telephone directory. Offer a 24-hour support service for all people facing emotional crises – and you don't have to be suicidal to call them. They also provide face-to-face counselling.

The Tavistock Clinic**, 120 Belsize Lane, London NW3 5BA, tel. 01–435 7111. Provide psychotherapy for individuals, couples and groups.

Westminster Pastoral Foundation*, 23 Kensington Square, London W8 5HN, tel. 01–937 6956. Despite the name, this is not an evangelical organization. They provide analytically oriented counselling.

Women's Therapy Centre**, 6 Manor Gardens, London N7 6LA, tel. 01–263 6200. Offers group and individual psychotherapy with a feminist orientation, sometimes but not always restricted to women only.

Further reading

Argyle, Michael and Henderson, Monika, *The Anatomy of Relationships*, London, Heinemann, 1985.

Barnard, Jessie, *The Future of Marriage*, London, Yale University Press, 1982.

Bettelheim, Bruno, *A Good Enough Parent*, London, Thames & Hudson, 1987.

Davis, Gwynn and Murch, Mervyn, *Grounds for Divorce*, Oxford University Press, 1988.

Dominion, Dr Jack, *Marriage, Faith and Love*, London, Darton Longman & Todd, 1981.

Fisher, Seymour, *Understanding the Female Orgasm*, New York, Bantam, 1973.

Friday, Nancy, *Jealousy*, London, Fontana, 1987.

Garlick, Helen, *The Separation Survival Handbook*, London, Penguin, 1989.

Hite, Shere, *The Hite Report*, New York, Macmillan, 1976.

Kitzinger, Sheila, *Pregnancy and Childbirth*, London, Penguin, 1986.

Knight, Lindsay, *A Consumer's Guide to Therapy*, London, Fontana, 1986.

Kovel, Joel, *A Complete Guide to Therapy*, London, Penguin, 1978.

Lawson, Annette, *Adultery: An Analysis of Love and Betrayal*, Oxford, Basil Blackwell, 1989.

Mansfield, Penny and Collard, Jean, *The Beginning of the Rest of Your Life*, London, Macmillan, 1988.

Masters, William H. and Johnson, Virginia, *The Pleasure Bond*, Boston, Mass., Little, Brown, 1974.

Pearson, Ethel Spector, *Love and Fateful Encounters*, London, Bloomsbury, 1989.

Peck, M. Scott, *The Road Less Travelled*, London, Rider Books, 1985.

Scarf, Maggie, *Intimate Partners: Patterns in Love and Marriage*, London, Century Paperbacks, 1987.

Skynner, Robin and Cleese, John, *Families and How to Survive Them*, London, Methuen, 1983.

Trachtenberg, Peter, *The Casanova Complex*, London, Angus & Robertson, 1989.

Zilbergeld, Dr Bernard, *Men and Sex*, London, Fontana Books, 1978.